# VIOLENT CARTOGRAPHIES

# VIOLENT CARTOGRAPHIES

## Mapping Cultures of War

Michael J. Shapiro

University of Minnesota Press
Minneapolis
London

Excerpt from the poem "He alo ā he alo (Face to face)" by Puanani Burgess reprinted by permission of the publisher, AFSC-Hawai'i.

Published by the University of Minnesota Press
111 Third Avenue South, Suite 290, Minneapolis, MN 55401-2520
Printed in the United States of America on acid-free paper

Library of Congress Cataloging-in-Publication Data

Shapiro, Michael J.
    Violent cartographies : mapping cultures of war  /  Michael J. Shapiro.
        p.     cm.
    Includes bibliographical references and index.
    ISBN 0-8166-2920-X (hc : acid free paper).  —  ISBN 0-8166-2921-8
(pbk. : acid free paper)
    1. War and civilization.   2. War and society—United States.
I. Title.
    CB481.S42     1997
    303.6'6—dc20                                                96-31509

For Alana, Kam, Miranda, and Noah

# Contents

# Preface

This book is not an attempt to provide an explanatory answer to the question, Why war? Indeed, some of the "explanations" are the subject matter of my analyses, for they participate in the rationales that encourage regarding warfare as a legitimate political practice. My aim has been to achieve analytic, discursive, and ethical distance from the objects of analysis typical in social science approaches to war. In various ways, the very grammar of such analyses—subject/investigators seeking to illuminate things such as national objectives, strategies, logistics, and enmities—inhibits the kinds of disclosure I seek.

While resisting such epistemological and strategic thinking, my questions concern how historically developed, socially embedded interpretations of identity and space give rise to the objects scrutinized in both policy discourse and the disciplinary conceits of international relations and foreign policy analysis (among others). More specifically, because my focus is on ontological commitments rather than strategic aims, I examine the ways that enmity-related global geographies and ethnoscapes emerge as collectivities try to achieve, stabilize, and reproduce their unity and coherence.

Geographic imaginaries are especially central to my analyses as I attempt to unread one that is particularly dominant. My investigations seek to counter a preoccupation with international enmities. An emphasis on internation violence presupposes the institutionalization of the dominant nation-state geographic imaginary. Organized on the basis of national boundaries, this map privileges international violence as an almost exclusive subject matter; other forms of war escape analysts' attempts at conceptual mastery, for their grasps are energized by their cartographic commitments. Certainly many identifiable enmities and violent engagements are "international," but rather than treating the way nations produce defensive and offensive strategies, I treat the way the discourse on war tends to be exhausted by a framing of the world in terms of state practices of violence.

My attempt to elude such a framing necessarily involves me in a continuous struggle over the language of analysis. For example, inasmuch as I am locating the framing problem as one who resides within the United States, I occasionally resort to a "we" and note that to raise such questions about framing involves "us" in a critical analysis of our imaginaries, of who we are and of "how" we are—that is, of how we (the dominant and unreflective "we") practice the construction of space and history in producing the aggregates that attract our allegiances and those that we deem threatening or antagonistic.

While I would like to represent that "we" as divided rather than consensually located in *an* interpretive practice, I must accept the limits of a language that can hold only a limited number of ambiguities and contending meaning practices per statement to remain intelligible. At a minimum, my aim is to make the already-intelligible appear less exhaustive of the available options. I approach this aim at times through juxtaposition and at times through rhetorical or grammatical impertinence.

For example, for those preoccupied with the geopolitical strategies of violence, the current system of global jurisdictions, represented by the boundaries of nation-states, constitutes an unproblematic grammar of policy action; it is the basis for educing the "explanatory variables" in their studies of either the onset or the prolongation of war.

Exemplary of this preoccupation is a contemporary analysis of the importance of geography for understanding war. The analysts concern themselves with the "mapping" of "spatial and geopolitical contexts within which decision makers must calculate and make choices."[1] But despite showing a sensitivity to a subjective dimension of this mapping, recognizing that it has shifting meanings for "decision makers," they treat the state configuration as the only spatial reality, failing to recognize that, as Etienne Balibar has put it, the real—for example, the nation-state structure as a whole—is also an imaginary; it is one way among others of organizing the significance of space.[2] And most significantly, space for such "security"-concerned analysts provides a perceived context for explaining decision making related to violence; they produce a world whose focal points are the power centers of states.

In this investigation I also turn to geography, but not to provide an explanation of state-level decision making. As I noted, I want less to understand war, in the traditional empirical/explanatory sense, than to effect a political and ethical resistance to the enmities upon which it feeds. To do this I emphasize an approach to maps that provides distance from the geopolitical frames of strategic thinkers and security analysts. Geography is inextricably linked to the architecture of enmity. But rather than an exogenous "explanatory variable," it is a primary part of the ontology of a collective. Along with various ethnographic imaginaries—the ethnoscapes that are a part of geographic imaginations—it constitutes a fantasy structure implicated in how territorially elaborated collectivities locate themselves in the world and thus how they practice the meanings of self and Other that provide the conditions of possibility for regarding others as threats or antagonists. Grammatically, then, it is appropriate for me to recognize cartographic violence instead of speaking of the geographic causes of violence.

Therefore, at the same time that I have sought to make intelligible the way that ontological aims construct a map of enmity, I have had to mount a resistance to many familiar languages of analysis, in particular the rationalistic discourses that dominate "security studies." My aim has been to juxtapose such rationalism to a more ethnographic mode of thinking, to make rationalistic and logistical thinking appear to be a peculiar preoccupation rather than an edifying pedagogy. While the particulars of my ethnographic focus are elaborated in the first chapter, here I want to provide an example of a particular misrecognition animated by the security analyst's way of constructing global problematics.

To render modern security thinking peculiar, it is useful to take a brief historical excursion to the Roman empire. Such excursions can be edifying, for as Paul Veyne has noted, "Roman history . . . takes us out of ourselves and forces us to make explicit the differences separating us from it."[3] More specifically, Veyne glosses a difference that highlights the radical contingency of contemporary security thinking:

> Rome incarnates an archaic form, not of imperialism but of isolationism. She denies the pluralities of nations: she behaves, as Momsen said, as if she were the sole state in the full meaning of the word. She does not seek a semi-security from day to day in equilibrium with other cities, but wants to live in tranquility and to obtain for herself once and for all a whole and definitive security.[4]

Heeding Veyne's advice, we can take another brief Roman holiday and visit the frontier of the old Roman empire. In so doing, we will discover that an appreciation of Roman "security" must necessarily displace a strategic approach to geographic strategies with an ontological approach to geographic imaginaries. Rome's territorialization of its collective identity turns out to have been as much related to its emerging construction of its moral/cosmological significance as it was to its strategic concerns. Nevertheless, one "security analyst," fixated on mechanisms of managing and securing boundaries, has provided an egregious misreading of Roman practices of imperial space.

Succumbing to a temptation to read Rome on the basis of contemporary strategic frames, Edward Luttwak interprets Rome's ecumenical drive and subsequent policing of its empire as strategic in the modern, territorial sense. For him Roman spatial practices, such as, for example, the Julio-Claudian expansion, constitute an epoch of "forceful suasion."[5] But if one recognizes more generally that a people's geographic practice can be understood ontologically as well as strategically, it becomes possible to recognize more specifically that Roman frontiers were not precise lines of defense or enforcement that radically separated what was Rome from non-Rome. Indeed, despite how often Rome's fall as an empire has been attributed to the "barbarians" at the gates, Roman frontiers were more zonal than wall-like.[6]

Paradoxically, as C. R. Whittaker points out, although Rome was a society organized by its frontiers both spatially and ideologically, at the same time it is almost impossible to discover where the limits are. Roman perceptions of cosmology and social space projected themselves on their concepts of imperial boundaries; the Roman cosmology of order was more ideological than rationalistic. As a result, Romans radically underestimated distances between center and periphery in their empire and tended to see unknown regions between center and periphery in terms of power rather than territory.[7] Most essentially, from the time of Caesar Augustus, who inaugurated the Roman ecumenical fantasy—the ambition to Romanize the globe—they divided the world into what was Roman and what was the barbarian periphery, which ringed the *oikumene.*

Contrary, then, to Luttwak's security-oriented reconstruction, the Roman boundary was less territorial (indeed, Roman mapping of territorial extension was very imprecise) than cultural, based as it was on the radical distinction between the cultivated and the barbarian. In effect, the Romans had a markedly ontological model of space. Roman limiting boundaries had a more symbolic or religious significance than a geometric or scientific one. The practice of the Roman geographic imaginary was aimed more at enclosing sacral space than at establishing military strategy.[8]

In effect, Whittaker's reconstruction of Roman spatiality and elucidation of the aggressive blindness of strategic thought, based on a contemporary, geopolitical cartography and a rationalistic version of state practices, unmaps a widely held view of imperial space. In the chapters that follow, unmappings and unreadings of a legacy of strategic and rationalistic thinking are central features of the analysis. Beyond that, the provocations initiating my concern with the cartographic dimensions of representational violence as well as violence under arms and the more specific modalities of my analysis are presented in chapter 1.

# Acknowledgments

I was fortunate to have spent a sabbatical leave on the University of Wisconsin campus during the 1994–95 academic year, which afforded me access to an exceptional library system. The art history collection and a separate Historical Society library on the campus, along with a vast collection of books and journals in the main library, greatly facilitated my preparation of this study. I am grateful to Gina Sapiro and her colleagues in the Department of Political Science for appointing me an Honorary Visiting Fellow and thereby providing an office and access to the campus facilities. And I am very grateful to the office staff for their hospitality and assistance.

Various friends and colleagues provided critical reactions either to my manuscript as a whole, to individual chapters, or to earlier essays that served as prototypes for chapters. Thanks are owed to Arjun Appadurai, Jane Bennett, Carol Breckenridge, David Campbell, Bill Chaloupka, Bill Connolly, Mick Dillon, Richard Drinnon, Tom Dumm, Kathy Ferguson, Kennan Ferguson, Merwyn Frost, Jim George, Michael Hardt, Sankaran Krishna, Rick Maxwell, Michael McKinley, Terry Nardin, Deane Neubauer, John O'Neill, Paul Patton, Sandy Schram, Phyllis Turnbull, and Rob Walker.

I am very grateful to my editors at the University of Minnesota Press, Lisa Freeman and Carrie Mullen, for their encouragement, support, and expert handling of the review process. I also want to thank Lynn Marasco for the copyediting and Mary Byers, Becky Manfredini, and Jeff Moen for managing the production process.

Finally, I am deeply indebted to my wife, Hannah Tavares, for loving support, intellectual challenge, and inspiration. She provides an exemplary model for encountering the world both critically and compassionately.

# ONE

# Violence in the American Imaginaries

## Beginning Close to Home

I grew up in Connecticut. Although my family's principal residence was in the town of West Hartford, my parents' love of the ocean, coupled with their growing prosperity, made it possible for us to first rent and then own a summer house at "the shore" (my mother's expression) in the town of Niantic, quite near the city of New London. For two months of every year of my childhood and adolescence, I swam, sailed, fished, and played in a place of names that had very happy resonances but very little historical significance for me. For most of that time, the names were mere labels. It wasn't until I was well into my teenage years that I began to hear the New in New London as an indication of the city's English patrimony. And it only became evident to me when local antique stores began spelling Niantic with the variation Nehantic that our "shore" was in a place formerly inhabited by the Nehantic tribe (among others).[1]

Apart from a few names—for example, the town of Niantic/Nehantic and two streets in New London, one named Pequot and the other Mohegan Avenue—there was very little evidence of the former Native American cultures in the vicinity. As in most of New England, English names predominated. New London even has a Thames River (although it is pronounced by locals as it is spelled). In elementary school I was taught that the original English settlers had enjoyed friendly relations with some local "Indian" tribes but had faced danger from some marauding, violent ones. This was represented mainly as a character-building ordeal for the early "settlers" and had the effect of increasing their moral authority. "Our"—the Euro-American's—place on the continent was established, we were told, by people whose courage matched their virtue. Of course my living spaces were remarkably safe. The seventeenth-century dangers were long since past, and there were no violent manifestations of class warfare because where I resided there was only one class. Although I grew up during the most intense period of the cold war, "war" was an abstraction, a designation applied to a history of battles in the past, on someone else's turf, and applied to violence that transgresses the borders of the nation-state map, which I understood to be "the world."

Nevertheless, I did in fact live more or less at ground zero in both winter and summer residences during the cold war. East Hartford, a few short miles from West Hartford, had the Pratt and Whitney Aircraft Company, which made engines for jet fighter planes, and Groton, right next to New London, had the Electric Boat Company, making the nuclear-powered submarines that carried Polaris missiles with nuclear warheads.

But I had no sense of imminent catastrophe. Somehow—primarily through a lack of reflection—I was able to preserve the venues of my childhood in the form of benign recollections, even as my political and scholarly interests gave me a less and less benign view of the emergence of the European dominance of the North American continent. Certainly the news about the violent conquest of the aboriginal population had penetrated the dense rhetorical defenses; there was increasing pressure on the discourses of discovery and civilizing that were central to my school curricula and on the discourses of comparative and international politics that were privileged within the mainstream of my (political science) discipline. Nevertheless, the more specific venues of the violence were vague.

When, however, more than a decade after its publication, I read Richard Drinnon's account of the Pequot War (in his study of European empire building in North America), my view of my former summer home was radically altered.[2] The leisure-oriented cartography of my childhood summer idylls lost its grip, and a place of enjoyment, whose names had simply indicated the English origins of the early settlers, had become a place of violence and erasure. The erasure was both totalizing and purposive. Drinnon describes what happened to the Pequot provenances after the slaughter of hundreds of them in the war and in subsequent attempts to exterminate them:

> The Pequots were "rooted out" as a tribe.... And there would have been no known living members of that tribe had the colonizers had their way. They sought as Mason ["hero" and chronicler of the war] said, "to cut off the Remembrance of them from the Earth." After the war, the General Assembly of Connecticut declared the name extinct. No survivors could be called Pequots. The Pequot river became the Thames, and the Village known as Pequot became New London.[3]

I had cavorted on a palimpsest, but there is a way to regain a respectful recognition of the peoples who preceded me in that space. Writing about it can serve as an act of restoration as purposeful as that of the sixteenth-century General Assembly of Connecticut. My account here is therefore meant not only to contribute to an understanding of the Pequot War but also to be complicit with other efforts to make a place for Pequots in the story of "America." Well before Drinnon's analysis, there was at least one early attempt to tell the Pequot story and, at the same time, assess its implications for the more general American story.

Roughly a century after the Pequot War and the attempts to efface the Pequots from history, the Pequot activist, philosopher, and writer William Apess worked strenuously to publicize the surviving Pequots and to bring to white public attention the sordid results of the violent confrontation between Euro- and Native Americans. Because his writings have been recently assembled and published by a major university press, that publicizing, which was more or less criminalized and rejected when Apess was read by his contemporaries, now participates in a new restoration of the Pequot imprint in Connecticut and the surrounding areas where they have dwelled.[4]

Apess's writings are disquieting. They act against the complacent, consensual understanding of American political evolution that most Euro-American narratives have perpetuated. In particular, in his eulogy to the leader of the intertribal league, King Philip, who led a last stand of Northeastern tribes against the Euro-American militaries, he "does more than disquiet a comfortably exclusive Euro-American version of the North American past";[5] he also reminds readers of the violence and theft associated with the "Founding" by announcing a competitor to the mythologizing of George Washington. As Barry O'Connell notes in his well-wrought introduction to the collection, "Apess cannily manipulates the rhetoric of patriotism" to place the American founding in a more contentious context.[6] But even a relatively straightforward rendering of the events surrounding the assault on the Pequots should go well beyond the effects of Apess's words.

The story of the "Pequot War" is ugly, disturbing, and especially devastating to the consensual narrative that has been a feature of the dominant representation of "American" history. Before the war, armed encounters between colonists and Native Americans were primarily skirmishes provoked by individual acts of violence, theft, or kidnapping. A series of such events provided the pretext for the genocidal attack on the Pequots in 1637. The Dutch and the Pequots had engaged in a violent trade dispute years earlier. A Pequot sachem was kidnapped and then killed, even though the Pequots had paid the demanded ransom. Subsequently, an English trader was killed at the mouth of the Connecticut River in 1633. The English blamed the Pequots for the killing, but the Pequots steadfastly refused to acknowledge responsibility.

In September of 1636 a large armed force left Boston by ship and anchored in Pequot harbor (on what is now the Thames River between New London and Groton). In a meeting with the Pequots' emissary, Commander John Endicott demanded that those responsible for the murder be turned over. As in their prior responses, the Pequots said that the killers were in fact Narragansetts, that the trader, James Stone, had tried to kidnap some of that tribe's members, and that in any case, the actual killers were now dead.[7]

Endicott refused to accept this version, and it became evident that the purpose of his expedition went well beyond a mission to punish those responsible for a crime. The Pequots were the most numerous and powerful tribe in the area and, most significantly, they controlled the production and distribution of wampum, the small shell beads that Eastern nations used as both a mechanism for storing wealth and for effecting exchanges. Wampum had mainly ritual and cultural significance; the exchange of wampum was not a money transaction. It was used to create sacred intra- and intertribal bonds. However, it came to be used inland by Euro-Americans to trade for Iroquois furs, which were then sold on European markets at great profit.

The role of European appropriation of wampum in the destruction of the Eastern nations is elaborated later. Suffice it at this point to note that more was at stake in the assault on the Pequots than righting a particular wrong or avenging an English death. When the Pequots would not capitulate, and various skirmishes against their highly mobile group of warriors proved indecisive—indeed, the encounters provoked their anger to the point where local settlers were endangered—Captains John Mason and John Underhill abandoned the skirmish model and led a force in a surprise attack on the Pequot fort in Mystic with the largest concentration of Pequot dwellings.

Although the surprise was total, the Pequots fought back so effectively that Captain Mason gave orders to set fire to the village. He ignited one of the tepees himself, and Underhill's force detonated gunpowder at another spot. Then the English retreated from the fort to watch the intense fire kill most of the five hundred inhabitants. Those who made it outside the palisades—men, women, and children—were shot at or stabbed with swords, and many of those who survived the English attacks were killed by warriors in an outer ring of Mohawks and Narragansetts allied with the English.

Although their Native American allies admired the English plan for surprising the Pequots and delighted in seeing their once powerful adversaries brought low, many were appalled by the genocidal result. Hearing the screams of those dying within the fort and seeing the deadly assaults on those who managed to flee the flames, many of those whom Underhill called "our Indians" "cried Mach it Mach it; that is, It is naught, it is naught, because it is too furious, and slays too many men."[8] But the English had a far more rapacious and totalizing view of war than did the Native Americans. Underhill had already expressed contempt at Indian warfare tactics, feeling that they lacked professionalism; "fight is more for pastime, than to conquer and subdue enemies," he said. And Mason concurred, stating that their "feeble Manner . . . did hardly deserve the name of fighting."[9]

At a minimum, the English did not share the Native American cultural constraints on violence. The decisive battle failed to satisfy their destructive impulses, and roughly two months after the burning of the fort, Captain Israel Stoughton traveled to the Pequot River with 120 Massachusetts militiamen and Narragansett guides to help hunt down Pequot refugees hiding in a nearby swamp. Finding themselves surrounded, the Pequots surrendered. Many of the male captives were killed (hurled bound into the ocean), and the women and children were sent into servitude either in the Caribbean or with local tribes.[10]

The attitude of the English commanders to the results of the destruction of the Pequots went beyond complacency; they saw their actions as morally vindicated. In addition to invoking the code of military professionalism to justify their genocidal approach to their hostilities with the Pequots, they found legitimation in their reading of Scripture. For example, allowing that the scene of the burning and killing at the fort produced a "most doleful cry," Captain Underhill, in response to queries about slaughtering women and children, responded: "We had sufficient light from the word of God for our proceedings."[11] And this view only strengthened during the colonial period. The prominent Puritan preacher Increase Mather, writing an account of the war forty years later, emphasized the power of prayer, which, he argued, delivered his people from "the rage of the heathen."[12] Mather ascribed the burning of the fort to the action of "the Lord": "The Lord burnt them up in the fire of his wrath, & dunged the ground with their flesh, it was the Lord's doing, and it is marvellous to our eyes."[13]

At least one prominent dissident voice among the colonists resisted the position that "the Lord" had it in for "the heathen." Roger Williams argued that "God" favored no nation. In his discourse on the name "heathen" in 1645, he said that the "elect" were not white and located in the Massachusetts colony, and he opposed the spatial imaginary that provided the major legitimation for European expansion, the view that lands used by the "Indians" were not occupied.[14] Although Williams resisted a variety of arguments used by colonists to assert their cultural superiority—land use practices, literacy, and so on—he consistently manifested horror at pagan religious practices, and he particularly hated and feared the Pequots. Ultimately he played a role in their destruction, working strenuously to convince the Narragansetts to avoid a federation with the Pequots just prior to the war. As Drinnon puts it, Williams was "a one-man office of strategic services," warning Governor Winthrop of Massachusetts of Pequot war preparations and sending a sketch of their forts.[15] But unlike the various enthusiasts for divine revenge, Williams expressed the view that "it would be pleasing to all natives that women and children be spared."[16]

## Economic Geographies

The Pequot War has virtually no place in the Euro-American telling of the history of warfare or in the story of gradual proprietary control over the North American continent. To give it a place of importance, it is necessary to analyze the forces at work that allowed the Pequots and their practices to be so devalued as to become targets of an attempt at total extermination. Moreover, such an analysis serves as a prelude to what I shall be calling an ethnographically oriented approach to warfare, one that is aimed both at disclosing the interpretations through which warring groups impose meaning and value on each other and at providing a critique of approaches to warfare favored by many contemporary historians and political scientists. The dominant, strategically oriented treatment of war, historical or contemporary, provides a rationale for violence rather than for respectful encounters. More specifically, a geographic imaginary, a nation-state–oriented geopolitical map, which provides the ground plan for what are known as "security studies," tends to frame conduct and events within a state-oriented cartography and thereby reproduces the structures of nonrecognition operating in the seventeenth century, when Pequots turned out to be easy prey for merchants, militias, and moral consciences.

To resist the nonrecognition built into the recognitions permitted by this cartography, two related aspects of the forces producing the cartography of North America imposed from Europe bear consideration; the first set of forces are economic and the second moral. The consideration of the economic forces requires a more detailed treatment of the European assault on wampum, which preceded the armed assault on the Pequots.

By the seventeenth century, a relatively new Euro-centered economic map had developed. The most efficient way to describe it is to follow

Immanuel Wallerstein and note that as the European world economy came into being in the fifteenth and sixteenth centuries, there developed a European core, a "periphery" that was a zone for the "production of lower ranking goods . . . goods whose labor is less well rewarded," and "the external arena," which "consist[ed] of those other world-systems with which a given world economy has some kind of trade relationship, based primarily on the exchange of preciosities, and what was sometimes called the 'rich trades.'"[17] As the external arena was pushed outward from Europe by the primary, mercantilist powers—the French, English, and Dutch were those who settled and traded extensively in North America—they brought about the beginnings of a "production of spatial configurations" that was later to be part of "the historical geography of capitalism."[18] In the Connecticut region, it was first the Dutch and then the English—operating out of a mercantilist cartography that saw the world through the eyes of the trader—who played a major role in incorporating the North American territories into an external trading zone.

The trade was triangular: the European traders acquired wampum from coastal tribes in exchange for manufactured goods—iron implements and textiles—and then traded the wampum inland with the Iroquois in exchange for furs, which were then very profitably sold in Europe, until the market was glutted late in the seventeenth century. The appropriation of wampum use was so effective for the Euro-Americans that after Isaac de Rasieres of the Dutch West India Company sold fifty English pounds worth to the pilgrims at Plymouth, their sale of the furs they acquired with the wampum greatly reduced their debt to the English sponsors of the *Mayflower* voyage. It had been de Rasieres who, in 1624 as the treasurer of the Dutch West India Company, had suggested trade based on the shell beads after requests for silver coins by Dutch colonists had been denied by company officials back in the Netherlands.[19] By 1627 the trading triangle had been established, and furs could not be obtained unless wampum was part of the deal.[20]

It was also the case that by 1627 and throughout the decade preceding the Pequot War, Dutch and English competition for wampum pushed the price up dramatically. The relatively abrupt appropriation of the wampum, that is to say, the pressure that European traders exerted to change it from a repository of local value and an instrument of cultural transactions to a money form, was not the single-handed achievement of de Rasieres. The appropriation began in the Virginia colony and diffused northward as trade relations in New England achieved the same frantic pace they had in Virginia.[21]

Most significantly, the use of wampum as legal tender in Connecticut was a prime initiating condition of the Pequot War.[22] It was evident that the English were keenly aware by 1627 that wampum had contributed to the Pequots' dominance in the region. In addition to being warlike and numerous, they were situated in between the wampum producers of the coastal regions (primarily Algonquins) and the inland Iroquois.[23] However, the Pequots' political effectiveness was not merely a function of their ability to deliver violence. They were a highly organized, complexly differentiated society. In addition to their leadership posts, with tribal units run by the hereditary positions of sachems (or sagamores), they had various councils—of elders and of women, among others—who shared in the decision-making process. And like those of other Eastern nations, their intra- and intertribal relations involved a highly norm-governed pattern of gift giving that helped maintain their systems of authority and provide for indigent tribe members.[24]

Most important for the wampum connection, the Pequots effectively controlled its supply and distribution. And it was especially valued by the main suppliers of furs, the Iroquois, who valued it for a variety of reasons. As a repository of value it was measurable on the basis of the labor required to shape and bore the beads. It was regarded as aesthetically pleasing while being easy to assemble into ornamental garments, and because wearing wampum in various forms was controlled within the tribe—with more elaborate belts and other garments allocated to higher-ranking persons—it served as an important social sign.

Beyond these dimensions of value, wampum also played an important role in Iroquois cultural and intertribal practices. Wampum exchange established reciprocal obligations between tribes and was involved in the founding and maintenance of various peace treaties, most notably the Iroquois League. Wampum was therefore precious on several levels. It played a role within tribes as a part of the system of social recognition and between tribes as an expression of bonds of reciprocity and obligation. Moreover, it extended the life of a tribe into the spiritual domain, for wampum had a pervasive existence in the mythologies of several of the Eastern tribes. Most tribes in the region told wampum stories that ascribed a mystical power to the beads.[25] For example, although they knew that wampum was manufactured by coastal tribes, the Iroquois gave it a pseudo-origin by telling a story about wampum issuing from the noses of pipe-smoking sorcerers at councils, with the effect that peace treaties were created with its subsequent use. Similar stories were told by other tribes, suggesting a degree of shared value for the wampum at a spiritual level.

Apart from deriving its significance from stories, the wampum itself, when it was arranged in belts, told stories. Wampum belts were therefore a form of writing. Although for the Euro-Americans wampum belts did not carry the authority of their inscriptions, for the Iroquois they were land deeds and treaty records. As noted in an analysis of Euro- versus Native American writing, "the length and shell configuration of Indian wampum belts represented the specifics of Indian land treaties."[26]

In short, strengthened by cultural practices and commitments, wampum served as a communication technology and a mechanism of symbolic exchange. These aspects of wampum made it an important instrument of the cultural resistance to intertribal violence. Prior to the Dutch and English pressures to transform wampum into money, its cultural significance was in effect integral to Native American identity at tribal and intertribal levels. During the period in which it was controlled wholly by the tribes, wampum was not strictly speaking "money," for as Marcel Mauss notes in his analysis of gift exchange: "There is money only when precious objects, condensed wealth or tokens of wealth are made into money—when they are named, impersonalized, detached from relationships with moral, collective or individual persons other than the authority of the state which mints them."[27] But wampum was clearly money-ready in that it was located at what Mauss identified as an intermediate stage between wholly subjective gifts bestowed to create bonds and items with both subjective and more extended value dimensions, what he calls "certain things, most of them magical and precious," that "circulate within the tribe and far outside it" to "serve as a means to count wealth and make it circulate."[28]

With the wampum story as background, the destruction of the Pequots, and ultimately Eastern tribal life as a whole, can be seen to have been overdetermined by the colonial expropriation of wampum, its capture and conversion into a money form. Once the Pequots were vanquished in the War of 1637, the English pushed up the price of wampum, gave it a specific, bead-per-penny value, and accelerated their demands for wampum tribute payments from Eastern nations by charging them with various "crimes." The records show a tribute total of seven million beads, valued at roughly five thousand English pounds, for the period 1634 to 1664.[29] While the extracted wampum helped underwrite the cost of colonization, it also was a disaster for the wampum-producing tribes. For example, Algonquin labor was totally absorbed into the colonial economy, with the expected destructive result on the Algonquin way of life.

The wampum assault thus effectively accelerated the breakdown of cultural traditions and relationships among coastal tribal communities, for the trade in general and the wampum exchange system at the center of it were bound up with the intra- and intertribal social web as a whole. The Iroquois nations, like other Eastern nations, were fundamentally structured through their relations of reciprocity rather than dominance. As Francis Jennings has put it, "to speak of trade is to speak of the whole public existence of the trading tribes."[30]

In addition, although the increased flow of wampum from the coast to the Iroquois produced a temporary prosperity for them, by the end of the century they too were attacked by Euro-American settlers and traders, for they stood in the way of the expanding political-economic map. The "external arena" of trade was being pushed westward, beyond their territory, and the push was not a function of merely local rationalities; it stemmed in part from an altered trading context in England. In the 1620s the House of Commons enacted laws that broke the monopolistic control of the Merchant Adventurers of London and the Shrewsbury Drapers over the trading of manufactured textiles, thereby unleashing formerly pent-up expansionary forces.[31]

As for the Pequot part of the story during this period, the Pequots who survived the war and were distributed into servitude in local tribes rather than being sold into slavery in the Caribbean turned out to be expensive chattel. Wampum tribute was extracted from these tribes on a per-Pequot basis. There were roughly two hundred Connecticut Pequots remaining in 1638, a year after the war. Eighty had been given to the Mainatonomo and seventy to the Ninigret (both Narragansett tribes) and one hundred to Uncas of the Mohicans. The "crime" of harboring Pequots was the pretext for payment demands.[32]

The "Pequot War" can be subsumed into a more general story of the assault on "Indian" identity. The relentless push of the cartography of the state-oriented political economy, which moved the external zone across North America in the seventeenth, eighteenth, and nineteenth centuries, destroyed the tribes not only through direct warfare (and of course the even more lethal effects of European diseases) but also through the war on indigenous cultural systems of meaning and exchange.

The special attribute of tribal exchange, as Mauss has pointed out, was the irreducible value of exchanges themselves. Thus, for example, even as the wampum flow into the Iroquois tribe increased, its value was not degraded within the tribe because its cultural significance remained the same. However, the wampum became more scarce among the tribes as the demands for tribute increased. By the eighteenth century, the English took over its manufacture on their lathes, and thereafter the tribes lost not simply the beads but also the major instrumentality of their cultural exchanges as well as historical memories, for their writing implements were being expropriated.

It should also be noted that expropriation of wampum constituted an attack on another important tribal practice. Wampum also served among the Iroquois as an instrument of condolence. It was invested not only with the power to instill like-mindedness in order to diminish grievances but also with a healing power to comfort those experiencing grief.[33]

As a result of the disturbance to the Eastern nations' source of peacemaking at all levels as well as the disturbance that the trading created in the preexisting pattern of their territorialities, intertribal violence increased among them. The appropriation of the wampum and the European inward movement created, between tribes that had managed to reach agreements that inhibited violence as well as maintained territorial boundaries, a violent animosity that produced more destructive intertribal wars than had been previously experienced. The intervention of European trading practices shuffled tribal alliances with the result that often tribe and colony were pitted against tribe and colony. For example, Hurons had adapted to French dominance, while others (Mohawks, for example) resisted.[34]

Thus, while the English militias and the Connecticut Assembly had virtually erased Pequotness, English political economy went on to play a major role in the erasure of Indianness. The roughly century-long process through which the Eastern nations were almost totally destroyed constituted a paradigmatic example of "war," if war is regarded as something aimed not only at causing death and injury but also at destroying collective integrity. Warfare, on this account, is effected "to destroy the very way the enemy perceives itself, the way it forms its identity."[35]

In short, the process of destroying Indianness was accelerated by destroying or appropriating the resources of Native American common identity practices. Certainly, tribal relations were often violent before Euro-American intervention altered their priorities. The prior Pequot dominance in the coastal region was aggressive and conflictual, but at the same time it helped maintain the stability of wampum as a cultural resource.

In addition, the manipulation of legalities provided a supplement to the war on Indianness once wampum had been wholly appropriated. The "General Laws and Liberties of Connecticut Colonies," revised in 1672, contained a provision against yet another Native American consensual process, the powwow: "It is hereby ordered that no Indian shall at any time powaw."[36]

Nevertheless, the powwow has survived, and a recent one is implicated in contributing an ironic turn to the story if we take it up to the present. The Connecticut Pequots have survived their holocaust and are thriving financially as a result of their federally mandated control over casino gambling in the state. A *New York Times* reporter expressed puzzlement about the way the Pequots have channeled their largesse into political campaigns.[37] The descendants of the Connecticut Pequot tribe, the Masantucket Pequots, have made millions of dollars with their casino and had put $315,000 into Democratic Party campaigns as of 1994.[38] The reporter notes that the Pequots were impressed not only because local Democrats helped the tribe gain federal recognition but also because President Clinton participated in a powwow. He held an

"American Indian Summit at the White House, which the Pequots viewed as symbolically significant." What the commentator and apparently others are puzzled about is that the tribe is financing candidates throughout the country who have no direct connection with tribal interests. For example, it is noted that they put $50,000 into an Iowa campaign, where Democrats said "the Pequots had asked for nothing in exchange for their $50,000 donation."[39]

Although the extent to which contemporary Pequots retain a broad range of seventeenth-century cultural practices is unclear, it appears that they consider themselves culturally coherent and distinct and retain elements of the practice of gift exchange.[40] In the context of tribal culture, the donations are gifts freely given, not exchanges meant to produce tribal profit. They establish a firm bond between tribe and Democrat, a form of solidarity-building, not a transaction in the ordinary commercial sense. Having largely obliterated cultures that use gifts in this way, and having failed to negotiate new practices in confrontation with incommensurate practices of others with whom they have shared space, Euro-Americans remain puzzled by a practice that has survived their destructive assault. The *Times* reporter's reaction is symptomatic of how destructive the encounter was not only to peoples but also to possible modes of comprehension.

Among the questions that this part of the story raises are, What has driven this persistent failure of comprehension? Why is it that Euro-American peoples have remained relatively impervious to learning about tribes and thus about themselves in relation to them? The Indian/Other has, in various ways, haunted Euro-American identity politics but has produced relatively little effective self-reflection. To pursue this issue, it is necessary to turn to the other forces behind the European-imposed cartography of America. The political economy cartography, which formed the interpretive and practical structures behind the Euro-American pursuit of land across North America, was aided and abetted by a moral geography; there has been a moral/political imaginary that has complemented the historically evolving map of nation-states and has been complicit in the withholding of recognition and respect from indigenous nations. In order to understand the moral and political status assigned to tribal peoples during the European advance in North America, one must therefore appreciate the moral and political dimensions of cartography.

## Moral Geographies

Michel Foucault put the matter of geographic partisanship succinctly when he noted that "territory is no doubt a geographical notion, but it is first of all a juridico-political one: the area controlled by a certain kind of power."[41] Now that global geographies are in flux, as political boundaries become increasingly ambiguous and contested, the questions of power and right are more in evidence with respect to the formerly pacified spaces of nation-states. The "pacification" was violent, but the violent aspects have been suppressed because the narratives and conceptualizations of familiar political science discourses of comparative politics and international relations, which have been aphasic with respect to indigenous peoples, have been complicit with the destruction of indigenous peoples and their practices. While these discourses now appear increasingly inadequate, it is less the case that they have been made invalid by changes in the terrains to which they were thought to refer than it is that the extended period of relative geopolitical stability during the cold war discouraged reflection on the spatial predicates of their intelligibility. Statecentric academic, official, and media political discourses approached adequacy only in their role of legitimating the authority of nation-states. Helping to contain ethical and political conversations within the problematics that served the centralizing authorities of states and the state system, they were complicit in reproducing modernity's dominant, territorial imaginary.

To recognize that the dominant geopolitical map has been imposed on the world by power rather than simply emerging as an evolutionary historical inevitablity, as the dominant consensual narratives would have it, one needs to achieve an effective conceptual distance, to think outside of the state system's mode of global comprehension, outside of the spatial predicates of its structures of power, authority, and recognition.[42] As Henri Lefebvre has noted, space, especially for those occupying it, tends to have an air of neutrality, to appear empty of normative imposition, as "the epitome of rational abstraction . . . because it has already been occupied and used, and has already been the focus of past processes whose traces are not always evident in the landscape."[43]

To the extent that the nation-state geography remains descriptive (what some call "realistic") and ahistorical, the ethics and politics of space remain unavailable to political contention. More specifically, this resistance to the geographic imaginary's contribution to ethical assumptions makes it difficult to challenge the prevailing political and ethical discourses of rights, obligations, and proprieties that constitute the normativity of the state. Nevertheless, the spatial practices of the state—its divisions into official versus unofficial space, local versus national space, industrial versus leisure space—are commitments that are as normative as the spatiality of the Christian imaginary, which divided the world into sacred and profane spaces.

Although they do not appear on the map, cultural and political struggles accompany and continue to challenge the political consolidations of space that comprise modernity's geopolitical map. The alternative worlds destroyed and suppressed within modern cartography become available only when the global map is given historical depth and alternative practices are countenanced. In sum, although the dominant geopolitical map appears uncontentious and nonnormative, it constitutes what I am calling a moral geography, a set of silent ethical assertions that preorganize explicit ethicopolitical discourses.

Although there is increasing pressure on the statecentric frame of understanding, as the state system's ability to code and contain actions associated with "large-scale ethnic mobilizations"[44] has been attentuated, the geopolitical map of states remains the primary model of space. Despite its increasingly active competitors for identity and affiliation, it continues to dominate the determination of how things are valued, actions are interpreted, and persons are assigned identities. Representing the structure of approved sovereignties, it is the primary force determining recognized political subjectivity.

In order to illustrate how the state system's normativity functions, consider two different glosses on events associated with the elimination of the border between the two Germanys in 1991. During the same month that the *New York Times* was reporting the trial date for former East German leader Erich Honecker for allegedly ordering East German border guards to shoot to kill anyone seeking to escape to West Berlin,[45] an advertisement appeared in the *New Yorker* magazine for "Warsaw Pact Military Binoculars"; the first full sentence began, "Used by East German border guards along the Berlin Wall . . ."[46]

Thus two social texts, generated from one of the globe's primary information-disseminating centers, performed a similar function. Both participated in the process of inscribing in social memory the significance of the recent cold war. Although multiple meanings can be derived from each, perhaps the most encouraged readings, given the genres and interests of the two expressions, are these: the advertisement, focusing on the deadly acuity of the guard's visioning equipment, the "astounding optical clarity and brightness," promotes a reading of the cold war in terms of the information it can still supply to shoppers interested in acquiring the technology with which it was associated. The news report on the trial aims the reader toward a reflection on the cold war's contribution to an ethical problematic, the contention between norms deriving from reasons of state and codes that transcend or transgress state boundaries.

That the two expressions can appear, if not side by side, at least in a situation of territorial adjacency is testimony to how easily minds can wander from recent horrors, how unstable is a particular ethical focus. Perhaps, as Don DeLillo has represented it, those living in contemporary industrial societies are disoriented by dangers and tend to regain their equilibrium by shopping.[47] Certainly a kind of forgetfulness impedes an effective ethical focus, but it is not the kind I have described. The forgetting that has global ethical import is less a product of wandering minds than it is a structurally induced amnesia, positively constituted by the dominant modes of global comprehension. Contemporary global understandings remain attuned to historical narratives that naturalize a particular, territorially oriented view of sovereignty, reinforce it with a political economy story that disparages precommercial systems of livelihood and exchange, and substitutes myths of evolutionary development for histories of violent confrontation and usurpation.

Forgetfulness is thus less a matter of distraction than it is of historically structured angles of vision. In order to elaborate the ethical and political implications of the institutionalized forgetfulness surrounding the Honecker trial, it is necessary first to locate Honecker's alleged orders in a more general political space, that of state practices of population control. At one extreme of this political problematic was East Germany's sedulous and violent patrolling of its borders. The state as a whole had constituted itself as a vast penal colony. Accordingly, the trial makes the statement that it is illegitimate, indeed unlawful, for a political leader to become a warden. And implicit in this statement is the recognition that ethical concerns transcend national borders; they are not contained by the geopolitical imperatives with which regimes claim dominance.

Looking at the issue from up close—that is, in the context of the contemporary practices through which states hold onto their spaces and the vitality (bodies) within them—the Honecker policy appears as an individual pecularity. Although there are ready-to-hand ambiguities in the assigning of responsibility, the implication of the legal codes deriving from war crime conventions favors a focus on the mentality of a particular perpetrator, one that is relatively easy to individualize and criminalize.

However, if we achieve some historical distance, "mentality" becomes not an individual orientation but a set of practices attached to the governing of the modern state. It is, in Michel Foucault's terms, a "governmentality."[48] More specifically, Foucault pointed out that the governmentality concerned with the management of populations, with surveillance and calculation of the various dimensions of vitality within state borders, did not emerge until the eighteenth century. Treatises on the art of government under mercantilist thought throughout the seventeenth century were preoccupied with sovereignty. In the eighteenth century, forces such as demographic expansion, monetary abundance, and agricultural growth encouraged governments to turn to the problem of managing an economy and to "security," the policing of the boundaries within which this management of people in relation to things was to take place. They became preoccupied, at least in the case of Europe, with the "population . . . as the ultimate end of government."[49]

So novel was this emphasis that prior to the eighteenth century there was no such persistent discursive identity as population:

One of the great innovations in the techniques of power in the eighteenth century was the emergence of "population" as an economic and political problem. Population as manpower or labor capacity, population balanced between its own growth and the resources it commanded. Governments perceived that they were not dealing simply with subjects, or even with a "people," but with a population.[50]

In the eighteenth century, then, various forces produced "the emergence of population as a datum, as a field of intervention, and as an object of governmental techniques."[51] For purposes of situating the practices related to population control in the present, it is therefore necessary to recall that they were already taking shape at least two centuries ago. The modern disciplinary state and society—carried to extremes in the East Germany of Erich Honecker—developed its primary conditions of possibility in the eighteenth century, when a new governmentality formed around its primary target, the "population," which had "as its essential mechanism apparatuses of security."[52]

What made the Honecker technique of population control untoward was less its rigor and brutality than the sudden shift in its spatial support. With the crumbling of the Berlin Wall and the subsequent dissolving of the German Democratic Republic as a sovereign unit, former actions were reevaluated within the new ambiguated ground plan rather than within the rationales of the old territorial state. Although, as a result, Honecker's violent strategy for incarcerating his "population" ran afoul of positive law practiced within nations as well as at a supranational level, in the context of the cold war, with its heightened levels of international enmity, excesses occurred within both strategic power blocs as the concept of "internal security" supplied reasons of state for interventions in academic, artistic, and athletic as well as political domains.

In particular, the nuclear face-off, which raised stakes and, accordingly, tensions, created what Paul Virilio termed an "inversion," whereby the "true enemy" became "less external than internal: our own weaponry, our own scientific might which in fact might promote the end of our own society."[53] While modernity's strategic religion, "nuclear faith," produced no worldwide catastrophes (but significant regional forms of danger from testing), recognition of the dangers that the weapons posed produced an "endo-colonialization,"[54] a serious constriction of the spaces of open, unimpeded exchanges in various societies. As surveillance tightened, forms of otherness within the order became increasingly read as signs of disorder, and states in the West as well as the East had become increasingly carceral.

It is important to recognize, however, that the normalizing power of the state, its control over identity and the interpretation of space, has always had competitors. Insofar as it has maintained control over its space and the identities of its citizens, it has done so through the continuous reproduction of its political identity. Among other things, its territorial map has been maintained with a series of containment strategies, which have ranged from force of arms to the literatures through which the territorial state has claimed coincidence with the nation it purports to represent. However, to say that the United States is a nation is to heed only the dominant cartography and to engage in a form of radical forgetfulness. Rather than forgetting, then, we can turn again to the historical construction of indigenous people within the European imagination and analyze it critically by exercising a genealogical frame to discern the emergence of the interpretations of space implicated in understandings of selves and others.

## Geographic Preludes: A Genealogy of Forgetfulness

The verticality of the premodern, medieval map has been described by Foucault as "a hierarchical ensemble of places: sacred places and profane places; protected places and open, exposed places, urban places and rural places,"[55] and in parallel to these places that "concern the real life of men" was a symbolic or cosmological geography that was similarly vertical: "There were the supercelestial places as opposed to the celestial, and the celestial place was opposed to the terrestrial place."[56]

That these medieval spatial practices had a markedly ethical coding is undeniable. This is evident in the comparison medievalist A. J. Gurevich offers between medieval and modern subjectivities and their spatial predicates: whereas the modern person in liberal democratic societies has "an 'individuality' which likes to regard itself as as completely autonomous and imagines itself as having sovereign rights vis a vis society," in medieval society a person's worth was derived from his or her place in the universal hierarchy with God at the apex.[57] The "individual" therefore has a moral subjectivity tied to national boundaries, to a horizontal, bordered world, which determines levels of autonomy and obligation. This bordered world has largely displaced the vertical one in which actions had trajectories toward a divine domain of judgment rather than a significance determined by geopolitical boundaries.

But we must not imagine that this vertical model is now wholly absent, for history is "conjunctural"[58] rather than linear; older forms persist along with more recent ones. Accordingly, although many contemporary state societies have left the vertical, spiritual geography behind, some nation-states, particularly those dominated by a religious cosmology, have incorporated the vertical axis within their geopolitical imaginary. Accordingly, in those states that owe their legitimacy to a hierarchical, spiritual ordering, all opposition to state authority receives an explicit moral coding as well as a political one.

For example, in the case of Sri Lanka, ethnic strife is read by the dominant Sinhalese Buddhist faction as an assault on the "nation," and thus on the moral integrity of persons and of the unity among persons embodied by the state. Ideological contention is moralized in this instance because it is drawn onto an ontological ground, derived from Buddhist moral geography.[59]

The contrast should not be overdrawn, however, for even in the case of contemporary, secular nation-states, which privilege a horizontal or territorial geography, actions within their bordered imaginary receive moral coding. Exemplary is what William Connolly has called "the moral isolation of nonstate violence," an isolation that "invests nonstate violence with a unique causality and danger" and "implicitly endows state violence with special sanctity."[60]

This moral isolation has encouraged a global ethic that translates the normalizing power of the state into a global normalization aimed at maintaining the legal and moral authority of the geopolitical world of territorial states. At issue at this juncture, however, are the legitimation narratives of state power that suppress the violence through which the territorial systems of states became virtually the only recognizable map. Without recognizing what this map has repressed, we cannot recover an important dimension of the history of warfare and therefore develop an effective ethical and political apprehension that engages peoples who are not easily coded within the dominant system of sovereignties. It is necessary, therefore, to elaborate the forgetfulness and repression that accompanied the production of the international imaginary, the dominant territorial moral geography.

To situate the narrativized forms of forgetfulness in the present, then, one has to return to their points of emergence, to the presuppositions within which the confrontations between different peoples took place. For example, Peter Hulme's discussion of some of the specific discursive commitments that Columbus brought to his Caribbean encounters can be applied more generally to those governing the North American invasion as well: "the panoply of words and phrases used to speak about the orient" (owed to Marco Polo) and the discourse of savagery (owed to Herodotus).[61]

Most significant for present purposes is how this lack of legitimacy of the indigenous system of provenance is connected to the way the "New" or Fourth World emerged in the moral geography governing the European invasions of the Americas. The "Fourth World" emerged as such from the persistence of the Babylonia Mappamundi, which was adopted by the Romans and thence by medieval Christian Europe. Because on this map as it evolved, Asia was the First World, Europe the Second World, and Africa the Third World, the Americas were located in the already available position as the Fourth and thus the "New World."[62]

To the extent that the Americas were the "New World," there could be no interest in the study of its antiquities. Although civilizations had existed there with huge populations for millennia, there was no attempt to recover their history. Moreover, this inattention was overdetermined by the European assumption that these peoples had no historical texts. Their literary media—for example, writing in such forms as knotted ropes and pictorial narratives like those on Iroquois wampum belts— did not fit within the genres of what Europeans recognized as texts.[63]

The sixteenth-century *World Atlas* constructed by Mercator constituted perhaps the most exemplary version of institutionalized forgetfulness of indigenous practices of space. As one commentator has noted, it gave the privileged Eurocentric view of geographic space that "instituted a systematic forgetfulness of antecedent spatial configurations."[64] More generally, since the time of the contact, the histories of the indigenous peoples of the "Fourth World" have not had an impact on the practices and representations constituting public and official cultures. They have not been accorded a significant narrative, and it has been recognized narratives that have been integral to the political subjectivity of the peoples who have commanded and organized the current territorial maps of the planet.

Two other structures of inattention are also implicated in the production of the indigenous peoples' nonrecognition. First, the European image of "culture" has for centuries used monuments and buildings as the most significant markers. Those, for example, who have dwelled in forests have had no significant culture for peoples whose gaze fails to discern the lineaments of culture in the spatial practices of peoples dwelling in areas with limited clearings.[65] Second, the spatial practices that count for purposes of producing citizenship in commercial and industrial societies have been based on the model of the "household." What began during nation-state consolidation and has been firmed up in modernity as recognition for citizens is the "legal address," for "households are . . . units in the political and economic organisation of society."[66] Thus, for example, much of contemporary political geography is preoccupied with such issues as electoral redistricting, for it is concerned with making sure that the institutionalized, legitimate forms of partisanship are equitably distributed.[67]

The influence of these two dimensions of the civilizational rhetoric are decisively represented in an engraved copperplate map of Manhattan Island produced in the late seventeenth century (Figure 1). The contrast between the gridlike regularity of the European settlement and the irregularity of the bodily comportments of the three Native Americans on the opposite shore is dramatic. While the Native Americans are represented as embedded in nature—indeed, in the case of one of the figures, clinging to it in a haphazard way—the settlers are shown to be organized in their proprietary holdings and commercial endeavors (the latter reflected in the ships shown in the middle ground). The Native Americans are also literally marginalized through their representation in the immediate foreground; they are depicted as existing on the margins of the colonial civilization. Moreover, these natives bear a striking re-

Figure 1. Seventeenth-century copperplate map of Manhattan Island

semblance to the European genre for representing Africans. The colonial gaze was clearly structured here by those previous encounters in which the discourse on "savagery" was elaborated.

To appreciate the signifying practices in this and other maps in the colonial period, one has to understand the auspices under which they were created. The Dutch traders, who established the first colonial settlement on Manhattan Island, were connected to a trading company—the Dutch West India Company—that was an "aggressive semipiratical body."[68] While the East India Company was controlled by Amsterdam merchants who were "partisans of peace," the West India Company was run by a coalition of Netherlanders who were "colonizing and warlike."[69]

This privateering spirit was reflected unambiguously in the language with which the West India Company's treasurer, de Rasieres, described the land around Sandy Hook (now Long Island) in his July 1626 landing. From his ship, not irrelevantly named *The Arms of Amsterdam,* he saw a sandy reef, which he described as "a musket shot broad," and narrows whose width was, he added, "about a cannon shot."[70] The trader's gaze, directed by the martial spirit evident in his figuration, belonged to a period in the imperial mapping of new worlds that Joseph Conrad percep-tively called "geography militant."[71]

As Conrad understood, English geographers, like the Dutch (and in the spirit of English political theory), mapped the world based on a belief, emerging during the centuries of the colonizing period, that it was "theirs by right of conquest."[72] Although, as was reported by many Europeans, the tribal nations in North America had complex social practices, agricultures, pharmacologies, and psychologies, Adam Smith, writing roughly a century after the production of the engraving, still referred to "naked and miserable savages" and "wretched natives," whom he regarded as "barbarous."[73] Given the political economy dis-course within which he operated, Native Americans had little worth or productive value without the help of European technologies and assis-tance (even though he lamented the cruel treatment they received from colonizers).[74]

The engraving's ethnographic imaginary was in evidence two cen-turies later. While much of the cultural cartography helping to produce the colonial view of Native Americans emerged from English political economy, it was also reinforced by nineteenth-century English liberal-ism. John Stuart Mill's discourse on the structures of sociability came out of the same civilizational discourse as Adam Smith's political econ-omy a century earlier. As though he were writing the pretext for the en-graving, Mill observed that "a savage tribe consists of a handful of indi-viduals, wandering or thinly scattered over a vast tract of country."[75] Denying that "savages" even had a society, he states that "in savage communities, each person shifts for himself; except in war . . . we seldom see any joint operations carried on by a union of many; nor do savages find pleasure in each other's society."[76] Mill went on to insist on the im-portance of "property" in the British legalistic sense as the grounds for creating both wealth and nationhood, and on this basis denied that "barbarians" have any rights as a nation, "except a right to such treat-ment as may, at the earliest possible period, fit them for becoming one."[77]

For Mill, as for the seventeenth-century engraver of the map, Euro-peans have an order and Native Americans are disordered. This view is clearly inscribed in the engraving through a contrast between the grid-like regularity of the European settlement and the seemingly aimless, unhoused, relatively unclothed, and sparsely distributed Native bodies shown on the fringes of the settlement.

It is important to recognize that the representation of Native Americans as disordered was less an observation than it was an ontological affirmation for Europeans. As James Axtell has noted, the finding of "disorder" alarmed Europeans in the seventeenth century, but it also confirmed their sense of virtue and their belief in the correctness of their own practices.[78] More particularly, the grid that characterized their urban domestic living arrangements spoke not only of virtue but also of the emerging space-time orientations of a commercial society. Paul Carter summarizes this spatiotemporality of the grid, which serves commercial societies:

> Rectilinearity . . . was a spatial stratagem for bringing space within the realm of communication . . . it was a means for speeding up the appearance of things, for hastening the nearness of distant objects. It was the most efficient medium of exchange.[79]

In short, the engraving is a device for translating the spatial practice of political economy into a moral economy. The result is a devaluation—nearly a denial—of the socioeconomic practices of indigenes. It is not a matter of people with differing practices reaching an accommodation. The Europeans' perspective on their encounter with American aboriginals in North America is very much like the one of which Carter wrote in the context of Australia: the aboriginals "constituted the rebellious nature which the authorities had to subdue."[80]

In addition to the moralizing of political economy that the engraving reflects, it also participates in the historical legitimation of "settlement," with all that settled inhabitation implies in a place once used otherwise. Landscapes are not constructed as objects of disinterest; the trading ship in the middle ground speaks of commerce, while the dwellings speak of settlement, and the trees and natives in the foreground represent that which has yet to be domesticated. The map as a whole is therefore one of the rhetorical mechanisms for translating a dynamic space of encounter into a fixed space of settlement, extended into the future.[81]

To settle in, as Carter has noted, has a pervasively linguistic dimension; it involves "a process of teaching the country to speak."[82] Carter's observation travels well from Australia to North America, for a markedly linguistic appropriation is evident in a map drawn roughly twenty-five years after the production of the engraving. In Cotton Mather's "Exact Mapp of New England and New York,"[83] while there are various sections labeled "Indian Country," "Nipnak," and "Country of Narragansett," it is nevertheless largely "ethnically cleansed";[84] it uses English names and church steeple icons to represent each town. Indeed, it should be read as an instrument complicit in a clearing away of indigenous practices of space in order to establish a colonial settlement.[85] By applying names, Mather was involved in the making of a new "spatial history," transforming space into a place of settlement while erasing prior naming practices.[86] It was part of a process of cultural conversion wherein "a negatively perceived place" is transformed "into a place of attachment"[87] as the perceived morally inferior life and culture of Native Americans is effaced.

If we accept the notion that war involves destruction of a people's source of identity, it must be underscored that names are not mere designations of place; they are complex cultural practices. For example, the western Apaches have had for centuries a practice they call "speaking with names."[88] Such speaking is not everyday discourse; "it is considered appropriate under certain circumstances only, and these conditions, which Apaches describe as socially 'taut' (*ndoh*) and 'heavy' (*ndaaz*), tend to occur infrequently."[89] The naming of a place when "speaking with names" involves not just a designation; it includes at least a vantage point for the viewing and a historical reference, and often an entire narrative expressing the location's historic significance. Like the Iroquois use of wampum poles, the speaking is meant to console someone suffering extreme stress; "it is a call to persons burdened by worry and despair to take remedial action on behalf of themselves."[90]

Therefore, to change a landscape, whether nominally or physically, can mean (and did mean in the case of Native American naming practices) to destroy resources central to cultural coherence and survival. Naming practices for Native American civilizations functioned at the same level as proprietory or landholding practices of Europeans. Cotton Mather (among others) was involved in the continuation of the wars

that he and his father, Increase Mather, saw as divinely legitimated affirmations of their culture's practices.

The erasures continued to the extent that by this century, the absence
of indigenous presence was regarded as a preexisting fact rather than an
aggressive spatial practice. By the early twentieth century, Native Americans, as they are constructed within the national imaginary, no longer
hover on the fringes of public space, as they do in the seventeenth-
century engraving, or have areas of habitation as they did on Cotton
Mather's map inaugurating the Christian commonwealth's eighteenth
century; they virtually disappear. An example is an early-twentieth-
century statement in a widely distributed civics text designed to teach
citizenship. As a lesson in political economy and history, the student is
asked to consider her/his inheritances: "When the first settlers came to
this country to live, there was nothing here but a few Indians, and
forests, soil, minerals, rivers, and lakes."[91]

The disappearance of most of the indigenous Americans here is handled by having them not exist in the first place (the Euro-American
"founding fiction"),[92] and what is allowed to become present—soil and
minerals—is the stuff from which modern "prosperity" was produced.
Instead of the violence that a commercial and sedentary people visited
on a more nomadic one, we have a story of the evolution of an economy,
as the authors go on to speak of "houses made out of forests" and "con-
veniences made from minerals."[93] Thus, while a political economy cartography helped launch the invasion of America, as the "external zone"
of commerce was pushed westward, the same political economy discourse is invoked to erase the deed. The Euro-American narrative of
space leaves the aboriginal peoples in prehistory. Those who used the
land for something other than commercial exploitation were not really
there in the first place.

As a result, Euro-Americans, from the entrepreneurial settlers to the
contemporary residents, have functioned within a history of space in
which they developed a vacant land and ultimately established the integrity of an entire continent while emphasizing their material practices
and ignoring the wars of extermination attendant to them. And of
course other media have reinforced the traditional civics curriculum in
this century; *Time* magazine, for example, while it was run by Henry

Luce, refused to print stories on Native Americans.[94] But most significantly for present purposes, Native American peoples, like other non-state nations, have not had a place in the history and cartography of warfare; the discourse on war, like that on political economy, has reinforced the geopolitical, statecentric map. Within the historical cartography of war, indigenous struggles still do not appear.

The omission of native peoples from the discourse on war is evident in a recent mapping of contemporary armed struggles. Bernard Nietschmann demonstrates that although in recent years there has been relatively little warfare between sovereign states, there continue to be enormous casualties and forced dislocations in the struggles between states and various indigenous nations (as well as between states and stateless peoples). Identifying 120 "wars" in 1987, Nietschmann found only 4 that involved conflict between two sovereign states, while 100 of the wars were accounted for by struggles in which states were at war with insurgencies and indigenous nations.[95] These struggles have received little attention, for "media and academia are anchored in the state. Their tendency is to consider struggles against the state to be illegitimate or invisible. . . . They are hidden from view because the fighting is against peoples and countries that are often not even on the map."[96]

Nietschmann's mapping practice is extraordinary because the dominant war cartography has opposed state to state. This dominance in representation is matched by a characteristic of narratives of warfare, "histories" that represent only interstate antagonisms. At the same time that European states were subjugating the peoples in the peripheral trade zones during the seventeenth century, their rulers "managed to shift the balance decisively against both individual citizens and rival power holders within their own states."[97] This led, as Charles Tilly has noted, to the disarmament of the civilian population while the state's "own armed force began to overshadow the weaponry available to any of its domestic rivals."[98]

The most important result, from the point of view of narratives of warfare, is that whereas the distinction between internal and external politics previously had been unclear, it became more distinct in terms of both power and representation. The state's domination of both coercion and its representation resulted in a discourse on war that trivializes what

is "inside," representing within-state violence in terms of law enforcement, the maintenance of domestic security, and so on. By ignoring
various forms of disorder within the national imaginary—that is, per-
petuating the fantasy of an untroubled and unitary order—practices of
violence maintain their ontological function. They operate to protect
boundaries between the "American people" and a dangerous world "outside," while the inside is depluralized as a unitary citizen body.

## War and Ontology

As I have noted, political science discourses on war for the most part are
dominated by a statecentric, strategic orientation. Indeed, so persistent
has been the statecentric, geopolitical cartography that security analysts
often end up reasserting it at the same time that they recognize its limitations. This is evident, for example, in Samuel Huntington's recent attempt to refigure global political geography. Speaking of the "cultural
fault lines" separating different "civilizations," he asserts that they are
displacing state boundaries as the geographic framing of political identity. His next move, however, is to reconstruct a nation-state map in
which civilizational affiliations have a more determining effect on international alliances (that is, nation-state political coalitions) than the old
cold war configuration.[99] Huntington's conceptual recidivism is telling.
Apart from his underestimation of the influence of secular bourgeois
classes in maintaining the strength of states against alternative forms of
solidarity,[100] he redraws the geopolitical map to make the new affiliations he sees conform to a state-oriented set of antagonisms. For such
strategic thinkers, the prevailing discourse on global power is so closely
tied to the traditional state model of space that the geopolitical map is
retrieved in the midst of a discussion aimed at departing from it.

Clearly the persistence of the strategic view is owed to more than reasons of state. Identity-related territorial commitments and the cartographic imaginaries they produce at the level of representation are tied
to ontological structures of self-recognition. The nation-state and its related world of Others persists in policy discourses because of ontological
impulses that are dissimulated in strategic policy talk, articulations in
which spatial predicates are unproblematic. To foreground the significance of ontology in warring violence and to heed the cartographic

predicates of self-Other interpretations, space must be treated explicitly as a matter of practice. Rather than naturalizing spaces of enactment by focusing on the actions by which boundaries are policed, defended, and transgressed—the familiar focus of war and security studies—the emphasis must be on the practices, discursive and otherwise, for constructing space and identity, on the ways that the self-alterity relationships are historically framed and played out. This emphasis requires an anthropological rather than a strategic approach to war, or, more specifically, ethnographic inquiries into how war is located among contending forces at social and cultural levels rather than strategic inquiries into how war is conducted logistically.

While strategic approaches to warfare tend to be explanatory in emphasis (and indeed tend to suppress their interpretive predicates), an ethnographic focus is more concerned with the interpretive practices that sustain the antagonistic predicates of war. Moreover, a critical ethnography attempts to disrupt dominant interpretations by locating the silenced remainders of various discourses. Rather than naturalizing the boundaries by which states maintain their control over the representations of global issues, the focus involves both criticism and recovery. It is aimed first at disclosing how representations of alterity (dangerous Others) reproduce the identities and spaces that give nation-states and nations in general their coherence, and second at disclosing other forms of affiliation uncoded in state-oriented interpretations.

A focus on ontological investments rather than the strategic aspects of warring violence turns our attention to the identity dimensions imposed on interpretations of enemy-Others. To elaborate this identity significance in terms of the Euro- and Native American encounters I have discussed, it should be noted that the erasure of indigenous peoples, in fact and in representation, has been part of the self-recognition by which state societies have territorialized and stabilized their identities. In recent years, however, instabilities in the territorial frames on which nation-states have relied have highlighted the identity stakes attached to state spatial practices, while at the same time making them more contentious. Given the heightened identity anxieties that this instability has produced, it is a propitious time to investigate the significance of those stakes in relation to modern state warfare. An examination of indige-

nous societies, which have tended to foreground the ontological investments and the identity stakes of warfare to which they give rise, provides
an effective, distancing strategy, a way to make that which has been all
too familiar appear strange, or at least historically contingent.

Accordingly, in the analyses that follow, some of those indigenous societies whose practices have been erased, ignored, or trivialized will be
accorded two kinds of recognition. First, unlike the English Captains
Mason and Underhill, who in the seventeenth century regarded Native
American warfare as unprofessional, and John Stuart Mill, who in the
nineteenth regarded it as aimless and disorganized, I take it seriously,
focusing on the war-related practices of space and identity. Second, I
turn in the last chapter to the issue of recognition to raise questions
about the possibilities for a global ethics of encounter between peoples
with incommensurate practices of identity and space, one in which respect for alterity is a primary predicate. The remainder of this chapter
focuses on some of the impediments to thinking through such an ethic.

As I have suggested, a primary inhibition to an elaborated frame for
extending respectful recognition is the state-oriented map, which continues to supply the moral geography that dominates what is ethically
relevant. In effect, states manage an ethical as well as a monetary economy, and, ironically, they have a stronger control over the former, because financial exchanges are more heavily influenced by trans- and
extrastate agencies. To be a subject of moral solicitude one has to be a
subject in general, and in the contemporary state system, the collective
imperatives attached to state-managed territories still hold sway over
political subjectivity. The neglect of ethnic minorities, women, and ves-
tiges of tribal and nomadic and, more generally, nonstate peoples, is tied
to the political and moral hegemony of the state system, which, living in
the perpetual present, has closed the book on the ethics of its cartographic predicates.

What is involved in reopening the book? The most important step is
to get out of the perpetual present where, for example, Huntington took
up residence in his analysis of "civilizational" confrontations as merely
current realities and exclusively in power terms, that is, as increasingly
salient forms of postsovereign global partisanship. The "cultural fault
line" imagery with which he builds the contemporary global map is both

historically and ethically impoverished. As the geopolitical map was formed out of violent confrontations, state boundaries developed and cultural ones were effaced. As a result, states and many nations within states have residual aspects of cultural alterity within them. Such aspects of difference cannot be resummoned by redrawing geographical boundaries, for they exist as invisible forms of internal otherness. Every boundary-firming practice will simply produce new modes of marginalized difference. It is therefore necessary, as Homi Bhabha states it, to change "the treatment of 'difference' . . . from the boundary 'outside' to its finitude 'within.'"[101] The production of a geography within which marginalized peoples can be recognized and accorded political status and moral solicitude requires both a resistance to state system maps that deny otherness within and narrative recoveries that add temporal depth to the global map.

To accord recognition in an ethical sense to peoples whose stories fail to mark contemporary global societies, it is necessary to return to the original imperially driven confrontations and revalue them. A clue to this process is provided in Aimé Césaire's reprise of the historical experience of colonialism. After remarking that it is "a good thing to place different civilizations in contact with each other, [and] it is an excellent thing to blend different worlds,"[102] he goes on to wonder whether colonialism actually produced "contact" and expresses sorrow at the loss of societies destroyed by imperialism: "They were the fact, they did not pretend to be the idea."[103]

Césaire's implication is clear. National societies that have operated within a utopian self-understanding, that have thought of themselves as a fulfillment of a historical destiny, could not be open to encounters. The original colonial encounters did not therefore supply the conquering collectivities with the attenuation, ambiguity, and uncertainty they deserved. But it is not too late. Despite those aspects of difference that have been effaced, the encounters can be imaginatively restaged.

The encounter between French Jesuits and the tribes in the Great Lakes region of North America in the seventeenth century provides an exemplary case. The Jesuit *Relations*, the collected accounts the Jesuits sent back to France, reveal their assumption that only one side had a civilization. For example, Father Le Jeune, who was one of the most prolific writers among them, wrote, "There is some pleasure in taming the souls of the Savage and preparing them to receive the seed of Christianity."[104] This approach to the encounter left Le Jeune and his readers with no vulnerability to indigenous practices and ways of world-making.

In contrast, in Brian Moore's recent restaging of the confrontation, in both his novel *Black Robe* and the screenplay for the film version, the fictional Jesuit, Father Le Forge, becomes vulnerable to native ontology and moral geography and ultimately ambivalent about the relative value of his cultural practices compared with those of the Algonquins and Hurons with whom he travels and dwells. Recognizing that at the time of the encounter, "the indian belief in a world of night and in the power of dreams clashed with the Jesuit's preachment of Christianity and a paradise after death"[105] and resulted in the domination of one world over the other, Moore restages the confrontation in a way that leaves an ambivalent and edified Father Le Forge. It also leaves readers and viewers with both critical distance from the history of Western domination and a new appreciation of the attempts at cultural coherence of a now obliterated society.

The Jesuit-Huron encounter is rethought in chapter 2, which focuses on a comparison of Huron and modern state warfare (while the ethical problematic is reserved for chapter 6). What remains for this discussion is a consideration of how to unread the dominant geographic imaginaries and forgetful narratives implicated specifically in the wars that victimized the first Americans and then to suggest how more attention to these first Americans as well as to other tribal peoples can help to elucidate the ontological dimension of warfare more generally.

## An Ethnographic Imagination

Two related analytic strategies are involved in responding to these issues of warfare. The first involves a critical ethnographic perspective and the second an emphasis on writing. Each analysis in the chapters that follow is structured around radical juxtapositions, often in the form of brief excursions into the ethnographic materials on tribal warfare (and state warfare in earlier historical periods). These excursions supply insights into the war-ontology relationship that is a primary focus of this study, and at the same time they allow those societies to stand against our own.

Moreover, the style of presentation, the writing, is meant to be disruptive to familiar modes of comprehension. Apart from disturbing entrenched interpretations, what the comparisons and contrasts are meant to provide is a "reverse ethnology,"[106] a way of allowing what is unfamiliar about the practices of Others to make our own practices appear peculiar or at least radically contingent.

Historically, ethnology, as it has been practiced in Western anthropology, has had two different foci. One has been aimed at objectifying both the self and alien-Others. While attempting to bracket or neutralize the influence of their own societies, anthropologists working within this perspective have attempted to classify the practices of others in order to develop universalistic codes of human conduct. The other focus has been reflexive or phenomenological, concerning itself with the subject engaged in the analysis and the background of practices in the society from which the analyst's gaze is aimed. After the excursion, the gaze is retrained in the direction from whence it came.

For example, Clifford Geertz's inquiry into the political structures of the nineteenth-century Balinese state was initially aimed at mapping a society in which symbolic actions dominated over instrumental ones. But the analysis was subsequently reflected backward to do a reading of the pervasive and underappreciated symbolic dimensions of interactions in contemporary industrial societies.[107] For those concerned with a reflexive self-understanding, an excursion into an exotic society is a distancing strategy. However, those governed by the assumptions of phenomenological hermeneutics ultimately move toward closure, toward a representation of the fundamental cultural meanings that the actions in their own societies express. In Geertz's case, the inquiry into Balinese symbolic practices was aimed at providing a better appreciation of who we are as a political culture. He concluded that our conversations about ourselves have been inadequate because of our failure to appreciate the expressive and symbolic dimensions of institutions, an insight he gained by examining a society in which those dimensions are more visually and discursively foregrounded.

My use of various historical juxtapositions contrasting current state warfare practices with earlier ones and with those of tribal societies has a similar aim: to show that U.S. warfare partakes of some of the same ontological impetus as that of other societies, particularly tribal societies, which did not overcode their violence with strategic rationales. However, while the result is meant to be disclosure of what tends to operate as a cultural unconscious, I depart from Geertz's hermeneutic tendency to conceive of an investigation as overcoming distance. In contrast to Geertz's aim of reducing the distance between his and other societies as well as between his society and itself, Michel Foucault's reverse ethnologies, which convey the sense of my analyses, were designed to maintain distance and resist resolution. Foucault's focus on the cultural unconscious was not aimed at showing that what lies under what we do is who we are. For him, the "who" is conceived as radically contingent and unstable.

Within a Foucauldian sensibility, discursive and other practices—for example, the discourse on national consensus through which states maintain their legitimacy—must be regarded as one production of a collective self-expression among a variety of possible ones, not an expression of something deeper. The question is not what they ultimately mean to someone or to a collectivity but rather what the political implications are when particular discursive objects emerge and maintain significance at particular times. For example, one could seek to disclose what is enabled and what disenabled by the emergence of "the Vietnam syndrome," which is an interpretation of the United States' post-Vietnam reticence to commit itself to violent international confrontations. The appropriate inquiry would be aimed at identifying the structures of power and authority organized around such a discursive object.

From a Foucauldian perspective, to maintain an ethnographic distance from one's own society is not to seek its ultimate grounds of coherence but to analyze the different forces that impose a particular representation of coherence as well as discerning those opposing forces against which they work. More specifically to the point of the investigations in this study, the point is to be able to gauge the forces that constitute a model of national space and national subjects as well as those that tend toward fragmentation and incoherence in the national imaginary. To do this, such forces have to be made to appear unfamiliar by showing that there have been different models of identity, space, and collective coherence and to show how the apparent stability of the dominant models is belied by the energy that must be spent to maintain them. To conduct such analyses is, in Foucault's terms, to do "an analysis of cultural facts which characterize our culture," to do "something like the ethnology of the culture to which we belong."[108]

The confrontations I stage in the following chapters on warfare are therefore not meant to be construed primarily hermeneutically, that is, as "acts of appropriative understanding."[109] The aim is less to achieve a deeper appreciation of U.S. warmaking by closing the distance between our rationales and conduct and thus to learn who we are than it is to provide a critical distance from the interpretive practices that seek to establish a dominant and unambiguous who.

## Writing against the "American" Imaginary

The second strategy involved in the analyses to follow is also aimed at providing critical distance. This strategy is a response to the observation, made at the outset of this chapter, that much of the construction of the more violent cartographies responsible for failing to respect indigenous Americans have only been more deeply inscribed by mainstream writing in the social sciences and other genres. This has been particularly the case in those genres that have incorporated the story of the advance and consolidation of the Euro-American possession of the continent as if it were an unproblematic destiny—much of the writing on "American history"—and in those that thematize the strategic concerns by which the progeny of Euro-Americans defend that continent by managing their "America" in the face of the dangers they perceive—much of the writing that might be called "security studies."

There are of course notable exceptions, and Richard Drinnon's *Facing West*, which chronicled the rationalizations accompanying the victimization of Native Americans, is a prime example. However, to set up the rest of the analysis in the chapters that follow, I want to focus on the nineteenth-century text that helped inspire Drinnon: Herman Melville's novel *The Confidence-Man*; Drinnon based his subtitle, *The Metaphysics of Indian-Hating and Empire-Building*, on the title of one of Melville's chapters.

Certainly Drinnon's history is a powerful antidote to the more triumphalist versions of the "American Incarnation,"[110] the projection of a destiny narrative on the European possession of North America, which still dominates curricula in the United States from secondary schools through postgraduate education. Would that the events speak for themselves, as the saying goes. But the saying is merely a pious hope. To disrupt deeply entrenched understandings that perpetuate violence and stories that repress it, it is necessary not simply to present historical accounts but also to recontextualize them; it is necessary to challenge the reigning structures of intelligibility that reproduce depoliticized and unreflective understandings. One must not simply present but also write.

Thus, Drinnon's inspirational predecessor, Melville, did not simply say what was happening; he mobilized ironic tropes, enigmatic characters, peculiar narrative structures, and disrupting juxtapositions to challenge the Euro-American imaginary—its views of space and stories of settlement and expansion—that positively moralized and celebrated the consolidation of white domination of the North American continent. The text's satirical edges were, and still are, too sharp for a facile grasp. And it remains inspirational for anyone who wants to engage in cultural criticism of the production of "America" rather than moralize its existence and present a harmonious and untroubled model of the forces that followed the violent founding of the United States.

I do not want to suggest that the chapters that follow approach Melville's achievement as disruptive writing, only that they are written with a similar disruptive aim and draw inspiration from the critical animus behind his writing. It is important to note that *The Confidence-Man* disturbs not simply because of what it says—Drinnon disturbs at the level of content, presenting events I earlier called "disquieting"—but also because "it disturbs the security of reading and communication in general."[111]

*The Confidence-Man* reflects Melville's disgust with the pious celebration of America's sense of community. Where some saw a healthy expanding democracy, Melville saw crass materialism and exploitation, slavery, poverty, and a continuing war of extermination against Native Americans. He saw a series of grotesque violent practices, masked by a dissimulating story of an "America" extending civilization by pushing across the frontier and bringing civilization to the "wilderness."

In the novel, Melville's "America" is a ship, the *Fidele,* headed down the Mississippi River, which divides civilization from the wilderness. The motley crew of characters are the objects in a series of dialogic interactions with a confidence-man, who shifts characters or masks throughout the story. War imagery abounds (the ship resembles a "whitewashed fort"),[112] for as Melville recognized, white America was at war with its indigenous population.

As the novel proceeds, no dominant narrative develops. The confidence-man adopts various personae and has a series of disconnected encounters that reveal nothing beyond the various illusions that constitute the American self-understanding. Having no coherent character of his own—Melville likens him to a "revolving Drummond light, raying away from itself all round it"[113]—the confidence-man serves to disclose the pretensions in the characters with whom he converses, illuminating a society that is essentially a confidence game: it prizes fidelity but has none; it is a society that is fragmented and immersed in violence while it tells itself stories that make it appear to be cohesive and pacific.

Most pertinent to my analysis is the encounter between the confidence-man in the guise of "the cosmopolitan" (representing the ensemble of American characters) and Charles Noble, a clearly false character (a man of "florid cordiality which flushed the man, something in the same fictitious way that the vest flushed the cheek").[114] Noble tells the story of Moredock, the Indian-hater. As the chapter title, "The Metaphysics of Indian-Hating," suggests, the tale is based on hearsay, prejudice, and fantasy; it has no experiential basis. Significantly, however, the Moredock story is called a "history," unlike the other vignettes, despite there being no real Moredock. He is given no biography and is described through a variety of analogies with historical personages. He appears to represent all the fantasies of a society that does not want to acknowledge its responsibility for the violence of its encounters with its indigenous population.

The "history" is full of contradictions. It places a mask of innocence over Euro-American conduct and makes explicit reference to the irrelevance of "Indian" testimony. Melville's text is therefore not, like Drinnon's, a recovery of the history of Indian hating and killing that accompanied the Euro-American push westward. Its object is as much the folly of confidence in a dialogic, consensual community as it is the deplorable, unrepentant, and delusional triumphalism of Euro-Americans.[115] This object is approached textually, through a pastiche of narratives and dialogues that defy facile interpretation. The reader must fall victim to the ironies and narrative involutions in which resolutions are promised and then withdrawn so that confidence in the ability to decipher the story (stories) is lost.

There is no easy political moralizing; the text mocks the very ideal of a simplistic ethics of communication. Its ethical force inheres in its performance of a language that impugns the discourses that provide historical vindication of Euro-American expansion, civilization, and democracy. Its war on such discourses discloses an America at war with its "Indians," at the same time producing a history that must be seen as a confidence game.

Melville's ironic novel plays into the hands crafting the analyses that follow. It helps me set up some issues in the inscription of the "history" of U.S. warfare treated in chapter 5; it encourages the consideration of the ethics of writing, which I discuss at the end of chapter 6; and it encourages a questioning of the place of the "Indians" in particular and tribal peoples in general in providing a critical examination of contemporary U.S. understandings of war, which I treat in the three chapters that follow immediately.

## TWO

# Warring Bodies and Bodies Politic

## Introduction: Desirable Enemies

In the Hegelian construction of human consciousness, self-Other relations are framed within the individual's striving for unity and coherence. The unity of the self results from the dynamics of negation. Because objects and other persons are forms of negation, the stuff against which the self establishes coherence, the human subject develops as a result of an "ontological rift,"[1] a striving to resist being absorbed by otherness.

Hegel regarded war as an especially significant arena of negation, referring to it as a "necessity."[2] This is among the remarks that have fueled debates over whether Hegel was an advocate of war. By *necessity*, however, Hegel meant not accidental. War can be explained philosophically by showing how it is organically linked to other aspects of civic and political association. Ever the theorist of organic connections—they are both what philosophy as philosophy must disclose and a form of life that a healthy society must achieve—Hegel saw war as explicable and as a vital opportunity both for individuals to maintain their ethical duty to the state and for the state to maintain its autonomy and connectedness in the world of states. The controversial section on war from the *Philosophy of Right* reads:

> War is not to be regarded as an absolute evil and as a purely external accident, which itself therefore has some accidental cause, be it in injustices, the passions of nations of the holders of power &c., or in short, something or other which ought not to be. It is to what is by nature accidental that accidents happen, and the fate whereby they happen is thus a necessity.

41

Here as elsewhere, the point of view from which things seem pure
accidents vanishes when we look at them in the light of the concept and
philosophy, because philosophy knows accident for a show and sees in
its essence, necessity.[3]

It is therefore Hegel's philosophy that led him to support war, for war
is organically linked to other aspects of civic, national, and international
life. Just as in his earliest writings he saw as a "necessity" an acceptance of
predatory commercial life, despite its troubled but nevertheless intimate
relationship with the ethical life (*sittlichkeit*) of the community,[4] Hegel
saw war as a necessity because its form of negation helps to maintain the
ethical life of the individual and the state.

Hegel's "advocacy" then, contrary to commentators pro and con, who
treat the issue as one of finding either a direct normative celebration of
war or a statement expressing repugnance,[5] was a consequence of his
philosophically constructed commitments to the state, to the organic
connection between the individual and the state, and, most crucially, to
the dynamics of negation in the maintenance of both.

For the individual, negation—an encounter with an aspect of alterity—strengthens the autonomy and coherence of the self. Hegel's wish
for the state is that it also experience negation in order to strengthen its
autonomy and maintain its coherence. In times of peace, according to
Hegel, civil life threatens the "health and unity of the [state] body,"[6] as
individuals, working for "particular Ends," pour their energies into
"their own special and independent associations."[7] Inasmuch as this
self-interested striving has the effect of "breaking up the whole," the
state must go to war to reestablish its ethical unity. As Hegel puts it,
"government has from time to time to shake them"—those systems that
"tend to isolate themselves"—"to their core by war."[8]

Making it clear that the "government" here is functioning on behalf of
a transcendent historical reason, Hegel shifts the agency of the move toward war immediately, substituting "Spirit" for government: "Spirit, by
thus throwing into the melting pot the stable existence of these systems,
checks their tendency to fall away from the ethical order, and to be sub-
merged in a [merely] natural existence."[9]

The state is therefore the individual in macrocosm for the purpose of
understanding the necessity for a coherence-inducing negation. And

Hegel is explicit about the analogy: "The state is an individual, and individuality essentially implies negation."[10] Hegelian (i.e., spiritualized and individualized) states need enemies for their health and solidarity. And Hegel extends this principle to groups of states. These aggregates are also like individuals, needing negation to maintain their coherence: "Even if a number of states make themselves into a family, this group as an individual must engender an opposite and create an enemy."[11]

Despite his position on war as a "necessity," Hegel disparages particular hostilities and registers himself in opposition to overzealous destruction during war. Again treating states as individuals, he emphasizes the mechanism of mutual recognition through which states are sustained in their autonomy. This exchange of recognition continues during war and functions to inhibit war's duration and destructive aim. Although his language is descriptive, Hegel's commitments to state interdependence and mutual respect, parallel with his views on civic life, should allow the reader to infer an advocacy of limiting war's aims so that "the possibility of peace be retained" and that "war not be waged against domestic institutions, against the peace of family and private life, or against persons in their private capacity."[12]

These inhibitions Hegel wants to apply to war, like his eager acceptance of war as a vital necessity, derive from his philosophy of identity, which he applies consistently across various levels of aggregation from individuals through states to state alliance groups. It is therefore misleading and simplistic to regard Hegel's advocacy of war as an attitude or a direct discursive performance. It is more appropriate to say that Hegel supplies an ontological justification for war. Whatever the claims particular states make to justify war—seeking to increase their protection, to settle grievances or acquire resources—Hegel's interest is in the affirmation they achieve as states by experiencing the "negation" of war through the violent confrontation with another autonomous entity.

We are therefore left with an apparent paradox: the Hegelian war enemy is an object of desire. But if we conceive of "desire" in its Hegelian sense, elaborately explicated in Alexandre Kojève's influential lectures on Hegel, paradox yields to consistency and comprehension. Hegelian desire is reflexive. It is not an emotional projection outward toward an object or person. It is aimed against the other in a way that allows its projection back toward the self. It is what brings a person back to herself or himself. It is animated by a resistance to being absorbed into the object.[13] Through desire a person becomes a conscious and autonomous "I."[14] The external object therefore serves as a force of resistance to be overcome through the action of negation. The individual negates alterity's independence and absorbs it into the I. Desire is not merely a "sentiment of self," something to be satisfied as in the case of an animal desire such as hunger; it is precisely resistance to a fall into animal (i.e., nonself-conscious) nature. Desire moves toward nonbeing or nonnatural dependence by revealing and creating the "I"[15] and thus achieving autonomy and freedom.

Rather than being enslaved by the object, one's confrontations with alterity are aimed at self-recognition, which is a nonbiological desire.[16] The Hegelian enemy, as an object of desire, is therefore an opportunity for the self-affirmation of the state body, an essential moment in the production of its coherence through a recognition of its autonomy and freedom.

The Hegelian ontological impetus toward war is exemplary. Hegel is both instructive about the significance of identity attachments and an exemplar of one committed to the kind of collective identity coherence that translates as a commitment to a strong nationalism. Therefore, rather than allowing Hegel to merely instruct as though he provides a detached philosophical stance, we can also treat his commitment as a datum and seek to discern the pervasiveness of his form of desire; we can learn as much from what he manifests as from the objects of attention in his writing.

Allowing Hegel an exemplary role, we can locate his kind of attachment to war in a more general cultural production of antagonism in which enemy/Others become acceptable—indeed, desirable—targets of violence for ontological rather than merely utilitarian reasons. Antagonistic Others serve as objects to perpetuate the identity of those who locate them as oppositional. This is the case for individuals as well as for collectivities such as peoples, nations, and states. Taking instruction from the broad outlines of this Hegelian model, Edward Said notes that the construction of identity requires an oppositional Other, for the struggles between peoples have involved contention over "historical and social meaning" as much as over territorial control.[17] In the case of war, the use of the oppositional Other involves a more intense and higher-stakes identity confrontation. But in the case of the modern state, this dimension of the antagonism is often difficult to discern because it tends to be overcoded with strategic rationales.

The prevailing orientations toward the study of war in the social sciences rarely attempt such a discernment, despite how pervasive ontological commitments are at various levels of social engagement, up to and including warfare. The ontological interests that Hegel both identified and expressed are nevertheless manifested in contemporary state violence. The modern state's warfare serves not only to maintain strategic interests, which are expressed in official discourses, but also to reproduce or maintain the coherence of the body politic as a whole. Enemy/Others in the case of warfare, as in the case of less violent forms of self-Other confrontation, are to be immobilized, dominated, or destroyed in the interest of the constitution of the national self.

Although the analysis that follows departs in important respects from the Hegelian construction of the ontological interests involved in the confrontation of warring bodies, the focus is nevertheless inspired by the Hegelian construction of desire as an ontological rather than a wholly strategically driven phenomenon. If we entertain the suspicion that an important impetus in modern warfare, in the case of state-dominated societies as well as in others, is both the individual and national body's striving toward unity and coherence, there must be a way to subject this suspicion to a provisional historical test.

The "test" that follows in this chapter is not rigorous. It is an interpretive thought experiment rather than an exercise in hypothesis testing. As is the case with all thought experiments aimed at understanding the dominant institutions of the present, it is necessary to achieve some institutional and historical distance as a first step. Therefore, in order to examine the implications of how the modern individual and collective body's striving toward unity and coherence relates to warfare, it is instructive to recover different institutional and historical bodies. To do this, the analysis turns to various nonstate societies in which ontological aims are more clearly in evidence. However, much of the focus is on seventeenth-century tribal peoples of North America, whose self-interpretations resulted in a body that was more divided and ambiguated, one that did not make the same coherence demands that many have discerned to be characteristic of many of the modern versions of the self and the nation-state.

As I noted in chapter 1, the novelist Brian Moore restaged a confrontation between the Western European self and the version of the self practiced by the Huron tribes of North America (or New France) in the seventeenth century. The Hurons, as Moore presented them, functioned within a self-conception remarkably different from that of the Western Europeans.[18] Moore focused especially on the clash of cosmologies in which "the Indian belief in a world of night and in the power of dreams clashed with the Jesuit's preachments of Christianity and a paradise after death."[19] Moore's restaging of the confrontation can be elaborated through an analysis of some of the same sources he consulted, especially Jesuit writings, which provide both an ethnography of the Hurons and a set of historical autobiographies of the Jesuits doing missionary work in the New France.

The Jesuit-Huron confrontation treated here is thus staged again, textually, with a focus on the articulation between the Huron body and the warring tribal body. Because the primary concern remains with the contemporary versions of this articulation, however, it is necessary first to elaborate some recent ontologies of warfare by receiving further instruction from Hegel, who in accord with his preoccupation with identity and emphasis on the ontological significance of confrontations provides a frame for regarding social, national, and international bonds as exchanges of recognition rather than, for example, mediations of interests or rationalistic decisions.

Hegel framed the self-Other encounters through which individuals and groups achieve coherence within an economy of recognition. Thus, as Kojève puts it, "the [man] who desires a thing humanly acts not so much to possess the *thing* as to make another *recognize* his *right* . . . to that thing, to recognize him as the *owner* of the thing."[20] Extrapolating to the violent encounters of war, Kojève notes that, in effect, "[Man] will risk his biological *life* to satisfy his *nonbiological* Desire."[21]

The desire for things, in the Hegelian construction of desire, is therefore merely a reflection of the more basic desire for recognition, the striving for autonomy and unity. Within this framing, individuals and collectivities are not isolated, self-developing forms of consciousness; they are dependent on each other for their self-consciousness. Just as being an autonomous individual requires recognition from others, the existence of a state's autonomy is a function of its ability to achieve recognition from other states. While this leads in both cases to actions, sometimes violent and intrusive, aimed at enforcing or extracting recognition, much of the exchange of recognition is semiotic; it is an exchange of signs.

Because sign exchange is in part an expression of desire or ontological dependence—the debts that identity has to alterity—any analysis of the ontological stakes of warfare must heed structures of expression, for the social body both reveals and conceals its relationship to warfare. Given the present situation of Western nations that are conflicted about their warfare, unlike those historical tribal societies that embraced their warring activities with little ambivalence, the contemporary revealing and concealing of America's warring past operates within a delicate and contentious structure of expression.

## The Faces of Warfare

Currently, the warfare of the modern state reveals two different faces. Its most prominent face is turned toward the light of official, public recognition, for its features are described primarily in official releases (and in those journalistic and academic discourses that slavishly reproduce official articulations). This is warfare as an instrument of state policy and, as such, the physiognomy of warfare represents itself as expressive of a deeper logistical "truth": the need for the state to approach a dangerously disordered world with force. Instrumental and rationalistic talk links the features of war with enduring projects of the state: maintaining security, clearing spaces for effective and vital functioning, meeting obligations to friends, and so on.

In time of war, this face is almost continually bathed in light. In time of peace it is illuminated only on occasion. Being temporarily out of work, it is unveiled at fleeting moments (for example, the Memorial Day parade) to wink at us as a reminder that although it is now largely unseen, it remains watchful and ready. If one takes the long historical view, however, this face is rarely out of work. Its nose is almost always to the grindstone. That many think otherwise is largely a function of the contemporary tendency to construe hostilities as temporary readjustments, as aberrations from the norm of peacefulness in policy as well as in fact. This tendency has been expressed as a historical narrative in which humanity's warlike tendencies, from tribal societies through imperial dynasties to the international system of states, have been mitigated by the rule of law.

The other face of warfare is ontological rather than strategic; as I noted earlier, it is focused more on the affirmation of identity than on the instrumental effects of the use of deadly force. The signifying practices associated with this face of warfare are episodic. For example, in the United States in recent years, the visibility it has achieved has been affected by changes in the symbolic status system. During a significant portion of the post–Vietnam War years, combat veterans became increasingly invisible. Having fought in a war that many wanted to forget, these veterans, and to some extent war veterans in general, moved to the periphery of the societal system of sign exchange. Their chairs on the podiums of public festivities became vacant as warfare lost its prestige. This second face of warfare had, for a time, to remain largely in the shadows.

More recently, however, what has been interpreted as a markedly decisive military victory for the United States and its partners in the Gulf War has coaxed this face out of hiding. Without reviewing all the features—not the least of which was the appearance of General Norman Schwarzkopf, the Gulf War commander in chief, on a television quiz program—it should suffice to note the proliferation of license plate insignia on motor vehicles. Throughout the nation, people stranded in lines of traffic going to and from work can read while they wait. Emblazoned directly on some plates are the words "wounded combat veteran," or on the license plate bracket "combat veteran."

It would be an exaggeration to say that military signs have become a pervasive part of contemporary social life. It is the case, however, that they have recently increased their visibility. They are now a more significant part of a national level of the exchange of recognition because the national mood in reaction to recent warfare has encouraged military signs to reenter the sign exchange process. Taken as a whole, this serves as a reminder that despite the prominence of the strategic face of warfare—its outward-reaching role as a projection of the state, its ontological face—its inward-reaching role as part of the constitution of identity remains significant.

This increased scrutiny of military signs was especially evident in a controversy that surfaced in late 1994 as the Smithsonian Institution prepared to exhibit the *Enola Gay,* the B-29 aircraft that dropped an atomic bomb on Hiroshima during World War II. Stirred to action as a result of an article in *Air Force Magazine* in April 1994, veterans' groups and ultimately several members of Congress objected strenuously to the planned accompanying narrative, which raised questions about both the morality of targeting a civilian population and the legitimation used for the decision to drop the bomb: preventing U.S. casualties that might result from a ground invasion.

The *Air Force Magazine* writer attacked the Smithsonian exhibit for being "political" rather than merely "aeronautical."[22] However problematic such a distinction might be, the resulting pressure led to a significant change in the exhibit. The narrative, which would have encouraged perception of the bombing as controversial, was omitted. As a result, a controversial military symbol was to be displayed without articulation of the ambivalence that has often accompanied the public expression of warring activities in the United States since the Vietnam War. Nevertheless, the controversy reflects a continuing national agonism over the place of past wars and current militarism, an interpretive struggle in which the interested parties emphasize both national and individual identity stakes.

## Tribal Societies and Military Signs

In order to place this dimension of warfare and its relation to a society's identity economy in perspective, it is useful to examine a society in which military signs played a more continuously prominent role. In sharp contrast to the modern state, for which warfare, however chronic it remains, has been disparaged in a variety of cultural media, are those tribal societies for whom warfare was recognized as intimately constitutive of the body politic. Given the prestige and ontological depth of warfare and, accordingly, the prestige of the warrior, these societies have tended to make the signs of warfare a continuous and legitimate part of everyday life.

The Mexica Aztecs, in a hundred-year period during the reigns running from Itzcoatl, in the early fifteenth century, to the second Moctezuma, provide one of the more extreme historical cases of the unabashed celebration of war, which they represented as a complex system of adornment.[23] Not all men were warriors, but a high percentage of the society's able-bodied men participated in war, and those who did wore dramatic, easily read signs of their personal warring history. The war-society relationship was both vocational and extensively semiotic; those connected to military affairs displayed that relationship. Parents who wanted their male children to be warriors struck a deal with a military instructor early in the child's infancy, and when training began at the age of fifteen, the inchoate warrior's body became a bearer of warring signs: "The hair on his head was shorn, but at the age of ten a tuft of hair was allowed to grow on the back of his head, and by the age of fifteen, it was long, signifying that he had not yet taken captives in war."[24]

By the time that inchoate warrior had become an adult fighter and had taken two captives, he went to the palace to receive a mantle with red trim from the king. For three captives he got a richly worked garment and for four, a special war garment as well as a complete haircut.[25] As a result, Aztec public space was dense with military signs, for "status achieved in war was marked by the honors one received, the way one's hair was worn, the jewelry one was entitled to wear, the clothing one wore in peace, and the arms, armor, and insignia one wore in war."[26] In short, there was nothing esoteric about the warring body; it was perpetually visible within the social body displaying its combat history.

For the Aztecs, then, it is hardly metaphorical to say that they wore their warfare on their sleeves. More importantly for conceptual purposes, along with this exoteric representation of combat biographies, Aztec society also wore its ontology on its sleeve. Although it was certainly the case that some of Aztec warfare was strategic and predatory inasmuch as it involved territorial conquest, the taking of captives, which provided the basis for the society's paramount military sign system, was primarily ontological. The enemy/Other seemed to have been there less to provide a managed space to be taken over than to provide

bodies as a resource for collective ritual as well as individual status striving. Captured enemy soldiers became slaves who served not only as
workers but also as iconic tributes to their captors. In addition, after rendering labor service and symbolic capital, they became the sacrifices for
feast days and other religious observances. Accordingly, they were the
adversaries against whom the Aztecs could develop not only their individual martial skills and prestige but also their collective identity, their
location in a cosmos occupied by the spirits nourished by the sacrifices.

This ontological service the enemy provided was most evident in a
particular, specifically demarcated form of war. "Flower wars" were dis-
tinguished from wars of territorial conquest in that their primary purpose was demonstrating martial skills and serving the subsequent prestige structure. Though at times these wars developed into territorial
wars, flower wars were used primarily to secure captives as well as to
provide combat training.[27] In particular, the securing and sacrificing of
captives and the role played by sacrificing them makes clear the ultimately inward, ontological aim of Aztec warfare. As the historical schol-
arship has shown:

> Whatever else it may have been human sacrifice was a symbolic expres-
> sion of political domination and economic appropriation and, at the
> same time, a means to their social reproduction. . . . The sacrificing of
> slaves and captives and the offering of their hearts and blood to the sun
> thus encoded the essential character of social hierarchy and imperial
> order and provided a suitable instrument for intimidating and punishing
> insubordination.[28]

Aztec as well as enemy death was part of the ontological impetus of
war. To die in a flower war "was called xochimiquizli—flowery death,
blissful death, fortunate death."[29] The flower wars therefore represented
the ontological part of the Aztec military repertoire. That they were not
strategic, as in the case of wars meant to appropriate someone else's
wealth or to expand territory, is evidenced by the formality surrounding
these wars—a set day, a sacred place, and accompanying religious ritual
such as the burning of incense between the two armies before they engaged. It would therefore be inapposite to approach this dimension of
tribal warfare with the traditional political apprehension that links violence with reasons of state, which are understood rationalistically and

strategically. But it is equally important to avoid assigning a wholly rationalistic structure to the warfare of the modern state.

## State Societies: An Ontological Clue

In the case of the modern state, the ontological dimension of warfare is more fugitive, for generally, most of the state's explicit articulations represent war as rational or instrumental—that is, as policy—and, as I noted earlier, the warfare-related identity markers are usually less prominent. Nevertheless, even in those rational/instrumental articulations, the ontological can be discerned through the cracks of the discursive facade. This is even the case in the writings of Carl von Clausewitz, who is often credited with fashioning the purely strategic and utilitarian discourse on warfare that still dominates the military thinking of the modern state. Indeed, Clausewitz's writings were evoked by the media continuously during the Gulf War. Despite Clausewitz's reputation as a utilitarian rationalist in his approach to war, however, his preoccupation with war is very Hegelian; it is driven by an ontological investment in both individual and national completion.

While the standard reading of Clausewitz represents him as an instrumentalist, it is possible to locate his widely quoted claim that "war is nothing but the continuation of politics by other means"[30] and his continual argument for the subordination of military reason to political reason in other than a simple utilitarian context. The deprivileging of a utilitarian reading becomes compelling with a focus on the way that war is an instrument of the state. For Clausewitz (as for Hegel) the growth of the modern state was virtually the end of history, the culmination of a historical movement toward the correct political form.[31]

More particularly, Clausewitz identified closely with the Prussian state and wrote of the importance of its maintaining a high level of military power. Certainly he thought that such military power was necessary for its security, but he was also invested in the symbolic significance of Prussia's maintaining its position as one of the most powerful states. This commitment was as much expressive as instrumental for Clausewitz, for he saw this state power as an expression of its "natural qualities."[32]

As was the case with Hegel, the state for Clausewitz was a spiritual as well as a territorial entity. His advocacy of a citizen army and his valorization of "the fighting power of the people"[33] were not simply an argument for efficiency. Popular participation in war evoked a warlike spirit that sanctified the bond between citizen and state and produced a sacred legitimation for the state and its territorial boundaries. Again and again he referred to "spirit" as the source of the strength of state institutions, and although efficiency was always a part of his equation, it is undeniable that the collective identification of a people with a state was primarily ontological for Clausewitz. Human life to be lived as it should be must be lived in the context of a martial commitment to defending the state. The military is thus an expression of the state through the willing participation of citizen soldiers and the consensual support of the population as a whole. Speaking of the need to maintain the position of the Prussian state, he asserted that "only great institutions, holding and channeling genuine forces and infused by a living spirit can maintain us at our present level."[34]

The same ontological commitment and spiritual reverence that Clausewitz expressed for the state's war machine is evident in his rhetorical choices. That Clausewitz is often constructed as an instrumental rationalist is owed to only one aspect of his language, his grammar. Grammatically, Clausewitz constructs a politically controlled military actor in pursuit of objectives. When the "objectives" are seen as simply ends in view, one is tempted to locate Clausewitzian discourse within a rationalist, means-ends epistemology. Military force is strictly an instrument aimed at defeating an external threat, identified as such by both the people's enmity and the discretionary thinking of their government. But although Clausewitz pursues this line of reasoning, and his writing is frequently punctuated with references to the "political objectives of war,"[35] it is being rather than doing that is the end in view. Through war, individuals achieve their appropriate consummated identities as men, and the state is sanctified.

This becomes evident when we heed the rhetorical rather than the grammatical Clausewitz. What emerges from the way that Clausewitz figures war is a passionate ontological commitment rather than cool political reason. Whereas epistemologically, war for Clausewitz is purely a form of acting in response to externally perceived threats in order to achieve subsequently educed objectives, ontologically, war is a major aspect of being. It creates the conditions for the production, maintenance, and reproduction of the virtuous self, a way (for men) to achieve an ideal form of subjectivity as individuals and for the state to achieve its ideal form of collective subjectivity, as an expression of spiritual power and virility.

That the achievement of an exemplary selfhood is what is primarily at stake for Clausewitz becomes evident in the metaphors with which he represents war as equivalent to both the benign and deadly interpersonal contests in which aggressive men achieve dominance and stature. For example, at one point he suggests that war is "nothing but a duel on a larger scale,"[36] and at another he likens war to a card game in which both chance and courage must operate: "In the whole range of human activities, war most closely resembles a game of cards."[37]

The realization and demonstration of masculine courage and daring is therefore at stake for Clausewitz. He waxes eloquent about the opportunity war supplies as a form of danger that is necessary for men to become what they must be. War allows their "courage [to] take wing" as they "dive into the element of daring and danger like a fearless swimmer into the current."[38] One's fundamental moral credentials are to be achieved as well. War is fighting, Clausewitz asserts, but what "fighting" most essentially involves is "a trial of moral and physical forces through the medium of the latter."[39] What is at stake is thus nothing less than moral virtue, which for Clausewitz seems to be almost exhausted (for men) by military virtue. Only war assures the opportunity to achieve it.[40]

Nowhere does Clausewitzian rhetoric do more to ontologize and sacralize war than in his famous trinity passage. Stating that war is not simply a neutral dynamic adapting like a chameleon to the characteristics of each immediate case, he continues:

> As a total phenomenon its dominant tendencies always make war a remarkable trinity—composed of primordial violence, hatred, and enmity, which are to be regarded as a blind natural force; of the play of chance and probability within which the creative spirit is free to roam; and of its element of subordination, as an instrument of policy, which makes it subject to reason alone.
>
> The first of these aspects mainly concerns the people; the second the commander and his army; the third the government.[41]

This remarkable passage remains central to neo-Clausewitzian think-ing. For example, in his reprise of the Gulf War, Colonel Harry Sum-mers, who performed as an "expert" commentator for television net-works covering the fighting, makes clear that the reconstitution of national solidarity through war is his primary hope. He begins his analysis with Clausewitz's trinity passage, calling it "primordial." He never mentions specific enmities or the spatial predicates of war's terri-torial struggle. What is primary for Summers is "reinvolving the Ameri-can people in the strategic equation," but it is clear that the "strategic" aspect for him is the reconstruction of a damaged "national will." In short, war for Summers, as for Clausewitz, is ontological. But also, as is the case with Clausewitz, there is a significant misrecognition in the midst of Summers's musings, for his ontological interest is overcoded with a strategic discourse. This discursive structure is especially evident in the trinity passage written by Clausewitz and admired by Summers, for it contains fundamental contradictions between the ontological yearnings throughout the Clausewitzian text and an emphasis on in-strumental reason. While the passage implies a narrative structure in which an initiating enmity on the part of a people is the first justifica-tion for hostilities, elsewhere in *On War* Clausewitz admits that what-ever enmity the people may feel for those in another nation is not "pri-mordial." He states explicitly that although "modern wars are seldom fought without hatred between nations," there is often "no animosity to start with." It is the fighting itself that "will stir up hostile feelings."[42]

Yet in his trinity passage, he suggests quite the opposite. He asserts that animosity is a primordial, blind natural force, and it is, moreover, located in the people whose originary hostility provides the impetus for the war. The military and political dimensions seem in the passage to be merely instrumental responses to implementing the people's passion.

The emphasis on the military subordination to political objectives and the idea of war-as-an-instrument-of-policy is reasserted here, but it is all dominated by an ontological interest in which a primordial hostile passion is assigned to a nation's collective subjectivity, "the people." De-spite the instrumental talk, war is a fulfillment not only for the virtuous fighters but also for the people as a whole. In short, Clausewitz's gram-mar is an aggressive misrecognition. Clausewitzian war is "policy," but not to be understood within a simple grammar of subjects acting on the external world to achieve objectives but rather as the process within which subjects are producing and reproducing themselves. This policy interest, which is reflected in Clausewitzian rhetoric, should be understood as a reflection of desire, where "desire" is Hegelian; it is a drive toward producing a coherent and unified self. The objective of action turns out to be internal, not external.

The uneasy disjuncture, evident in Clausewitz's formulations, suggests that his so-called objectives represent internal as well as external referents. More generally, in the domain of policy talk, objectives have a legitimating significance. Insofar as they can be evoked as collective goals, they serve as the end point of a narrative or strategic calculus and help to summon collective efforts. However, the story of objectives is not exhausted by this model. This becomes especially evident when the particular objects on which rationalized justifications for action are based become unstable as they have, for example, in the post–cold war world in which some traditional enmities have dissolved while others have been reasserted.

The interpretive activities through which national bodies have located themselves and projected dangers no longer enjoy the stability they had during the recent East-West bipolar power configuration. The degree to which an individual or collective is troubled by such an instability cannot be separated from structures of self-recognition. To recognize such structures, it is necessary to depart from the Hegelian model of the self and consider in more depth what I have termed Clausewitz's (and Summers's) "aggressive misrecognition." This expression summons a Lacanian rather than a Hegelian model for conceiving self-Other dynamics. A conceptual detour, in which Lacan's version of desire is elaborated, is therefore necessary before we look for the operation of Clausewitz's ontological impulses in both nonstate and state venues.

## The Lacanian Other

As I noted earlier, while Clausewitzian grammar mediates relations between warring bodies with rational calculations involving disembodied objectives and means toward them, Clausewitzian rhetoric reveals a dependence of bodies on other bodies for the development and coherence of their identities. When this dimension of Clausewitz is heeded, the antagonistic Other can be viewed not simply as something to be outplayed but as a resource, an object whose dangerous existence supplies the object against which the warring body maintains unity and consistency. As was the case with Hegel, Clausewitz can serve us as much through being a datum as he can by dint of his theorizing. Moreover, because of the misrecognition immanent in his account, his failure to perceive the debts to alterity built into his views of persons and states, his attachments are exemplary within a Lacanian model of the ontological dependencies of the self.

Although Hegel provides the initial relevant theorization, nowhere is this ontological dependence of bodies on other bodies better elaborated than in the approach to subjectivity of Jacques Lacan, who discerns this dependence very early in a person's transactions with the world. According to Lacan, psychoanalytic experience shows that the child constructs its initial coherence as an autonomous body by seeing itself in a mirror (or by viewing an-Other). Because one's own bodily existence provides only fragmentary experience, it is the sight of a whole autonomous Other that provides the basis for a sense of unity, coherence, and stable identity.[43] This construction of subjectivity as a function of contacts with alterity has obvious debts to Hegel's notion that objects and other subjects serve the developing coherence of the subject.

Operating within a linguistic rather than a mentalistic idiom, Lacan privileges the dynamics of representation rather than what is represented. Lacan accepts the Hegelian emphasis on subjectivity, asserting that "the constitution of the object is subordinated to the realization of the subject."[44] But while Hegel's model of desire privileges consciousness over the objects against which consciousness produces its self-reflection, Lacan regards the operation of desire as constitutive of signifiers whose coded structure renders the quest for being at home with oneself always undecipherable and thus always unconsummated.

The subject for Lacan does not achieve a totalizing self-consciousness that overcomes disjunctures between it and its object relations. Rather, the subject is constituted *as* disjuncture in that it misrecognizes the dependence of its identity on alterity. It knows itself through others while at the same time misrecognizing this dependence and assuming itself to be wholly self-contained. Thus, in Lacan's psychoanalytic mediation of the Hegelian view, the particular objects through which the subject strives to achieve identity coherence become the arbitrary and often unstable substitutes for interests that do not achieve clear recognition for the subject.

In combining the Freudian and Hegelian emphases on the problem of the subject, Lacan helps us to understand what I have called Clausewitz's aggressive misrecognition. Like the Hegelian subject, the Lacanian subject seeks a coherent selfhood and uses alterity in the service of that aim. However, unlike Hegel, who posited a wholly successful narrative of the development of a continuously more self-conscious and coherent subject, Lacan emphasized the Freudian dissimulating mechanisms whereby the subject dwells in misapprehensions, projecting meanings on objects as a result of irreconcilable incoherences within its aims.

These incoherences are related to the misrecognition of aspects of otherness within the subject—for example, the masculine subject who seeks to recognize its aspects of the feminine and at the same time to avoid that recognition and maintain an unambiguously masculine self-interpretation. This troubling disjuncture can produce aggressiveness as the subject focuses on the world rather than its own coherence problem, thus "throwing back onto the world the disorder of which it is composed."[45]

The turn to Lacan to investigate the ontological dimension of warfare is appropriate, therefore, because the various displacements and projections through which objects of violence are interpretively selected are at issue, and because this interpretive dynamic operates in relation to the ontological interest of the subject. This frame can be applied to collective models of subjectivity as well. Just as Hegel took his view of the necessity for negation from the level of the individual to that of the state, we can move the Lacanian model of aggressivity from individual to collectivity. The individual's symbolic participation in national enmities derives from identification with the national body. The nation's coherence-producing activities and boundary policing serve to affirm the coherence sought by the individual while at the same time projecting a collective unity that constitutes a denial of social antagonisms and other fragmenting domestic forces. At a collective level, the domestic negotia-

tion of a national identity, which is an ongoing historical and often contentious process, involves a continuous search for dangerous forms of
disorder, various Others whose dangers involve threats that are not
exhausted by merely strategic considerations; they are fueled by interpretations that cannot be comfortably focused on various contentious
dynamics involved in attempts to produce an ideology of national
coherence.[46]

One should expect, therefore, that a strong identification with unambiguous boundaries for one's collectivity—that is, a strong demand for
a coherent model of national autonomy and difference—can produce
adversaries, both within and without. These become national objects of
desire; they are both necessary for self-identity and a threat insofar as
they reflect a disorder too unacceptable to be recognized as part of one's
own order.

Finally, the turn to Lacan is not an attempt to ascribe the impetus to
violence to individual psychology but to point to the misrecognitions
inherent in a strategic mode of thought that radically separates subjects
and objects, fails to discern the involvements of subjectivity in objects,
and thereby dissimulates the ontological investments involved in producing violent aims (and their targets). The aggressive misrecognitions
discerned in Clausewitz's writings remain in the contemporary public
discourses associated with the warfare of the state. The ontological aspects of relations with alterity (other nations and nationalities) are overcoded with strategic, means-ends rhetoric, making it difficult to recognize the interests that antagonisms serve. What the subject/nation
represents as a hostile object of an aggressive aim is in part a stand-in for
an inward aim; its antagonistic status is produced by the drive for inner
coherence, an attempt to assemble harmoniously those elements of the
self or the order that defy this coherence.

When dealing with this use of alterity at a collective level—that is,
with the primary modes of otherness with which cultures, societies, and
nations police their boundaries—we must view the enmities involved in
warfare more ethnographically than strategically. A comparison of tribal
and state collectivities therefore suggests itself, especially because the
ontological aspects of enmity are more forthrightly expressed in the case
of the former. For example, ethnographic evidence suggests that for the

Huron tribes of the Great Lakes in the seventeenth century, for some of the Native American tribes of the U.S. plains at the same time, and, more recently, for the Anggor of New Guinea, cosmological commitments and other dimensions of the cultural or group ontology provide the collective coherence that determines the peaceful versus militant or violent apprehension of Others.

In the case of the modern state, a complex clash of interpretive positions, driven by interests, bureaucratic and institutional complexities, and ideological positions, plays a major role in the selection of dangers in general and foes in particular. As a result, the ontological aims, which are forthrightly expressed in tribal societies, are overcoded by official and bureaucratic discourses in modern states. Nevertheless, although warfare in the modern state is legitimated on the basis of a discourse of security interests, to which a variety of security-related agencies contribute, the ontological aims can be recovered despite the dominance of policy-oriented rhetoric, very much the way they were in Clausewitz's discourse. The ontological interests driving hostilities go unarticulated because a policy grammar commands attention, and the rationale for violence emerges as something like suppressing or destroying external threats.

Once the ontological aims can be discerned beneath the strategic discourse, tribal and state warfare become less dissimilar. Both rely on a discourse of danger based on a radical separation of a domestic order versus a disordered world. But in the case of the former, the agents of disorder tend to remain historically stable—the traditional enemy tribe, the other village, and so on—while for the latter, particularly of late, the map of danger is unstable, and identity-related violence and preparation for it must operate in a climate of uncertainty.

## Tribal Warfare and Stable Systems of Enmity

The Anggor of New Guinea provide an exemplary case of the tribal approach to warfare. For them intervillage violence is a stable "central feature of social life."[47] To locate this violence within their meaning system, one needs to appreciate their historically stable, imagined cartography. As Peter Huber has put it:

Each Anggor village can be considered a cosmos in itself, an autonomous and essentially harmonious moral system confronted by a uniformly hostile, dangerous, and chaotic outside world. Violence between these villages is consequently not a form of policy or a distinct kind of political situation, but an inescapable feature of man's existential condition.[48]

It is clear by this account that Anggor warfare has a markedly ontological impetus, based on the contrast between the inside and outside of the village order. This is highlighted further in the observation that "the integrity and solidarity of the village is further manifest in its contrast with the surrounding world. . . . Beyond the village boundaries, social and spatial safety gives way to danger, order to chaos, and peace to violence."[49] Therefore, central to the Anggor self-understanding is that the village is a "cosmos," an autonomous order that does not recognize its debts to alterity. As a result, the relations between the village and the outside involve "dangerous and ambivalent manipulations of the very boundaries of the cosmos."[50]

Insofar as a comparison between the Anggor and the United States is appropriate, one would have to select the cold war period because it supplies a level of stability similar to that experienced in the recent history of Anggor cosmology. What constituted the cosmos for the United States during the cold war was what was called "the free world." The outside, represented primarily by the Soviet Union, was the domain of danger and disorder. While the Soviet Union or, more generally, the East Bloc was represented in the strategic discourse as a "military threat," ontologically, the world of danger and disorder served as a stable identity support. David Campbell, in a remark that effectively locates U.S. cartography in the camp of the Anggor put it well: "The cold war was an important moment in the (re)production of American identity animated by a concern for the ethical boundaries of identity rather than the territorial borders of the state."[51]

What then can one make of the post–cold war situation for the United States? At a minimum, instabilities abound. The traditional enemy is absent, but the necessity for having one has produced an anxious search for a stable moral geography. The articulations from various branches of the enemy-producing establishment bear witness to this ontological angst. Before I elaborate this new, unstable discourse on danger, however, it is propitious to turn to the restaging of the Huron-Jesuit confrontation in order both to elaborate a different period of ontological angst and to examine its effects in the context of a different construction of both the individual and the collective body.

More specifically, by examining a confrontation between the European and Huron body at a moment near the beginning of the modern state system, we are in a better position to appreciate the ontological basis of violence.

## Jesuits and Hurons

Without examining all the elements that drove French Jesuits to "New France," we can say that they represented an aspect of French foreign policy. The Jesuits were involved in domesticating the "New World," and although in some ways they were a sideshow to the acquisitiveness of political and commercial authorities, they also represented a more general ontological concern. They sought to confirm the truth of their way of life and the spiritual commitments in which it was anchored. Unlike their Latin American counterparts, the missionaries who accompanied the Spanish and Portuguese conquistadors, the Jesuits in New France expended considerable effort to learn native languages. This was not, however, a comprehending regard and respect for alterity. These Jesuits wished to make the Other the same, to deepen the certainty of their own spiritual practices and confirm the view that they were on the right trajectory from this life into the next. Confirmation would come from convincing the "savages" that they had to accept the true God.

The words of the Jesuit Le Jeune leave little doubt that their aim was to deepen their own moral certainty:

> There is some pleasure in taming the souls of the Savages and preparing
> them to receive the seed of Christianity. And then experience makes us
> feel certain that God, who shows his goodness and power to all, has never-
> theless, for those who expose themselves freely and suffer willingly in his
> service, and succors them in the midst of their dangers with so prompt
> and paternal assistance, that often they do not feel their trials, but their
> pain is turned to pleasure and their perils to peculiar consolation.[52]

What is this "pleasure" but the inward-oriented, ontological communion of those whose confrontation with alterity serves only a project of self-confirmation, of a deepening of the identity coherences that are their major concern? And, more generally, what is the relationship of this kind of pleasure to "foreign policy"? If one recognizes the debts to otherness that identity both requires and abjures as part of what constitutes foreign policy, one can discern a similar pleasure in some recent, violent aspects of U.S. foreign policy.

This "pleasure" dimension of U.S. military policy was emphasized in an analysis of U.S. participation in the Gulf War that emphasized the symbolic connection between the coherence of individual body or identity and the satisfaction derived from a "unified national body."[53] Given this projection from individual to state, the appeal of the war lay in its ability to provide the state's subjects with "the illusion of being masterful agents of history."[54] In prestate, tribal societies, it was through participation in rituals that individuals derived their ontological connection between their individual bodies and the social body. In modern society, it is through consuming media representations rather than participating in festivals that the connection is established. The fixing on an enemy Other, in either case, is a major aspect of this ontological connection. In general, "Both external and internal enemies, or more precisely, enemy images that can be attached to 'alien' bodies within and without, are indispensable to the armament of the body politic and to the pleasurable experience of community."[55]

This experience of community provided ontological enjoyment for the U.S. public that watched the war on television. The Jesuits' pleasure in confronting an alien Other was similar, but in their case the pleasurable experience was one of deepening their attachment to the divine rather than to a secular, state-based community. Ironically, it was often the "savages," for whose reasoning the Jesuits had such contempt, who had a more critical comprehension of and respect for cultural difference. Perhaps the Hurons were exemplary in this respect. Because they were deeply attuned to respecting others, they were, in the words of one who has studied their epistemology, able to "receive the revelation of insights about the other in more objective fashion, that is, in terms of the other and not merely in terms of subjective claims and needs."[56]

A conversation between a Jesuit and a Huron that took place in 1637 is notable in this regard. A tribal leader named Onaconchiaronk was cooperating with the Jesuits and directing his tribesmen in the building of a chapel. They labored with the expectation of being paid in tobacco. On hearing that he and his tribe were expected to renounce their spiritual beliefs and worship in the chapel upon its completion, he spoke as follows:

> We have our own way of doing things, and you yours, as well as other nations. When you speak to us about obeying and acknowledging him who you say has made Heaven and earth, I imagine you are talking of overthrowing the country. Your ancestors assembled in earlier times, and held a council where they resolved to take as their God him whom you honor, and ordained all the ceremonies that you observe; as for us, we have learned others from our Fathers.[57]

This view was of course unacceptable to the Jesuits, and as the commentary goes:

> The Father rejoined that he was altogether mistaken in his opinion,—that it was not through a mere choice that we had taken God for our God, that nature herself had taught us to acknowledge as God him who has given us being and life: that, as for what concerns our ceremonies, they are not a human invention, but divine; that God himself had prescribed them to us, that they were strictly observed all over the earth.[58]

Exaggeration about the comprehensiveness of the observance of Christian ceremonies aside, what the rejoinder reveals is the persistence of a unitary and exclusively vertical view of space as well as an uncritical reading of history. The Jesuit's privileging of a single version of the sacred is intimately connected with a failure to countenance the ethical integrity and worth of the practices of alien-Others. For the Jesuits, the Hurons were not eligible to negotiate a code of conduct; they had to succumb to the Jesuits' coding of the world and of the propriety of sanctioned actions within it.

Ironically, at the same time that the Jesuits were imposing this particular vertical universe and mythic reading of history, it was under extreme competitive pressure back in France. Two years before this conversation took place, Richelieu had committed French forces to the Thirty Years' War, and at its end, the Treaty of Westphalia had helped establish the dominance of a horizontal, geostrategic version of space and, accordingly, a decisive erosion of ecclesiastical authority. The dissolving of the old Hapsburg empire, along with a more general end of attempts at maintaining religiously oriented empires, helped to consolidate a system of nation-states. And as reasons of state subsequently supplanted what remained of the power of spiritual proprieties, all codes based on personal commitments and group affiliations paled in comparison with the proliferating norms of the order of states and their interrelationships.

However, as reasons of state have overcoded the personal and collective, spiritual commitments behind violence, they have also monopolized the historical narratives within which warfare is currently understood. Most significantly, the tendency has been to represent modern war as solely an extension of state policy and as a less and less frequent resort.

Why the dominance of this interpretation when a relatively dispassionate historical overview reveals that (1) "the twentieth century has already established itself as the most bellicose in human history" and (2) "the nuclear age has not slowed the centuries-old trend toward more frequent, deadlier wars"?[59] One answer is that the contemporary account sheet privileges wars among the great powers and classifies other deadly quarrels as nonwarfare. The answer needs elaboration in terms of practices as well as discourse, however. First, the historical trend whereby the state has increasingly monopolized violence must be recognized:

> Since the seventeenth century ... rulers have managed to shift the balance decisively against both individual citizens and rival power holders within their own states. They have made it criminal, unpopular, and impractical for most of their citizens to bear arms, have outlawed private armies, and have made it seem normal for armed agents of the state to confront unarmed civilians.[60]

Thus, within the state, the rivalrous and violent struggles have lost their warfare-oriented coding as state social control and policing discourses dominate historical narratives. Then, as the international system came to be dominated by powerful states and their allies, the international discourse on warfare has been dominated by their narratives. And, most importantly, discourses that have dominated in the modern era are political discourses.

With the development of the modern state and along with it of specifically military institutions and their legal, bureaucratic, and political interfaces, the ontological dimension of warfare becomes dissimulated by a web of practical and discursive relations. The violent arm of the state is not directly connected with the state's articulations. In short, we are thrown off the trail of the ontological engine of warfare by the dominance of the legal, political, and bureaucratic discourses through which the state represents the harmony of its order. This institutional obfuscation has been accompanied by a discursive practice at the center of modern political orientations. Since Hobbes raised nonwar to the privileged position in the order of the state, warfare has been regarded as an aberration, a failure of politics rather than a result of the individual and collective identity drives that constitute the domain of the political.

Nevertheless, warfare in the modern state remains constitutive of its identity practices. Enemy/Others are ontologically just as important to the state society as they were to the prestate society. The primary difference is that the prestate society did not segregate its military operations in the same way the state society did. It is necessary, therefore, to overcome the dissimulating political discourse of the modern state with an ethnographic one that will show the ways in which individual and collective modern bodies constitute themselves through war. To recognize this relationship, however, it is important to look at it within a context in which the individual body is differently constituted. For this purpose, the Hurons serve admirably.

What is dramatically significant by way of comparison is that unlike the modern state, the Hurons manifested a remarkably straightforward understanding of the economies of their peaceful and violent proclivities and the relationships of these tendencies to their ways of constituting self and Other.

## Huron Uses of Alterity

I noted that the Hurons seemed to be better able than the French Jesuits to accept cultural difference. Perhaps this stemmed in part from their lack of pretension. The Hurons had only a local map of the world. Their spiritual life had a pervasive effect on their practical existence, but Huron self-confirmation did not require an external validation of the kind involved in universalizing one's particular commitments. A remark by Aimé Césaire is apropos here. In a lament about the many societies in the Americas that were effaced in the process of colonization, he states, "They were the fact, they did not pretend to be the idea."[61] However important alterity may have been in the Hurons' systems of self-recognition, their Others were not there to serve as confirmation of their transcendent and universal significance.

In addition, because they did not have a fictitious entity, the state, their extratribal relations did not have to be located vis-à-vis this particular symbolic entity, which serves in modernity as the general equivalent for what can be threatened in each individual. More generally, Huron-Other relations did not partake of any of the mediations at the level of the psyche or collective identity familiar in modern state societies. Although they had traditional enemies, whom they often treated with ferocious violence, they did not locate Others in a lesser moral space. Indeed, they believed that confrontations with the power and integity of their enemies strengthened them. In various ways, they strove to incorporate others—sometimes by consuming them as food and sometimes by adopting them as members of their tribe to replace their war losses.

The Hurons did not therefore represent their violence as "defense," "conflict management," or "peacekeeping." Like the Aztecs, they wore the ontological dimension of the violence on their sleeves. Warfare was an important, even vital, activity, an activity through which they completed, reproduced, and enhanced the self. To understand this ontological connection between warfare and the self or body, one must know how that body was assembled.

The Huron body had two "souls," the intellectual and the emotive. The former predominated during periods of deliberation and slumber and the latter, a sensitive-animating soul, was part of conscious life.[62] This dualistic approach to the body, a recognition of different and often opposing orientations and forces, which the French Jesuits found perplexing, translated into the body-warfare relationship. Specifically, the Hurons' intellectual and emotive souls operated respectively as peace and war souls: "Corresponding to the intellectual soul are the chiefs and councils of peace; corresponding to the emotive soul are the chiefs and councils of war."[63]

Whatever else such a divided body and its correspondingly divided practices might imply, warfare for the Hurons could not be totalizing, for the whole identity was not involved. And, perhaps more important for purposes of comparison with modern state warfare, there was a relative absence of collective stakes. In contrast, modern states have decidedly collective stakes with a peculiarly modern character. What makes the contemporary state-oriented war animus peculiar when it is placed in historical perspective is the structure of its rationale. The stakes of war are bound up with the survival of a kind of collective body that did not exist in the seventeenth century, the "population." Speaking of modern warfare, Foucault isolates the relationship of this new body to violence:

> Wars are no longer waged in the name of a sovereign who must be defended; they are waged in behalf of the existence of everyone; entire populations are mobilized for purposes of wholesale slaughter in the name of life necessity. . . . The principle underlying the tactics of battle—that one has to be capable of killing to go on living—has become the principle that defines the strategy of states.[64]

"Strategy" here does not mean the instrumental rationale through which violence is a policy to achieve various ends. It is meant ontologically, for it refers to the modern concern with the boundaries of individual and collective bodies that provide the predicates through which the globe is mapped and dangers are discerned. By contrast, warfare for the Hurons was individualistic; it involved the exercise of bravery and anger (parts of the emotive soul, for revenge was always involved), and the torture and cannibalism practiced on their captives stemmed from their notion that they needed the Other to nourish their soul: "To procure and deepen their courage, young men were encouraged to torture the flesh and minds of their victims, tear out their hearts and then partake of their roasted flesh and intermingle their blood with that of their victims."[65] The body-to-body relation here was literally one of incorporation.

Moreover, the symbolic meaning of this "nourishment" is underscored by the metonymical character of the eating of flesh. High-status members of the tribe such as chiefs ate the head, while those in lower positions got fingers or toes. The consumed body had parts with differential relations to parts of the Huron social body. While the postwar

cannibalism of the Hurons has deep symbolic and ontological resonances, it represents at the same time a relative absence of a representational mediation in the Huron-Other relationship. The differences between Huron transactions with human alterity and those of moderns in
the context of warfare would seem to operate at two different levels.

First, at the interpersonal level, Huron epistemology did not function
within the modern frames of interpersonal perception and interpersonal communication. The relationship of one body to another emphasized excursive rather than discursive activities.[66] For the Hurons,
the mind and body did not accrue data on the Other in an abstract way,
but moved toward it, even to the point of consuming it. The second level
is that at which self-Other relations animate warfare relations. The
Hurons' model of dealing with alterity is coherent with their tendency to
either eat or adopt captives, to incorporate them. The ontological significance of warfare thus was experienced primarily at an individual level;
each person who partook in the incorporation experienced a spiritual
nourishment. There remained, of course, a level of group recognition as
well. Warfare for the Hurons as for moderns had the collective ontological function of producing group self-recognition through radical difference with the enemy. What differed was the Huron practice of incorporation to overcome difference once actual contact was made.

In the case of the modern state, the individual does not consume the
enemy in a bodily sense. Because the distancing technology associated
with modern weapons and the separation between civil and military institutions dematerialize enemy/Others, modern citizens consume codes.
The self-enemy relationship in the case of most members of the body
politic is a highly mediated symbolic form of consumption. It is enemy
images rather than enemies that must operate for a culture that is discursive (and oriented toward conceptual mastery) rather than excursive.
In the case of the ontological investments associated with modern warfare, they involve "enemy images that can be attached to 'alien' bodies"
and provide "the pleasurable experience of community."[67]

Moreover, it is a stability in these images that provides the coherence
in the body politic along with a stable structure of symbolic identifications for its citizens. In this context, the end of the cold war has produced a frantic attempt in the United States to reestablish the sense of

coherence seen to be threatened by the lack of a stable adversary. To re-assert a stable orientation toward potential warfare, there is a need to construct the order on the basis of what is dangerous and disordered outside. A brief review of some recent, post–cold war articulations is therefore in order, for it demonstrates that the ontological stakes are presently very much in view. When instability reigns, as in the post–cold war circumstance in which the map and the distribution of subjectivi-ties is in flux, the ontological begins to assert itself; the problem of co-herence and the unity of the national body recommends itself with greater urgency.

## Conclusion: The Search for New Enemies and Dangers

The current problem was well represented in a post–cold war essay by the then U.S. Commander in Chief Colin Powell in *Foreign Affairs*.[68] In his opening gesture, he locates "America's armed forces" in an ontologi-cal rather than a strategic space, "as part of the fabric of U.S. values."[69] Thereafter, much of his discourse is strategic and Clausewitzian—he even specifically invokes Clausewitz's name—as he maps the world geo-strategically, while speaking in a means-ends, policy-oriented grammar. The ontological is the prime predicate, however, for all the policy talk is based on an ontology not unlike that of the Anggor villagers. There is the domain of order, which Powell designates as "the free world," and there is the domain of disorder. The map of the disordered world of dangers is undergoing alteration, however, the threat is now "regional" rather than global, and an even more alert and active posture with the expectation of enmity is appropriate.

That the "free world" is a cosmology rather than a specific set of insti-tutional practices is evident from how it functions conceptually. It gets elaborated not as a way of life but as a thing to protect against the non-free world. Regions are as close as Powell gets to designating the more dangerous forms of alterity against which the U.S. national body can de-fine its virtue.

Subsequently, however, General Lee Butler, whose approach is more immediately instrumental, provided some fine tuning. Butler, who headed the U.S. nuclear command, had a vocation organized around specific targeting. His job is not to speculate about enemies, but to aim nuclear weapons at them. Having been deprived of his primary "target," the Soviet Union, he and the like-minded evoked a new world of disorder filled with "terrorist states" and "rogue leaders."[70] History has not yet been able to provide the stability that logistical functionaries would like, but their rush to aim their weapons seems often to run ahead of the process of political deliberation. While national political leaders express uncertainties about the future of danger and the addresses of friends and foes, those with more specific responsibilities for violence are promoting a view of an increasingly dangerous world and are rapidly designating potential foes.

Butler therefore has many fellow travelers. For example, President Clinton's nominee to head the CIA in 1993 "described the world as an even more dangerous place for the United States than it was in the days of the Soviet Union," and after saying we had slain the large dragon noted that there still exists "a jungle filled with a bewildering variety of poisonous snakes."[71] Enemy bodies turn out to resemble a threatening bestiary. But Butler's list was geopolitical rather than zoological. His specifics included Third World nations with sophisticated weapons, ethnic and national conflicts such as the one in the former Yugoslavia, drug trading, and terrorism.

No doubt this is still an insufficient degree of specificity for those manifesting the higher levels of ontological angst. Happily, syndicated columnist Charles Krauthammer can be relied on as a spokesperson for those who need a more specifically dangerous world to constitute the symbolic pleasure that derives from being in the virtuous part of the world. Without a hint of irony, Krauthammer has designated Iran as "the New Evil Empire." He has overcome his ontological angst by designating Iran as an unambiguous substitute for the old world of disorder:

> Iran is the center of the world's new Comintern. It is similarly messianic and ideological, ruthless and disciplined, implacably hostile to Western Liberalism (though for different reasons) and thus exempt from its conventional morality. Hence, for example, that common thread, terrorism.[72]

Here is someone who needs an implacable foe, one who is unambiguously evil or at least an unambiguous threat to the order. To situate this radically antagonistic position, it is useful to recall again the Hurons' accepting reaction to a culture that was also outside of what Krauthammer calls "conventional morality." Without going into an exhaustive analysis of the Huron practices of the self, it should be noted that the Hurons' acceptance of a pluralistic moral universe was complemented by their recognition of a divided body, of different, opposing forces within the self—for example, peace and war souls.

To put the matter within the discourse of order, which emerged in the discussion of Anggor cosmology, sensitivity to the ontological dimensions of warfare should lead one to expect complementarity between the orders of the self and those discerned in the world. Those who regard any aspect of disorder within the self as intolerable—those who demand a totally coherent and unified body—must necessarily engage in a denial of the forces of disorder within the order of the self. Insofar as this is the case, external disorder, practices in the world that do not comport with the system of order within which one resides, will be particularly threatening.

When one recognizes in addition that the collectivity or nation serves as a symbolic extension—the individual body connects to the national body—the same structural logic linking self and other at the level of individual selves also applies to the link between the domestic and foreign orders. Denial of disorder within the order for the collective body as a whole should lead to an intolerance of an external order that fails to validate, by imitation, the domestic order. Thus a nonimitative order will be interpreted as disorder and, accordingly, as a threat. Moreover, the "threat" is dissimulated because of the misrecognition involved in the very constitution of the self, a failure to recognize dimensions of incoherence and otherness within the self. Accordingly, the threat is interpreted as a danger to the survival of the order rather than an affront to the order's interpretive coherence.

Having established a basis for the suspicion that the modern nation-state, like the prestate society, contains an ontological impetus to warfare and that in modernity this often takes the form of extraordinary demands for coherence within the orders of the self and the nation, the next move is to deepen that suspicion by pursuing a recent case. Accordingly, in the next chapter I pursue the ontological theme with special attention to the selection and targeting of dangerous objects during the Gulf War.

# THREE

# That Obscure Object of Violence

## Introduction: Virtual Warfare

Almost a decade before the Gulf War, Don DeLillo wrote a prescient short story titled "Human Moments in World War III." His construction of warring bodies and their spaces of deployment anticipated many of the implications of the "coalition's" Gulf War technology. Like many of the Gulf War combatants, DeLillo's warriors and their enemies are largely dematerialized, for attacks are mediated through remote laser guidance systems; the attackers never see their human targets. Moreover, the spatial imaginary organizing DeLillo's war effaces the boundary between the earth and the cosmos to an extent even greater than that in the Gulf War.

Only two protagonists occupy the space of DeLillo's narration and the venue of his story, the commander/narrator and Vollmer, his young assistant in a laser shooting capsule, orbiting the earth. While the narrator allows that "the earth is land and water, the dwelling place of mortal men," such "facts of life" are irrelevant, and it is already the case that for young Vollmer the earth has been reduced to a series of specular, aesthetic effects. For example, he sees "a silver ribbon" off the Irish coast, which, he is informed, is an oil slick.

The contemporary nation-state cartography is wholly absent, for territorially speaking, these warriors are disengaged from antagonisms based on geopolitical boundaries. The war is a fact without any hint of territorially based interests or grievances. Moreover, there are no antagonists in any traditional bodily sense. They neither see nor hear enemies; indeed, they have no sensual evidence of other bodies. Similarly, their sense of their own bodies, both personally and in terms of their affilia-tions with compatriots, is absent. The "human moments" in this war consist of such banalities as the fact that they wear their bedroom slip-pers at their firing panels and have enough room in their capsule for each of them to have small "personal preference kits."

War-relevant affect is also absent. There is no evidence that these war-riors feel antagonistic toward their targets or even have feelings of exhil-aration about the rigors of combat. Vollmer appears to be a misplaced adolescent. He wears "suction clogs," resembles "a high school swimmer, all hairless," and takes pleasure in the simple routines of his military du-ties. He says at one point, "I am happy," and the narrator responds with a soliloquy on the irrelevance of emotions:

> What does he mean he's happy? Isn't happiness totally outside our frame
> of reference? . . . I want to say to him "This is just a housekeeping arrange-
> ment, a series of more or less routine tasks. Attend to your tasks, do your
> testing, run through your check lists" . . . I want to say, "happiness is not
> a fact of this experience, at least not to the extent that one is bold enough
> to speak of it."[1]

During the Gulf War, there were certainly more direct engagements between "warriors" than in DeLillo's war. Nevertheless, the technologi-cal mediations separating warring bodies, the irrelevance of passions and other bodily based forces on the part of combatants and citizen/spectators, and the distancing technology involved—laser-guided smart bombs programmed from space satellites, for example—constituted a giant step in the direction of dematerializing confrontations both spa-tially and biologically in a way that DeLillo anticipated.

If throughout history war at its most basic level has involved violent confrontations of bodies, the next level of defining conditions requires the specification of the bodies and the spaces of confrontation. In this context, the Gulf War involved such remote forms of enactment that the traditional languages of engagement cannot be unambiguously applied; the body and spatial dimensions associated with war through the cen-turies prove to be anachronistic, and they become increasingly so as each technological development produces a more prosthetically medi-ated warring body and an increasingly virtual geography.[2]

Spatially, the Gulf War was simply the realization of a trend that began after World War II, which can be regarded as the "last territorial conflict," last in the sense that "colonial management" had given way wholly to a "globalization of conflict"[3] in which satellite surveillance and the delivery of force from great distances had displaced the violence associated with wars of annexation. What had emerged is what Paul Virilio calls a "topographical amnesia."[4] The recording of information and the sending of communications and weapons operated in a virtual space that had displaced the venues based on visualization from generation to generation.[5]

Moreover, the technologies that permitted killing in the absence of seeing had removed specific, suffering bodies in a way similar to the way they are effaced in the theoretical language of war, as war discourse has increasingly moved from images of flesh to images of weapons and logistics. Indeed, the enactment of the war bore a closer resemblance to theories of war than to actual violent engagements. The view that the U.S. combatants had of their targets was so mediated that the attacks were aimed at abstract targets in highly schematic spaces. The "battles" were thus very Clausewitzian inasmuch as Clausewitz spoke always in very abstract terms about the "battlefield" and avoided speculation about particular historical battles, particular antagonisms, and the actual bodily registers of violence. His discourse, in short, was as bloodless as the fighting must have seemed to those who operated on the control side of the contemporary technologies of battle.

There was of course what the geopolitically minded regard as a specific adversary, "Iraq." From the point of view of the U.S. population of television spectators, however, the media's history and geography lessons during the Gulf War never effectively constructed Iraq as a wholly plausible enemy. Iraq's identity consistently lacked historical depth, for among other things, the U.S. public had never had a firm grasp of historical or contemporary Middle Eastern jurisdictions. Unknown to a public with an anemic political discourse on the Middle East—which includes "militant Arab regimes," Israeli security practices, and such—is the way in which petroleum interests helped to construct the contemporary system of sovereignties in the region. What is now a familiar Middle Eastern political cartography had a decidedly commercial impetus, generated from the capitals of the "great powers."

The current geopolitical map of the region originates in 1928 with what was popularly referred to as the Red Line Agreement, an oil cartel arrangement in which the great powers and their oil companies marked access to the Iraqi oil fields. Subsequently, much of the system of jurisdictional boundaries reflected in the political map of the area has been owed to the struggle for control of oil fields. What is now a geopolitical cartography, respected by Western states and regarded as endangered by cross-border movements, was constituted out of a predatory set of commercial interests during a period of egregious Western disrespect for traditional boundaries.[6] And popular understanding of the Middle East in the United States has supplied no countercartography. In the United States, both the official and the popular Middle Eastern imaginaries impose a marginality on the significance of each geographic entity.

Geopolitical maps are static. No longer available to the gaze are older territorialities and the aggressively expansionary codes that spurred conquests that displaced them. Iraq, under Saddam Hussein, was certainly extremely aggressive in a contemporary, cartographic sense; it engaged in violent expansion outside its designated place on the map. And Iraq's violence was legitimated within the hostile cartography Saddam has helped to produce: a world of Zionist imperialists and Arab apologists for and collaborators in the neocolonial configuration. But Iraq would not have earned the popular ascription as aggressor if the official map had been disrespected as much by the U.S. public as it was by Saddam, even if Saddam's Manichaean substitute was not embraced as an alternative.

However, the U.S. public received virtually no effective history of international political economy lessons. The media resorted to a biographical genre, a simplistic history of individual global villains. For example, Saddam Hussein was likened to Adolf Hitler: "Saddam Hussein is not Hitler," said columnist George Will (before the "storm"), "but the dynamism of its regime is Hitlerian."[7] And the media cartography was almost wholly military in its orientation; they even used the strategic maps released by the U.S. Command.

The Hitler analogy and strategy maps dominated attempts to produce an effective antagonism. Saddam Hussein, his "Republican Guards," and the area of the Iraqi troop concentration constituted the bodily and spatial antagonisms of the war. But those bodies and spaces remained relatively nonfigurable and certainly not very palpable as the war was seen through the sighting devices of U.S. weapons during the telecasts of video footage of the war.

In the absence of an enduring antagonism and given the lack of both historical association with and proximity to antagonists, it becomes necessary to rethink the various aspects of the satisfactions and legitimations the war had for the U.S. public and its political and military leaders. What bodies and places were at stake, and what kinds of stakes were implied when the meanings of antagonistic selves and Others lacked traditional foundations? If we recognize that despite the strategic, Clausewitzian discourse in which war continues to be framed—it is part of military discourse in general, and Clausewitz was often explicitly evoked by media commentators during the war—war retains a significant dimension of both individual and collective identity affirmation, how can identity affirmation operate from such a remote contact with such a vague form of alterity?

Without elaborating all the developments that have produced modern warfare as a virtual and derealized form of confrontation lacking the face-to-face tradition of battles in earlier periods, it is important to recognize various ways in which discursively mediated enmity—the language of war, the discourse on weapons, and the media reports of confrontations—have removed the body from violent encounters.

The significance of the disappearing warring body becomes especially evident when one examines earlier antagonisms that required bodies for the fulfillments that were expected. For example, the presence of palpable bodies was essential to the intertribal battles in North America before the European invasions. The European introduction of the gun into North America disturbed not only the precarious balance of power among tribal antagonists but also the understanding of the significance of warfare. Consider the following scenario in which a European gun, one of the first distancing technologies of warfare, interrupted an antagonistic encounter in which what was primarily sought was close physical contact.

Traveling in canoes in July 1609 with a group of Montagnais, Algonquins, and Hurons in the New France, Samuel de Champlain and his
party of sixty sighted some canoes full of Mohawks. With Champlain on
the sidelines, the traditional antagonists arranged a fight. Based in part
on Champlain's account, a history of the period describes the conference:

> Each side withdrew from the water, uttering loud cries, and barricaded
> itself as darkness set in. In a conference that night, the opponents agreed
> to fight the next morning, in daylight, "so as to be able to recognize each
> other." To be anonymous and to miss the meaningful gestures and verbal
> discourse of battle would be to undermine the encounter's significance
> for each party.[8]

The tale continues: "the entire night was spent in dancing and singing
on both sides with endless insults and other talk."[9] It is evident that the
"fight" was intended to be a ritual confrontation aimed at symbolically
representing antagonism rather than producing casualties. The point for
each side, as explained in Joseph-François Lafitau's account of "American Indian Customs," was to draw together, body to body, and fight in a
series of duels.[10]

Misunderstanding the rules of the encounter, however, Champlain
joined in and discharged his arquebus, killing two chieftains, who were
clad in textile armor to avoid injury from the Indian weapons. Champlain's use of a killing power with greater "standoff capability" (as contemporary armament manufacturers put it) than tribal weapons disturbed the event and was only a small preview of a more systematic
disturbance that European fighting technologies and purposes were to
introduce into the economies of violence and peace seeking among the
original North American nations.

As the history of "American" warfare has proceeded, nothing is more
exemplary of the change from tribal dueling to modern remote killing
than a comparison between indigenous tomahawks and the Tomahawk
cruise missile used in the Gulf War. In contrast with the original, handheld version, which required close proximity to the enemy, the missile
namesake is fired from battleships at unseen targets and tracked "with
onboard television cameras and radar sensors that correct the paths."[11]

No disparagements are uttered and no hostile gestures are exchanged before missiles are launched. At the beginning of the Gulf War these Tomahawks helped to initiate the highly mediated hostilities:

> In the leading wedge of an air assault against Iraq, the Pentagon said, more than 45 Tomahawk missiles fired from the battleship Wisconsin and other warships in the Persian Gulf zeroed in on key military installations and communication centers around Baghdad and destroyed many of the targets.[12]

Of course bodies were affected adversely—many were killed and wounded in and around the "military targets"—but the discourse of the battle here is as derealized and bodiless as the more general logistical talk with which contemporary warfare is framed. Common to both the discourse of the "armed forces" and their mimics in the subdiscipline of "security studies," for example, are references to "theater missile defenses" rather than bodies.[13] As one security analyst put it in his post–Gulf War ode to the Patriot missile, "The Patriot was given center stage on television."[14]

Ironically, the introduction of machine technology in warfare two centuries after Champlain's disruption of the intertribal encounter was to have a similar dampening effect on the pleasures of battle confrontations for European antagonists. For example, the machine gun, used extensively for the first time in World War I, antiquated the warfare based on muskets, bayonets, and horses, which had allowed "the individual officer and gentleman" to feel that "he counted for something."[15]

The "pleasure" of battles henceforth became increasingly vicarious, a pleasure of identification with the collective outcomes of battles, as warfare became a corporate, collective effort in the production and conveyance of firepower and the evasion of its effects. That pleasure of collective identification owes more to a sense of national affiliation for both combatants and citizens reading and viewing the news reports of battles than the pleasure of being an exemplary champion, which harks back to both indigenous American battles and those of the early Greeks.

What have been displaced, in the Americas as in Europe, are the specific identity affirmations involved in the physical encounters between bodies. Indeed, Norbert Elias's "civilizing process," the historical withdrawal of affect and physical contact in sociability since the Middle

Ages, has been paralleled in the conduct of warfare between states.[16] Both normative codes and distancing technologies of instrumentation and vision have separated adversaries from each other, while the rationalization and professionalization of war have separated combatants from their own emotional investments. At a minimum, modern warfare has moved alterity outside of the boundaries of vision, affect, and historical significance. Just how dematerialized and bloodless the encounters were for the U.S. combatants in the Gulf War is indicated in this description of U.S. bombing missions:

> American bomber pilots flew missions over Iraq with the heavy metal music of Van Halen pumping through their headsets. Graphic simulation displays helped guide their bombs to their targets. Back on deck they could describe strafing retreating Iraqi forces as a "turkey shoot." In short, everything appears as in a video game.[17]

But there is a force other than technology mediating the encounter of bodies. I will argue that the ontological functioning of desire always makes alterity in some way remote. In the contemporary situation of increased technological mediation of interpersonal encounters, however, it is necessary to rethink the complicity of the two forms of mediation, the bureaucratic/technological on the one hand, and desire on the other, in order to locate the Gulf War as an exemplary episode in contemporary ontologies of violence.

## Abstract Enmity

As the Gulf War progressed, it became apparent that the identification of friends and foes relied on media coverage (in the broadest sense) not only for television viewers but also for combatants, for the targets of lethal violence were glimpsed primarily on video devices and were rarely available to direct vision. Although it has always been the case to some extent that during large-scale hostilities the enemy/object of violence is familiar neither to the antagonistic populations nor to the combatants, in modern warfare, the visioning and weapons technologies render the antagonists even less familiar by derealizing or dematerializing them— by apprehending and targeting them primarily through remote visioning devices.

One of the most familiar theoretical narratives describing the trend toward the derealization of the objects of violence in modern warfare is Weberian. Max Weber's well-known account of modernity emphasizes the intensification of the process of rationalization where instrumental rationality displaces the intersubjective, reciprocal aspects of social relations in which participants can personally enact the values that link them with others. Not incidental to this process are such technologies as printing, which renders writing rapidly reproducible and therefore makes possible the general systems of accounting and recording in which large numbers of persons are grouped within the same abstractions. I elaborate this dimension of derealization later. The Weberian insights require more attention.

The Weberian narrative achieves a new level of relevance in the case of modern warfare because the modern warrior is even more removed from reciprocal human interactions than was the bureaucrat, who was the exemplar of rationalization for Weber. Although Weber noted that modern systems of bureaucratic rationality had their origin in military codes of discipline—a combination of weapons technologies and new disciplinary codes encouraged systems of massed forces to displace cavalry-type individualistic heroics of battles—his emphasis was on the rationalization of industrial forces, for which "military discipline is the ideal model."[18]

However, Weber also recognized how disciplinary practices and new forms of mechanization were creating a human body that was less and less attuned to its emotions and other aspects of its embodiment. He recognized this attenuated and reshaped body particularly in the context of the new industrial technologies:

> The individual is shorn of [his] natural rhythm as determined by the structure of [his] organism; [his] psycho-physical apparatus is attuned to a new rhythm through a methodical specialization of separately functioning muscles, and an optimal economy of forces is established corresponding to the conditions of work.[19]

The contemporary warring body has been modified and attenuated even further than the working body central to Weber's observations. Revelatory in this respect is the weapons manufacturer McDonnell

Douglas's post–Gulf War advertisement for one of its "attack missiles," the SLAM (Standoff Land Attack Missile). The ad refers to the missile's "man-in-the-loop" guidance system, a description that constitutes the totality of the warring body as an assembly of human and machine components.[20] The grammar reflects the situation. In modern warfare, devices shape and use persons.

Accordingly, the Gulf War soldier was not merely influenced by the weapons technology but modified to fit it. Drugs were administered to enhance night vision and make the pilot's body compatible with the night-visioning equipment in the fighter planes. Anxiety depressants and other contributions from the disciplines of molecular biology, biocybernetics, neurochemistry, psychopharmacology, and so on were also employed, along with various other person-extending prostheses, to make the soldier into an effective fighting machine, into a virtual "cyborg soldier."[21] Weber's rationalization of the factory and reshaping of the industrial worker, which was a product of disciplinary practices arising from militarization, has come full circle as the biotechnics of industrialization have fed back into military activities.

In Weber's narrative, as well as in others in the classic sociological tradition, the process of rationalization is a relentless force, not effectively resisted by the human desire to achieve coherence of and control over meaning. In this story, persons are imagined as striving against the pressures of an institutionalized instrumental reason so that their choices can be made responsive to a substantive rationality that accords with personal values.[22] In contrast, the argument here is that the process of derealization of the warring subjects (their cyborgization) and of the objects of lethal violence is overdetermined because human valuing procedures tend to aid and abet the process of derealization associated with technological rationalization rather than oppose it.

Complementing rather than opposing the Weberian rationalization process, which is driven by the structures and forms of modern society, is a Lacanian dynamic based on Jacques Lacan's view of the dynamics of desiring. In this narrative (elaborated in chapter 2), the structures of apprehension provide a conceptual currency within which objects of desire and violence are substitutable. They are identified within a valuing process that the valuing subjects do not understand and control, for the meanings of the objects resonate with dimensions of subjectivity that are not parts of a conscious and rational choice procedure. I discuss this dimension of derealization later. As a first step, we move in the direction of explicating the first narrative and rendering the process for producing abstract enmity peculiar by going back to an ancient and very different condition surrounding warfare, part of Thucydides' account of the Peloponnesian War.

## Identification of Friends and Foes

The immediate provocation for turning to Thucydides is a particular post–Gulf War representation, an advertisement by an affiliate of the Raytheon Corporation that appeared in a coffee-table book commemorating Britain's participation along with the McDonnell Douglas advertisement.[23] The ad refers to Raytheon's device on attack planes known as the IFF (Identification Friend or Foe) system, a piece of technology with which persons and objects are determined to be military targets. The ancient Greek "system" for distinguishing friend from foe differs markedly from Raytheon's. Speaking of what he regarded as "the first among the causes of the Peloponnesian War,"[24] Thucydides tells the story of two naval battles between the Corcyraeans and the Corinthians. Stung by the loss of the first naval battle, the Corinthians spent a year building ships and assembling a navy by recruiting in the Peloponnesus and throughout Hellas.

Alarmed by this threat, the Corcyraeans sought an alliance with Athens, emphasizing the common threat of the buildup in the Peloponnesus. In response to this, the Corinthians sent envoys urging at least neutrality and possibly alliance with them. They reminded the Athenians of their prior nonaggression pact and of the time when Corinth had rendered military aid to Athens in the midst of a crucial battle, a time when one must "deem him who assists them a friend though they may have previously been a foe."[25] Having heard both sides, the Athenians held two assemblies. After the first, they were influenced by the position of the Corinthians, but during the second they swung over to the Corcyraeans,[26] and as a result participated on their side in a subsequent naval battle between the Corinthians and Corcyraeans. Although the battle was indecisive (both sides erected victory monuments), it had the effect of moving the Greek world closer to the larger war.

Especially significant for present purposes are the two Athenian deliberations. It took two assemblies and many days for the Athenians to decide who were to be friends and who foes. It was ultimately a political decision in the full (Greek) sense of the term. The deliberative mechanisms of the polis were engaged as legal, political, and moral dimensions of the choices were examined within the political space of Athenian society.

If we now do a fast-forward to the present, the Greek example provides a context for recognizing what is extraordinary about electronic "friend or foe" identification systems: they represent the disappearance of political space. Spy satellites and electronic ship- and aircraft-carried information systems, which not only determine threats but also automatically send hostile responses, constitute what Paul Virilio has called "the intelligence of war that eludes politics."[27]

Certainly some of the relevant decisions about the Gulf War were politially initiated. But as the codes constructed around the process—Desert Shield, the code name of the initial deployment, and Desert Storm, the code name of the attack on Iraq—imply, the political process was displaced by a language of environmental disaster. The conflicts between persons and collectivities was therefore derealized by the war's media-oriented tropes. Lamenting such tropics of war, Avital Ronell noted the ambiguated cartography that resulted from the various American battle zones—in the Gulf, against drugs, and elsewhere. The representations of war produce "a number of atopical zones that require an altogether new mapping of the world, neighborhood, proximity."[28]

In short, the various instrumentalities—militarized language, environmental tropes, dehistoricized geopolitical language, and technological apprehension of the forces involved—mediating the significance of events in the Middle East for the U.S. public and Congress amount to a shrinking of the space of political deliberation. Accompanying this diminution of political space has been the destruction of geographic inhibitions. Such innovations as the all-terrain vehicle, which dissolves the earth, and the supersonic speed of travel of persons and weapons, which, along with assists from night vision technology, ends the significance of the meteorological day, mean that war, once dominated by the enclosed cities and later the territorial states that kept it close to the spatial divisions of politics, no longer functions within traditional geostrategies.

By way of contrast, we can consider a period in which military and political space and time more or less coincided. For example, the inhabitants of the Renaissance city were keenly aware of the relationship of political and administrative space to the space of war, for the city was a fortress as well as a domain of habitation and a governmental unit. The design of its walls—often a pentagon shape—emerged from the plans of some of the Renaissance's most notable artistic talents, including Leonardo da Vinci and Albrecht Dürer. The coincidence of aesthetic and defense design reflected the recognition of the city as the ultimate in a political aesthetics, a place for harmonious living as well as protection.[29]

The city's designer/architects "had close connections with cartographers or were actually cartographers themselves," and they used "accurate topographical site plans" to fit the fortifications effectively into the landscape.[30] At a minimum, the design of the city was manifestly connected to a militarized view of cartography as well as the coherence of the political and social order. As weapons technology imperiled the wall structures, designs evolved with increased layers of fortfication, with the aim of increasing the time period in which a city could hold out against a siege.

Fortification designs had begun taking cannons into account by 1550,[31] and a deepened rationality of design developed. Once the mobile siege cannon made the high walls of fortresses obsolete, design shifted to a concentration on depth and complicated geometries.[32] Driven no doubt by urgency, by the seventeenth century the rationality of design was reflected in a shift from an Aristotelian model of space, which emphasized a cosmological harmony reflected in "a differentiated set of innerworldy places," to a Euclidean model attuned to the "real space of the world."[33]

Throughout the Renaissance, the space of war was not the battlefield but the city. As is reflected in the names of battles of the period—Breda, La Rochelle, and so on—the "real space of the world" was conceived on the basis of the dangers of armed assaults on cities and the structures needed to buy time.

The center of the embattled city, comprising the essence of its political and military self-understanding, was the ultimate center of its defenses, the citadel, a fortress within the fortress:

> Composed of a single geometrically pure form, containing a city's best ammunition and devoted entirely to its military presence, the citadel is the paradigmatic representation of the fortress, modelled upon the ideal city—Euclidean form and central planning, with total social control represented in its architectural composition.[34]

And ultimately, the military mentality behind the construction of the city colonized other dimensions of social and cultural life: "The defensive imagination, applied to securing the impregnability of the fortress, was translated into a mental habit of accounting and enclosing which eventually pervaded the approach to every human endeavor."[35]

The fabled enemy at the gates, who was far more figurable for those in the Renaissance than to contemporaries, is still motivating today's militarized cartography. Now topographical calculations produce the programming and direction finding for intercontinental missiles, rather than for designing cities as fortresses. The speed with which and directions from which destruction can be delivered have outmoded visible defenses. Indeed, time and the technology of remote vision have almost wholly displaced geographic extension in military significance. And, accordingly, defenses have been dematerialized: radar and other visioning technologies replace walls and other material defenses.[36]

Accompanying the dematerialization of defenses has been a change in the structure of decision making. With the displacement of traditional geographical inhibitions and the "dwindling of the last commodity: duration,"[37] logistically oriented decision-making procedures, which depend on electronic information systems, displace political processes such as those described by Thucydides.[38] Certainly logistical systems are not randomly deployed. They function as an adjunct to already-determined, often historically conceived, threats. For the contemporary United States, for example, there is a rough (although lately unstable) cartography of danger. The geopolitical world at any given moment is divided into friends and potential foes, and violence is expected more from some quarters than from others.

And still the decision to commence hostilities is based on national (and sometimes international) deliberations. These deliberations, however, designate "enemies" only in gross geopolitical terms. Once hostilities are begun, the more significant determinations, particularly the identification of the "combatants" versus "noncombatants," which is implicated in who shall survive, do not always pass through human deliberative assemblies. Increasingly, extrapolitical and, to a large extent, extrahuman information systems replace deliberation. This was most apparent during the Gulf War when a civilian air raid bunker was destroyed after it was "read" (from data stored in a computerized database) as a military target.

Such technological dyslexia has been in evidence for some time and was dramatically illustrated in the recent record of one particular IFF system employed on U.S. ships in the Persian Gulf. The navy's "Aegis battle management system," as described by a group of military journalists, "draws on the latest technologies in digital computers and radar signal processing technologies to create a total weapons system that will automatically detect, track, and engage multiple targets simultaneously"; *engage* is a euphemism for *destroy*.[39]

The navy and some of its celebratory media were excited about the Aegis system before it had had anything but simulated "engagements." Expressing enthusiasm over its ability to "track more than 200 missiles and aircraft simultaneously," one reporter described the system of representation that the Aegis system employs: "Everything over, on, or beneath the ocean in the immediate area is identified. Small symbols differentiate ships from subs, indicate whether the object is friendly or hostile, and plot object, course, and speed." Even in 1986, however, there were indications that the Aegis system might be seriously dyslexic. The excited reporter admitted that one Aegis-equipped ship in the Gulf of Sidra "did fire missiles at a radar contact the Navy has yet to identify," and a navy source thinks that it is likely that the Aegis-equipped cruiser *York Town* "may have blown up a low flying cloud."[40]

Two years later, despite this foreboding, the commander of the cruiser *Vincennes* relied on the Aegis identification system and allowed it to shoot down a passenger plane carrying 290 Iranian civilians (Aegis will automatically fire on targets that meet a predetermined level of threat unless it is manually overridden).[41] Among other things, the Aegis reading and representational systems cannot distinguish a 177-foot airbus from a 62-foot F-14 Tomcat fighter. Apologists for the commander point out that there had already been hostile engagements in the area, that the ship's crew had been put on alert to expect attacks, and, further, that the commander, whose primary responsibility is for the safety of his crew, had very little time to make a decision. But however one might want to interpret the responsibility of the people on the ship, the technology for identifying threats cannot, according to one "specialist," distinguish between "an unknown threat, friendly aircraft, [and] hostile aircraft."[42]

Clearly, the device plays a role in a decision process that was once allocated to human, political deliberation, and the attitude of national security bodies, from the U.S. Joint Chiefs of Staff and the Pentagon through the "hands-on," Nintendo-type warriors, is resignation. As Don DeLillo has noted, in the context of a meditation on military intelligence practices, "devices will drain us, make us pliant."[43] But one must go beyond the recognition that there are pieces of technology identifying friend and foe on the modern, hypermilitarized globe to understand how the contemporary targets of violence are selected. There is a more fundamental historical process of derealization at work, one that transcends mere technological innovation, although the electronic coding systems are a coherent piece of the narrative.

## Derealization: Ontological and Discursive Mediations

The concept of "derealization" is the process by which increasingly abstract and distancing modes of symbolic representation mediate the relationships through which persons and places acquire meanings. In the case of targets of military violence, the modern stage was achieved during the Vietnam War, when, in Virilio's words, "the target area had become a 'cinema location.'"[44] Targeted persons and places were selected by pilotless planes whose imaging devices created data, which were sent back to computer-processing centers. The earth and its inhabitants became a series of strategic coordinates and various symbolic entities within the coordinates. In the absence of direct vision, the targets had been derealized. "Enemies" had become wholly and continuously invisible to those who, relying on electronic identification systems, had to strike at what can be seen only as symbols rather than as discernible bodies.

The beginning of this dimension of derealization—the displacement of direct vision by aerial imaging devices—occurred in World War I, when, with the use of aerial photography, "a terrain was reduced to a set of coded topographical features, 'grounded' by the digital logic of the grid."[45] Photography is simply part of a more general implication of technologies designed to speed up and intensify the reading of signs for military-logistical purposes. Virilio speaks of the production of a "delocalized language which can now be grasped via brief and distant glances." These digitalized and highly symbolic languages have replaced the earlier condensations of military signs, the "signal flags, multi-colored pennants, schematic emblems . . . that replaced faltering voice signals."[46]

As a result of the reigning abstractions and distancing technologies, there has been a representational change from earth and bodies to coor-dinates and symbols arrayed by digital logic. Although this logistically driven move to abstractions to speed up reading was originally devel-oped during specifically violent historical episodes, it is no longer episodic. Because the modern notion of national security is linked with a militarization of the globe, imaging from space satellites and high-altitude aerial reconnaissance, with at least potential hostilities in mind, is a continuous, everyday phenomenon.

Nothing testifies to this more vividly than the cover illustration of a pamphlet published by the National Defense University: a "computer-generated image of the Los Angeles area." It is noted that "Earth data ('quantified and codified information about the earth and its surface features') was used to produce the image and is a critical element in the use of many new weapons."[47] This view of the earth, which shows a digi-talized, contour map–oriented cityscape of Los Angeles with a super-imposed target-sighting symbol, produces Los Angeles as a simulated target zone. In the language of information processing, the authors tell us that "digital earth data" are "information about the earth needed for accurate positioning, targeting, and navigation."[48]

The pamphlet is at once a nontechnical discussion of the concepts implicated in the visual surveillance aspect of the militarization of the globe and a call to arms (the authors complain that at the moment of their writing there were large gaps in information provided by the Defense Mapping Agency, which is responsible for supplying the "data" needed to guide weapons to their targets). Anticipating the logistics of the Gulf War, they point to the specific need for advanced photographic surveillance to provide cruise missiles with a "point positioning data base," because this weapon operates with a proleptic map, a "prestored digital scene of the target."[49] Apparently their dire warnings were not heeded, for one surveillance expert admitted (on a television reprise of Gulf War intelligence), that the Lacross spy satellite was pressed into service to feed the "hungry brains" of the Cruise missiles with terrain maps just before the actual hostilities commenced.[50]

Where does human subjectivity enter the "earth data" scene? Although the "earth" is still produced within a variety of discourses or symbolizing systems—aesthetically oriented landscape paintings, satellite-generated weather maps, and so on—for some societies at certain times, the targeting praxis provides the dominant images of parts of the earth's space. This was the case in U.S. network television coverage of the Gulf War, in which viewers were given pilot- and missile-eye views of targets, complete with sighting crosshairs, and were even treated to actual detonations (but not in "real" time).

The value significance of the abstractions through which warring populations view each other can be discerned when the trend toward military derealization is compared with other historical narratives with similar effects. Perhaps the most apposite is Karl Marx's discussion of the significance of the money form. Marx designated two basic stages in the evolution of the production of equivalents. The first is the development of extended equivalents in which, to employ his metaphor, one commodity serves as the "mirror" of another, as when "the value of a commodity, linen for example, is now expressed in terms of innumerable other members of the world of commodities. Every other physical commodity now becomes a mirror of the linen's value."[51]

But this system of extended equivalents has obvious limitations when the forces at work begin to require a rapidly and widely dispersed exchange system. Therefore, from such extended equivalents, in which one commodity serves as a mirror for another, there develops a generalized equivalent, a universal, substitutable type of value, realized in the form of a single commodity that allows all others to be socially recognized and located on a single register of value. Once this generalized equivalent had become gold, the money form had arrived in a stable, enduring, and pervasive way.

For all the gains to be achieved from the facilitating of exchange that the money form allows, there are obvious losses, and the one Marx lamented was the obscuring of the human involvement immanent in the production of value when commodities are read only on the basis of exchange value. Elaborating Marx's narrative of the displacement of barter by the money form, J. J. Goux notes explicitly the disappearance of the body in the process of exchange: "In barter a harmony of desires and a reciprocity of ties implies that the exchange is also a commerce of bodies," whereas "in capitalist monetary economies," legal tender creates "a differentiated, depersonalized asignificant relation between abstract individuals."[52] As a result, the identity dimension of exchange is removed. The "harmony of desires" is replaced by desiring consumption, and interpersonal connections by person-object valences in which the subjective connections are repressed.

There is an analogous process discernible in the development of the technologies of language—various modes of writing—in which a similar depersonalizing narrative can be glimpsed. As one account has it, as writing developed historically, it moved roughly through stages that can be designated as the pictographic and the ideographic before it achieved the present phonographic stage.[53] At the stage of pictography, the drawings work on the basis of a resemblance between the signifying marks and the things and actions to which they refer. In the next stage, in which ideographic notation takes over (as in hieroglyphics), writing has moved to the extended form of value in that the written signs now represent aggregates rather than individual entities.

Once writing moves to the more abstract stage in which signifiers represent sounds, the stage of general substitution or equivalence has been reached. A small number of linguistic entities, assembled from the units in the alphabet, can be arranged to stand for the entire range of objects and relations, thereby allowing for a more universalistic form of representation. Arbitrary signs produce a system for generating and transmitting meaning.

There are important implications in the narrative of the development of writing technology for the economies of violence. The logic of writing functions to produce and convey an abstract level of hostility. Now, with the narrative of writing technology as a frame, it is possible to deepen the appreciation of abstract enmity. Ironically, this can be done by turning to some pertinent observations on the relationship between the logic of writing and religion.

Jack Goody's inquiries suggest that religions with written texts, unlike those with wholly oral traditions, tend to produce an ethical universalism because "written formulations encourage the decontextualization or generalization of norms." More specifically, religions with written texts produce more general injunctions against violence—formulations such as "thou shalt not kill," rather than thou shalt not kill unless under special orders from this or that leader, or thou shalt not kill other tribal members.[54]

The mediation of the written text produces not only more universalistic codes but also a more mediated authority structure. "The relatively close accommodation between religion and other aspects of the social system in oral societies [although there are contradictions] may give way in written religions to a considerable lack of fit," and to a situation in which religion influences the social system rather than simply expressing aspects of it.[55]

Referring to the demonstrable influence that Christianity has had on marriage laws, and in ways advantageous to the church, Goody insists that "the presence of the text of the word . . . favors a partly independent role for ideology, giving it a measure of 'structural autonomy' which it doesn't possess in oral societies."[56] Adding to Goody's analysis the observation that the written word enfranchises an interpretive elite, we can infer that a writing technology can overdetermine both the distance and the power of abstractions over those subject to them.

It takes only a simple reversal to switch from the effects of the abstracting and universalizing of ethical codes to the effects of the way that a geostrategic form of inscription achieves autonomy from other dimensions of the social system and allows for the imposition and mobilization of enmity toward remote peoples.

To appreciate the effects of these mediating inscriptions, however, it is necessary to consider also the role of machine technologies, which add an additional depersonalizing layer of mediation. For example, with the alphabetization and phoneticization of language, mothers' voices became involved in teaching reading (attenuating the control over reading formerly situated in the patriarchal school). But with the invention of writing apparatuses, "alphabetization-made-flesh" (in the form of "the mother's mouth") gave way to technological media. [57]

For example, the typewriter removed writing from aspects of bodily engagement in the writing process. In place of control by eye and consciousness, the typewriter "institutes spacing as the precondition of differentiation"; it "unlinks hand, eye, and letter," and, ultimately, the subject is removed, for "the word has ample room to be able to do without any help from thought."[58]

These technological effects on abstraction articulate with the effects of desire. Both technologies of communication and vision and the ontological drive toward coherent subjectivity combined to frame the construction of enemy/Others during the Gulf War.

As I noted in a previous chapter, within a Lacanian frame, the objects of desire are substitutable signs related to the subject's attempt at self-constitution and coherence. They are thus never destined to provide the self with satisfaction. Accordingly, during the recent Gulf War, discursively engendered understandings and desires found distant objects of attention, not only for those involved in combat—however technologically mediated that involvement was—but also for the viewing public, who watched the war on television and experienced the destruction of people and things at another technological level of remove. The highly mediated relationship, in which both linguistic and weapons technologies intervened, rendered the relationship between viewing and fighting subjects complex, for the targets of violence were rarely available to anyone's direct vision and were hardly ever available for direct contact. There was very little actual touching.

It was indeed telling when one air force pilot praised his sighting devices and weapons by remarking of his recently vanquished enemy, "We

could reach out and touch him, but he could not touch us" (a bit of discursive flotsam left over from AT&T advertisements for long-distance
telephone service).[59] The remote touching of "someone" was involved.
In most senses, then, the objects of violence in the Gulf War were obscure and remote, both in that they were removed from sight and other
human senses and in that they emerged as appropriate targets through a
tortuous signifying chain. More generally, they were remote in terms of
the *meanings* they had for their attackers as well as the audience/viewers
of the atttackers: those watching the war on television.

To treat the implications of how hostile actions can be understood
in such a peculiar, modern condition, it is appropriate to turn to Luis
Buñuel's film *That Obscure Object of Desire*, which contains not only a
structure and dynamic that fit the array of subjects acting in as well as
following the story of the Gulf War but also is implicitly structured
within a Lacanian frame that fits the approach to interpreting the Gulf
War emphasized here.

## This/That Obscure Object of Desire

At the level of its primary narration, Buñuel's film is the story of a failed
seduction, told in flashbacks by the middle-aged Mathieu Fabert to his
(accidental?) traveling companions, sharing a compartment in a train to
Paris. At a more abstract level, the film is governed by a Lacanian view of
the opacity or deeply encoded noncomportment between desire and its
objects. Ambiguities abound from the outset, not the least of which is
the absence of a designation in the title that a woman is the object in
question. This absence of gender marking adds to the this/that (close or
remote) ambiguity of *cet* in the French title (*Cet obscur objet du désir*).

Moreover, as is shown (but is necessarily evident to all viewers of the
film), Conchita, the object of Fabert's amorous quest, is two different
women (she is represented by two different actresses), and this is seemingly never apparent to Fabert and is of course not known by his listeners in the train compartment. Apart from the various mediations between the various desiring subjects and objects in the film (Fabert's
audience in his train compartment is straining with attention to the narrative), we as viewers also have desires, and they remain unconsummated as the narrative and images frustrate our attempt to attain com-

pletion, to grasp a coherent episode, unless we work to help make it coherent. Despite the seeming confidence with which Fabert delivers his
story, what we see, especially the dualistic Conchita and other enigmatic
images and events, deprives us of confidence that we have a story we can
understand.

Ultimately, the imposition of meaning (by the viewers, among others)
on the ambiguous and arbitrary aspects of Fabert's story is organized
within the frame of a Lacanian view of the functioning of desire. Buñuel
leaves many hints that Lacan hovers in the background, and, most significant for the purposes at hand, the lessons of the film transfer to the
U.S. actions in the Gulf War, for a similar functioning of desire complements the narrative of the derealization of the targets of violence I have
developed.

Because Lacanian desire operates through a series of substitutions,
there is a compatibility between the functioning of desire and logistical
abstraction as they work together to locate targets of violence in modern
warfare, despite how recalcitrant those targets may actually be to the
meaning frames that direct the enemy-perceiving gaze. Of course, the
functioning of desire in a war works on the basis of a process different
from that of an individual's search for erotic completion. It is connected
to national-level rather than individual-level work on the production of
a coherent self. As has already been suggested in my analysis of Clausewitz's duplicitous discourse, what is represented as a quest for accom-
plishing political and military objectives obfuscates a more fundamental, ontological quest, the attempt for the national subject to achieve
completion, to become a wholly coherent identity, through the display
of courage and the lack of inhibition against using force in a violent confrontation with an enemy.

For a deeper appreciation of how desire complements the historically
emerging, logistical narrative in which the enemy/object has been derealized, it is necessary to recognize that within the Lacanian view desire is
formed at the time when the subject first enters the realm of the symbolic.[60] Residing as an infant in the domain of the imaginary, where
there is no recognition of oneself as separate from others, the subject's
entry into the symbolic is a dual alienation. First, it is a separation from
the maternal source of satisfaction and, second, through becoming a

named being within language, it is a loss of control over meaning and the bonds of affect; it amounts to a subjugation to the law of the signifier.

The compensation for this alienation is the ability to participate in the domain of the symbolic, but it is also the birth of desire, which, given the unlawfulness of achieving the satisfactions longed for but lost, takes the form of a series of substitutions. It is the always-obscuring acts, based on the ways in which the subject is divided from itself, that impose significance on the objects of desire, and within the Lacanian model these impositions follow the twists and turns of linguistic, figural mechanisms. More specifically, Lacan notes that "desire *is* metonymy, however funny people may find the idea."[61]

For Lacan, then, desire is not a mere drive or impulse; it is a transformative phenomenon. The seeking after the lost object of desire articulates itself in the form of a representational practice. "The structure of representation is present in the very process of the drive," as Lacan puts it.[62] The demand for fulfillment that the drive expresses is addressed to an "Other" who stands in for the attempt by the subject to achieve a coherent, untroubled sense of identity or self. The Other seems to hold the truth of the subject, but is, according to Lacan, merely arbitrary.

To apply these insights to violence, we must add another transformation, making the object of desire an object of violence. As I noted in chapter 2's reprise of Hegel on war, however, this transformation is always already involved in the ontological work of the self in its projects of coherence. As a first step, moreover, we must recognize that objects of both desire and violence are similarly arbitrary. Both derive their ascriptions as desirable or dangerous from prior interpretive expectations in which the subject (individuals and collectives) already have places for them, places for appealing Others or enemies. Nowhere is the relationship to objects mediated through a metonymically organized representational practice better elaborated than in Buñuel's film.

The mechanisms are most apparent in the film when Conchita gets in bed with Fabert in a chastity-protecting undergarment tied tightly with little knots that he cannot undo. As he weeps in frustration, she names the various parts of her that he already possesses and expresses puzzlement that he is so resolute in his quest for the one part that is denied him. During the Gulf War, President George Bush and many television commentators seemed caught in a similar signifying structure. What eluded final consummation in their case was not someone's maiden-head. It was the destruction of Saddam Hussein. All the parts associated with him were possessed. Kuwait was freed, his army was routed, his "weapons of mass destruction" were largely eliminated. But as long as Saddam remained the ruling leader of Iraq, the "victory in the desert" seemed empty. The narrative was left uncompleted.

But perhaps "Saddam Hussein" (the "Hitler," the "Arab fanatic," the "ruthless dictator") needed to survive. Without him, there would have remained no archenemy. Without Saddam Hussein, the United States might not have been able to justify remaining so armed and alert. Indeed, this is precisely what Fabert says in response to his cousin, the arbiter/judge who asks why he doesn't just marry Conchita. Fabert says, "Si je l'epousais, je serai desarmé" ("If I married her, I would be disarmed"). If Saddam had been destroyed or removed, no sense of fulfillment would have lasted because the conditions of possibility for producing desire would reemerge. For example, there is of late in the United States (as I noted in chapter 2) a national debate over toward whom the reduced nuclear weapons arsenal ought to be aimed. National desire is searching for new dangerous objects.

At this moment, at least, Fabert seems to understand much of what is driving his narrative, but there is also much evidence that the more fundamental part remains obscure, for his story continually turns the incredible—for example, encountering Conchita almost everywhere—into the credible. This is because the object of desire for Fabert (Mathieu for one Conchita and Mateo for another), like the enemy/object of violence for the United States, is in part a product of a damaged subjectivity in search of reestablishing coherence as an effective and virile male entity. The nonrapport with the self, which is fundamental to obsessive forms of object identification within the Lacanian model, is especially exacerbated in both instances.

In the case of the United States, the damaged collective subjectivity (often called the "Vietnam syndrome") is a result of a lost and muddled war in the recent past. In the case of Fabert, his manly subjectivity is similarly uncertain. First, his wife of many years is recently deceased and he has had no substitute prior to his pursuit of Conchita. Second, he is a law-abiding, obviously well-established and well-off citizen and in his pursuit of Conchita uses his spending power rather than his male strength (until the very end, when he is driven to the limit with frustration). Meanwhile, all around him, he witnesses a series of acts of violence: car bombings and political assassinations, apparently carried out by youthful terrorist groups. At one point we overhear a radio report claiming that the bombings, which are randomly dispersed in his narrative, are attributed to coalitions of political groups that form the acronyms PRIQUE and RUT.

The virile young terrorists, with which one version of Conchita seems to be associated, serve as an affront to Fabert, who cannnot show his potence (cannot use his prick). Similarly, the collective subjectivity of the United States prior to the Gulf War (the Vietnam syndrome) and its leader's potence (the "wimp factor") had been affronted by the violence of others not restricted by law-abiding inhibitions. Hence the increasingly frenzied complaints from the White House against terrorists (similar complaints issue from Fabert about the terrorist acts around him). Thus the comparison: two levels of incomplete and increasingly provoked subjectivity in need of an episode of completion.

But perhaps the major similarity that suggests Buñuel's film as a model of the Gulf War is the similarity in the dynamics governing the meanings of the objects of attention. In Fabert's narrative, Conchita appears as both lack (as an elusive object of desire) and excess (she appears everywhere Fabert goes). At one point, Fabert's servant likens women to a *sac d'excrement*. Rather than simply a sexist disparagement, this can be read as reference to the object of desire's excess, of all that is imposed on it by a restless, driven subjectivity. Conchita flees Fabert's employ as a servant after his initial advances, and then he encounters her as a restaurant coat check person, as part of a youthful gang in Switzerland, as a flamenco dancer in Seville. She is excessive, inexplicably appearing everywhere. With each encounter, she seems to promise herself to Fabert and then does something extraordinary to frustrate him. Similarly, as the Gulf War progressed, Saddam's resistance capability was easily overcome, but U.S. air superiority and the decisive land battle left Saddam where he was, a defiant leader of an Iraqi nation that was badly bruised but had never been completely possessed. What substitutes for a final and telling violence in the Gulf War is a fitful and ambiguous attempt to force the object, Saddam, to comply with the law (the United Nations resolution).

Within a Lacanian frame and, accordingly, in Buñuel's film, the relationship between the law and desire is complex. The law cannot still the operation of desire in the direction of seeking consummation. It may even provoke it. In a telling episode, Fabert atttempts to use the law—his cousin the judge—to send the object of desire away. The judge uses his influence to have the police exile Conchita and her mother, sending them back to Spain. As the decree is read, we learn that Conchita is a name related to her legal name, which is Concepción, and that her mother's name is Encarnación, deepening our suspicion that their existence and significance are largely a function of the work of the subject, Fabert and his desire-driven imagination.

Fabert decides to take an arbitrary trip to forget his frustration, but after he chooses Singapore by pointing to a map while he is blindfolded, he ends up traveling to Seville, where Conchita is. The arbitrary is always controlled at some level by desire. It is not wholly clear what the signifying elements are that turn Singapore (etymologically, "lion city") into Seville (etymologically, merely "city"). Perhaps it is that the lion represents virility and reminds Fabert of his quest to enact it. What emerges most significantly is the need for a woman to complete Fabert's self (in the way that the United States needed an enemy and George Bush needed to get tough for self-completion), and here again the law does not quiet desire; it seems only to inflame it. Moreover, the love object or object of violence is arbitrary inasmuch as it does not summon on the basis of what is intrinsic to it. It acquires its force from the signifying practices that erupt out of a subjectivity pursuing it, a subjectivity that lacks a reflective rapport with itself.

Once the objects are fixed upon, they need to be justified (to be changed from the arbitrary to the relevant), and here the subject can count on a lot of help. One of the most apropos comparisons between the Buñuel film and the Gulf War would situate both the war's media interrogators and their interviewees in the place of the traveling companions on the train, and the television viewers in the place of the film viewers.

The traveling companions in the compartment are complicit in a variety of ways with Fabert's narrative. One is a dwarf who, upon first entering the compartment, is accosted by a little girl who leaps up and tries to assist him as he struggles to climb up onto his seat. He turns and says he needs no help, but it emerges that he needs no help understanding Fabert's incredible story. He needs no discursive assistance, for he is always already at work rationalizing the arbitrary. He is busy reproducing a world within which the arbitrary becomes the expected. Such is the case with the rest of the travelers as well. After seating himself, the dwarf turns to the man next to him, offering him his copy of *Le Monde*, and the man declines, saying he has already read it. Fabert's story, which is elicited when the passengers see him pour a bucket of cold water over Conchita's head outside the train, is about to unfold within a widely shared pre-text.

It is the dwarf (who needed no help) who poses the question for the rest of the travelers (and for the film viewers) about the meaning of Fabert's act of drenching Conchita. How can he justify the sudden violence?: "Je voudrais savoir l'origin de votre geste." We viewers need more of the narrative as well, for the film has opened with a room in disarray, blood on a pillow, and wet panties on the floor. There are many signs that Fabert has violently raped a woman, whom his valet says has already left the scene. The viewers are thus as expectant of a vindicating narrative as the traveling companions. The viewers are helplessly remote, however, while the travelers increasingly appear to be complicit. It turns out that as they speak, they recognize each other as neighbors or have seen each other in Paris at public events. They are old hands at discursive complicity, and the most complicit is the dwarf, who turns out to be a professor of psychology. He is available to all, for, as he puts it, he gives "private lessons." Accordingly, at one interval, he fills in part of the story for Fabert.

The primary parallel between the film and the television narration of the war should be apparent. First, we return to the derealization or dematerialization of the object of violence. Like Conchita, Fabert's object of desire, the targets of violence emerge from a combination of subjective identity—striving practices coupled with a technology that constitutes targets logistically—that is, within an automated, digitized discourse that makes the objects symbolically abstract or remote and obscure while the distance between the objects and those who deploy the weapons also contributes to the dematerialization of them.

Throughout Buñuel's story, the two Conchitas and the arbitrary venues of her appearance dematerialize her; she is indeed more of a conception (Concepción) than living flesh. But, as in the war scenario, actions must be vindicated, and therefore the arbitrary must be turned into the the nonarbitrary (what has been dematerialized must be rematerialized; what has been derealized must be rerealized). Fabert has a lot of help in this regard. To his listeners on the train and to the viewing audience of the film, *That Obscure Object of Desire* is an intelligible narrative, but this intelligibility, this recognition and familiarizing of Conchita as an appropriate and understandable object of desire, despite her arbitrary appearances, physiognomy, and conduct, is a function of the way that Fabert's narrative is aided by those to whom it is addressed. Like Fabert, his viewers/audiences already have a place for such an object. It is a Lacanian object inasmuch as for Lacan "*the place logically precedes objects which occupy it.*"[63]

This Lacanian logic applies equally to the mechanisms by which the media and their audiences welcomed the targets of the Gulf War, for again, the places for such objects were already there. As is well known, the narrative and images of the Gulf War were tightly controlled by the military. Like Fabert, the military was in charge of the narrative, and, as in the film, the images followed the story line from the perspective of the narrator. In the case of the war, control over the images was only partly a function of the military's media censorship. As a result of technological developments in weaponry, particularly laser-guided bombs and missiles, there are videos that provide pilot- and missile-eye views of the war. The military provided the media and their audience a war seen from the point of view of its battle strategy. And, provided with the most exciting images available—military videos of strikes on targets—the media picked them up and showed them to an audience increasingly on the verge of switching back to their regular television-viewing habits. The media then reinforced this strategic orientation and did their own logistical version of the war.

Most of the informant/interviewees upon whom the media called were logistical experts, former military and intelligence personnel who supplemented the missile- and pilot-eye views with strategic talk. The war was thus told and seen from the point of view of the military's electronic prostheses, the digitizing visioning equipment that selects and destroys their derealized targets. Even the television viewer's ability to see explosions was a result of military seeing. The television audience saw the initial attack on Baghdad in the light of the tracer bullets and missiles guiding pilot vision,[64] and they saw some subsequent night strikes with the same thermal imaging devices that had provided the pilots with night vision. Truly, the war was seen through the squint of the sovereign eye. Through media control, coupled with the development of sighting with weapons, those with the power to wage war displayed "war" through the sighting dimension of its killing devices. Nothing was available to show for those with the will and potential power to resist the interpretive imperatives that the logistical displays entailed.[65]

The weapons-eye view became sovereign, then, in the sense that it was authoritative, controlling, and largely legitimated by the perspectives of the subject/viewers. While with respect to some public policy dynamics sovereignty is constituted through a contentious process over the significance of various objects—that is, eligibility to determine significance is dispersed among scattered perspectives—in this case the range of possible contention was diminished and "channeled" through the medium of television, the modern sovereignty device that welds intelligibility constituencies to authoritative images and voices. The coverage ultimately encouraged an identification with "our weapons," for through its logos, images, interviewees, and so on, it reproduced what Elaine Scarry has argued is the injury-sequestering tendency of military representations of war, which are effected through an "exchange of idiom between weapons and bodies."[66] In short, the war was described and shown by reference to the weapons rather than to the affected bodies. Accordingly, violence emerges as a kind of "disarming rather than injuring,"[67] and the reading of its significance is abstracted to make it appear to be a technological contest, a series of exchanges whose outcomes amount to imbalances of logistical expertise.

In discursively reproducing this orientation to war, the media were turned into linguistic dwarfs (to return to Buñuel's metaphor), smaller versions of the same thinking as it slavishly helped to turn arbitrary vio-

lence into rational action. At televised press conferences, reporters posed
questions that encouraged logistical responses. When, for example, the
viewers were "put in the cockpit of an F-115E for one of the air to ground
sorties," the reporters asked about the key to such successful targeting.
"We've been able to execute [no pun intended] because we've been
training very hard," responded the commander of the air war (Lieutenant General Horner). Flanked by both ancient and modern tactical
devices, a map and a video machine, Horner showed a video replay of a
"successful strike" on the headquarters of his "counterpart." A question
was posed about whom we were trying to kill—any "specific persons"?
queried a reporter. But the discourse returned immediately to abstract
technical/spatial talk, the derealized imagery of such locations as "the
war theater."[68]

For the most part, eliciting details about the delivery of technological
might was enough for the media. The national team was winning, and
one CNN commentator describing the initial attacks on Baghdad linked
the attack with the primordial violence of the emergence of the United
States as a nation. "The sky was filled with a star-spangled display of
lethal force," he exclaimed. While the dominant orientation of the media
was in the direction of the military's tendency to both technologically
and discursively derealize the objects of violence, a few scenes of actual
human carnage were shown. There was video footage of bodies being
removed from an air raid bunker that had been penetrated by a missile,
killing scores of civilians.[69]

The bunker was selected as a target (as was a baby-milk factory) by
satellite-level surveillance and targeting mechanisms. The destruction of
these "targets," which produced some of the few discernible human moments and consequences available to television viewers, resulted from a
data-gathering routine that involves minimal human discretion. One
intelligence officer admitted that the targets were "in the database," but
that the data were not current.[70]

The arbitrariness of the resulting deaths from these incidents can be
traced to the derealization of the targets, which in this case involved
temporal judgments suspended in the interface of human-machine target identifications. The media responded by simply covering the military's discourse within which the arbitrary was again turned into the

reasonable and rational. "Allied intelligence had detected military personnel moving in and out of the building,"[71] said a Pentagon official. "I'm here to tell you that this was a military target," said an air force spokesperson at a televised press conference.

The controlled narration produces the same result Fabert's story produces in Buñuel's film. After the viewers (and train travelers) see a beaten and bruised Conchita and are horrified to see what appears to be an undeserving victim, the controlling narrator, Fabert, reconstructs her as a deserving target of the violence, indeed, as "the worst woman in the world." But both stories, that of the film and that of the war, do not end. The possibility of consummation is ambiguous. Indeed, in this respect the war and the film are strikingly parallel. In the film, after producing, with some assistance, a story for those sharing his compartment that effectively anathematizes Conchita, making her man's worst enemy, Fabert is seen leaving the train in Paris with Conchita. They get in a taxi and are later seen walking arm in arm. Despite how contentious, fractious, and violent their relationship has been, the suggestion remains that Fabert needs his object of desire—his lack and his excess—to complete himself, or at least to carry on with the project of maintaining the masculine identity he presents to the world.

The Gulf War leaves us with a similar suspicion. Saddam Hussein, our archenemy, remains in place, occupying a position that national desire would nevertheless reproduce were he to be removed. Despite the trumpeting about our "victory in the Gulf," the discourse on the danger from such enemies reasserts itself. Even now, the media dwarfs are busy helping the militarized national consciousness fix on an antagonism. The problematic at present is how to justify armed preparedness in a world of dissolving power blocs that have until recently reliably supplied antagonists. Unable to use the old ideological discourse that required the existence of implacable communist regimes, one inventive commentator has provided a geopolitical category that is aimed at saving our identity-affirming cartography. There exists the dangerous entity he calls "the weapons state," which possesses "weapons of mass destruction"; examples are such feisty little places as Libya, North Korea, and Iraq. He argues that the antagonistic structure of response to such enemies must be "unipolar"—that the United States must be the sole geopolitical unit taking the responsibility for managing the dangers.[72] It turns out that national-level hostility still needs its objects, but the rationale remains duplicitous.

As in the case of Clausewitz's discourse, the objects only appear to be the result of an epistemologically oriented kind of thinking, a thinking that locates dangers as external objects to be met by the endangered subject. Despite the strategic coding, then, the more significant frame is ontological. The commentator is fixing on objects, but their meaning derives from the concern with maintaining selfhood.[73] This is made even more evident when an adjacent dwarf, writing in the same issue of—appropriately—*Foreign Affairs*, writes of the need for a new "self-justification" now that the United States lacks the one it had "for nearly a half century," until the East Bloc dissolved.[74] Lest there be any doubt that it is the maintenance of a coherent subjectivity, not rationality in the old external means-ends sense, that is at stake, the commentator is explicit, and here his remarks support the case for the operation of a desire whose restless quest is aimed—*through* its objects of attention—at its own constitutive identity: "The great lesson of the cold war ended may be stated in these words: being is superior to doing. What a nation is, is essential. What it does can only express what it is."[75]

# FOUR

# From the Halls of Moctezuma to the Tube and Silver Screen

## Introduction: Recruitment

A modern society's warfare organizations, like its other agencies, need to be intelligible and appealing in order to recruit employees. However, contemporary military recruitment functions within an agonistic environment. First and foremost, there are extraordinary delicacies involved in representing the positions. Contemporary popular media, with differing levels of cultural authority, emphasize how lethal the work can be for both the recruits and their adversaries. And more generally, now more than ever, U.S. armed services recruitment efforts must struggle against various political, social, and cultural criticism of military work in general and of particular "missions," both acknowledged wars from Vietnam through the Persian Gulf and various "peacekeeping activities." Various media represent values that conflict with cultures of militarism and therefore complicate the design and dissemination of recruitment appeals.

Further complicating the recruitment process has been a disruption of what was once a relatively stable basis for promoting the military management of a dangerous world. The cartography of interstate antagonism is now radically unstable, and even the statecentric model for enmity, the state-oriented geopolitical map, is contested by alternative mappings of peoples, tribes, and nationalities. Since the demise of the cold war, enemies do not have fixed addresses. Despite these delicacies and inhibitions that affect representational strategies in recruitment messages, the general approach to attracting recruits has been comparable with that of other agencies. Social and cultural codes evoking broadly distributed stocks of signs within the social order are the predominant mechanisms used to locate the work. More specifically, the images and texts in military recruitment ads function within two quite distinct kinds of codes. One kind is rationalistic or utilitarian. The appeal is to a match between what are projected as the recruit's personal career objectives and the ways that the military unit can provide resources and a context for achieving them.

There is a venerable historical tradition associated with this kind of appeal. For example, recruitment into the Roman army promised land in exchange for military service.[1] More recently, the utilitarian appeal has been characteristic of U.S. Army recruitment television ads, which urge young people to join the army now for free job training or to obtain financial aid for college later.

The other kind of appeal is more ontological. It describes the military unit as a place in which the self can be realized or perfected. However, the implication is that the primary "self" exemplified is masculine. Although the various armed services are increasingly less gender-typed, qualities that tend to be understood as masculine—strength, toughness, perseverance, and individual distinction—are emphasized. The prize is not something exogenous for the self to use but the making of an exemplary (male) self. What is offered is a way to *be* rather than the fulfillment of preferences or the acquisition of valued things.

In this second domain of codes, the effectiveness of military recruitment advertising has to be a function of the plausibility and centrality of the codes with which the armed services identify themselves and of the general cultural disparagement of those codes from which they distance themselves. In a contemporary state society such as the United States, as contrasted with both traditional, tribal societies and some state societies earlier in this century, military recruitment is not wholly facilitated by the surrounding culture. In many contemporary nation-states, the sources of ontological commitment are fragmented. Many citizens are or are descended from refugees; they have diasporic identities and locate themselves with respect to more than one global nodality. Such conditions produce significant contention over the value of various territorial identities. Thus, in addition to contention between military codes of daring, honor, and discipline and alternative cultural codes that are specifically antimilitaristic, there is resistance to official frames for mapping antagonisms, owing to divided territorial loyalties and senses of attachment.

To appreciate the impact that this deepened level of fragmentation has on military recruitment, we can examine political cultures that have been, at least in some periods, relatively undivided in their support of military establishments and their projects. While the identity commitments of armed services in contemporary nation-states are often contentious, subject to critique, and disjunctive with other domains of societal distinction, two contrary cases help to situate the recruitment environment created by such contention. First, in some Mesoamerican subcultures just prior to the Spanish invasion, there were periods in which military honors were almost universally applauded as the highest possible distinction. I discussed this martial culture briefly in chapter 2, and I will elaborate on it here.

Second, the recruitment of the Australian (Anzac) military contingent during the "Great War" provides an exemplary case of virtually universal complicity among cultural, social, and organizational sectors in support of national participation. Although the pressures that the war experience ultimately placed on Australian society created substantial fragmentation—"the war provoked class conflict and religious and racial hatred; it confirmed the male dominance of society and produced massive displays of confrontation"[2]—patriotism and loyalty to empire were encouraged early on by virtually all Australian institutions. Almost universally, the clergy supported the call to arms; academics were largely united in their support (the University of Melbourne convened a series of prowar lectures); schoolbooks emphasized duty to empire and along with other popular texts produced a romantic imagery of war; and the Australian press, unlike some British papers (such as the *Manchester Guardian*), urged a quick and unrestrained Australian military response.[3]

In addition, the Australian sports establishment, which had an especially significant place in Australian male culture, played an indirect recruitment role. Sport analogies and metaphors were a major part of recruitment appeals, and they helped to forge the codes of manhood that translated into military adventurism. This intimacy of sport and war in pre–World War I Australia is picked up in Peter Weir's film representation of Australian recruitment. The opening scenes of his *Gallipoli* focus on the cultural context and present the Australian version of preoccupation with achieving manhood. The story begins as Archie, an aspiring sprint champion, is being coached by his uncle (a former "manly" adventurer). After a training scene in which the uncle behaves like a drill sergeant, the narrative cuts to a challenge to Archie from other young ranch hands with whom he works. "Girls run, men box," says one contemptuously. The ensuing contest between Archie on foot in a race against the taunter on horseback emphasizes the masculinity struggles, expressed through athletic competitions, that surround the interactions of many Australian young men.

The media that convey the masculinity codes within which their self-preoccupations function are especially notable. One is oral and the other textual. The crucial scenes with regard to the interaction of the masculinity codes and media begins with a conversation in which Archie's uncle tries to dissuade him from joining the army, saying he is underage. Archie protests that his uncle was also at least this young when he went out as a young adventurer. Shortly afterward there is a shift from the oral—stories of his uncle's adventures—to the textual. Archie overhears his uncle reading Kipling's *Jungle Book* aloud to his younger siblings. He walks into the room just as Bagera is saying to Mowgli, "Now I know that thou art a man and a man's cub no longer."

Immediately afterward, Archie is in his room opening *Every Boy's Book: Sport and Pastime,* into which he has tucked a newspaper clipping with a report on the British campaign in Gallipoli right next to a page with this heading: "Splendid Gallantry, Magnificent Achievement." As Archie traces his finger around Turkey, he is seemingly locating the place where his manhood can be tested (as his boyhood is left behind). And not incidental to this process is the newspaper whose daily existence provides a textual mechanism for Archie to identity himself as an Australian and member of the Commonwealth as well as to identify Turks as his enemies. The newspaper is the major vehicle for constructing the national imaginary.[4]

This print medium is important in the next scene as well. The other young ranch hands are sitting around while one reads a report in the

Western Australia press about the war on the Turkish front. As he reads an account of the Turkish tactic of digging pits with false bottoms to catch foot soldiers, another shouts "bastards" and adds, "That's it, I'm going to join up." Another adds "Me too" and "How about you?" shortly followed by "Hey, we could all join up together." And lest the extent to which masculinity codes are central be forgotten, one who is undecided for a moment is reminded: "Hey, the girls go wild over a uniform."

Weir also includes reminders that lives as well as manhood are at stake. The film deploys many signs of death, particularly during the Anzac prewar exercises in Egypt, where scenes of the pyramids supply much of the death imagery. Ultimately, Archie and many of his young friends die in Turkey, driven there by, among other things, the cultural codes that motivate them to become men by finding a violent adversary and by the way in which the textual form, the print media, help them to forge their identifications with an extended "imagined community," Australia and the British Empire.[5]

As assault troops trying to dislodge well-entrenched Turkish troops on a hillside, the initial Australian attackers were a virtual suicide squad. This unusual vulnerability of the Australian troops evokes an immediate comparison with the U.S. Marine Corps, for throughout their history, the marines have been a highly vulnerable assault force. For example, one in every sixty marines (including noncombatants) serving in Vietnam died in combat, a death rate of more than double that of army personnel and roughly seventeen and nineteen times the death rate of air force and navy personnel respectively.[6] Marines are especially at risk, for as assault troops, they are relatively ill equipped to hold territory once it is taken. The manhood appeal, which is foregrounded in marine recruitment, has thus had a similar deadly consequence.

The U.S. experience in the Vietnam War, including the extraordinarily high marine casualty rate, resulted in a fragmented political culture with respect to U.S. participation in armed conflicts. Attitudes toward military vocations were divided. Although public support for militarism has made a strong comeback since the Gulf War, this fragmentation, much of which is reflected in various media, at the levels of both popular and official culture, nevertheless provides the current context for the recruitment of the most ontologically oriented of all the military services, the

U.S. Marines. An identity concern, what it means to be a marine, has been foregrounded in recruitment appeals.

## The Chessboard in the Sand

In contrast with the recruitment of Australians during World War I, the contemporary marine is recruited at a time when visual forms have tended to displace textual ones. In this context, my analysis turns to one of the more remarkable television recruitment ads for marines. It began running frequently during the football season in the fall of 1992 and continued to run, in various versions, adjacent to sports news telecasts well into 1995. It was doubtless positioned to reach the maximum audience of recruitable young men and at the same time to take advantage of the relays between sport and war on which masculinity codes thrive.

In response to one of the standard critiques of marine values, physicality and brute force rather than intellection, the advertisement adds smartness to the package. A marine recruitment magazine that anticipated the ad's debut noted that "the Marine Corps decided that adding the element of mental strength to the already pervasive Marine Corps image of being tough and elite would heighten the appeal of the Marines to today's school and college graduates."[7]

In the most elaborate version of the ad, the scene opens on an Arthurian-looking wizard in black, carrying a huge sword (Figure 2; the costumes are taken from the film *Excalibur*). A fadeaway shows that he and other white and black figures are on a chessboard in a desert landscape. The black wizard propels himself magically (there are no strides; he almost seems to be on wheels), and he strikes down the flag holder of the white side, who disappears in a magical poof. The scene cuts to the white king, who gestures for retaliation. A white knight on horseback goes into action and vanquishes the magician, who also disappears at a laserlike sword stroke (reminiscent of scenes from *Star Wars* films and Nintendo video games).

Next, a female magician/wizard in black shows up and directs various foot soldiers in medieval costumes in the direction of the white knight. These soldiers are also vanquished with swift sword strokes, and as the white knight moves to meet their attacks, a long view indicates that he is advancing in an orderly patterned way across the chessboard; his move-

PUBLIC SERVICE ANNOUNCEMENT

Figure 2. Marine recruitment television advertisement

ments conform to the pattern of the contest. After the white knight vanquishes various kinds of foot soldiers, the female black wizard raises both arms as if summoning evil cosmic forces, and then a black knight on horseback enters swinging a mace against the white knight's sword (a familiar scene from film culture—both *Ivanhoe* and *Excalibur*, among others).

Although the female wizard keeps supporting the black knight with various gestures, he is also vanquished as a voice-over says, "To compete, you've got to be strong." The white knight then approaches the black king with sword pointed toward him and the king bows in a gesture of capitulation, showing a skull on his crown, as the voice-over adds, "To win, you've got to be smart" (which accords with the chess imagery and thus the new cerebral emphasis the corps wishes to add to its image). Then the white knight rears back on his horse and draws lightning (the forces of good from the cosmos) with his raised sword. The camera then closes on the arm clad in armor, which changes to a modern marine dress uniform. Then, with the camera drawing back, we see a young marine doing parade maneuvers with his sword. A shift to a profile shot shows that the young marine is standing very stiff and straight (particularly his neck), as the voice-over says, "Maybe you can be one of us: the few, the proud, the marines."

Two different domains of codes must be addressed if we are to appreciate the conveyed meanings of the recruitment ad. One is the set of codes from which it is constructed, and the other is the set belonging to the culture of the viewers, helping to mobilize their interpretive reactions. Looking first at the construction of the ad, the historical codes are perhaps most evident.[8] The costumes of all the figures and, in particular, the strikingly upright posture of the white knight evoke those past ages in which soldiering and individual moral character were inseparable. The individualistic nature of the fighting reflects a tradition of individual distinction in battle going back at least as far as ancient, prehoplite Greece, where combat took place between exemplary champions. Battles were "a mosaic of face-to-face duels between *promachoi*" (champions) with the purpose of producing "a wholly personal superiority," in contrast to the subsequent age of hoplites (citizen soldiers), who massed together in phalanxes that experienced collective victory or defeat.[9] And the U.S. Marine Corps seems to hold onto such an individualistic model of valor, in contrast to the team codes characteristic of the U.S. Army's self-representation.

The other notable historical code connects the bearing of the knight with a history of body culture associated with being a soldier. As Georges Vigarello noted:

From the Middle Ages on, every failure of physical uprightness has been attributed to two main categories: the stigma of deformity, sanctioned by the attention given to strength and aesthetic qualities, and the lack of proper deportment prescribed mainly by socialized ethics.[10]

Michel Foucault offered a similar observation about the semiotics of the soldier, which he identified as persisting into the seventeenth century. The soldier's body comportment "bore certain signs of his strength and valour"; he displayed "a bodily rhetoric of honour."[11] The extraordinarily strict control over bodily posture, which is characteristic both of the marines' training and of their representations of who they are, thus goes back to the era in which outward deportment was supposed to say something about the inner depths.[12] Inasmuch as the body posture continues to convey these codes, recruits are being invited to join, at once, the strong and pure of form and the morally proper. And this recruitment ad maintains a continuity of the military body from the erect posture of the knight on horseback to the erect posture of the young marine, whose extraordinarily stiff and straight neck has stood as the primary coding mechanism for strength, honor, and morality since the Middle Ages.[13]

The imbrication of the historical and bodily coding provides the central tropes of the ad's expressed meaning: the marine is not only strong and morally correct but also part of a noble historical tradition (it was indeed the noble caste who followed these strict rules of posture). There is therefore a continuity between the noble courtly caste and the modern marine. Both operate with an "ideal of physical violence"[14] with parallels in their posture.

Significantly, the recruitment ad emulates a second important dimension of the strict rules governing the deportment of the courtly noble caste. Vigarello points out that by the sixteenth century, books on deportment for the nobility established not only "a stricter control over posture and the right position" but also strictures on the spaces of that deportment. He quotes one of the influential treatises from that century:

"The plan for a perspective is a checkerboard: in the construction of sketches we start with a regular grid pattern, and identical rectangles juxtaposed to each other generate, as they become more distant, similar triangles. Nothing is better suited to marquetry."[15]

Viewed in historical perspective, the chessboard in the ad therefore has resonances beyond the metaphor of the game. The marine's discipline has a noble history not only through its body culture but also through its disciplined uses of space.

The presence of other strong codes serves to overdetermine the morality standing of the marine. In addition to the nobility with which correctness and deportment are associated, a good-evil polarity permeates the rhetoric and narrative structure of the ad. The white knight versus black sorcerers, soldiers, and knights is of course coherent with the chessboard metaphor, which locates the marine in a strategic situation, reinforced by the voice-over saying "You've got to be smart." But in addition, the white-black code is unmistakably a good-evil one, which is underscored by two additional signs, one obvious and one subtle.

The obvious one appears near the end of the brief narrative, when the black king bows in capitulation and reveals the skull on his headgear. The subtle one is a gender code, represented by the choice of a sorceress instead of a sorcerer to direct the attacks against the white knight. While her upraised arms seem to be summoning an extraworldly evil source, the fact of her gender cannot be ignored. The evil beguiling woman of the other tribe appears often in the Old Testament (Delilah is an example), and from the Arthurian legends there is Merlin's counterpart, the evil sorceress Morgan LeFay (more likely the explicit model for the recruitment ad).[16]

However, there is another level at which an oppositional woman has meaning in the context of recruiting marines. Since ancient times the meaning of the soldier's strength has been constructed through its opposition to the feminine, and the unisexuality of military units has been jealously guarded. In the case of the U.S. military, the marines were the last to let women maintain active status in peacetime (1948). In general, as Barbara Ehrenreich has noted, warrior castes regard women as "a threatening intrusion in the unisexual world of war."[17] The gender code in the ad therefore has important resonances with the self-creating practices of marines (a theme to which I will return in a discussion of films).

What becomes especially significant at this point, however, is the highly symbolic representations and therefore unrealistic and anachronistic historical scenario of an ad that seeks to recruit "real men." The

various inhibitions of the ad address various necessary political delicacies and at the same time represent a frustration that modern warriors
experience. One important delicacy relates to the white-black, good-evil
polarity for an agency that must recruit African-Americans. This problem is handled in one version of the ad, in which the cut from the knight
to the young marine in full dress doing parade maneuvers reveals a black
marine.

The larger political issue, however, has to do with the ad's inability to
refer to specific enemies and hostile territories. Given the breakdown of
historical partisanships and traditional enmities, geopolitical spaces and
national identities can no longer be unambiguously allocated to friendly
and unfriendly categories. Marine recruitment ads must therefore eschew
geopolitical and national partisanship lest they offend various foreign
and domestic sensibilities. The chessboard and mythic figures provide a
visual representation that codes the marines in terms of a contest. Power,
morality, and the disciplinary postures and structures for the shaping of a
virtuous self are involved, but the resources for specific enmities, which
make possible warfare as a vocation, are not supplied. The ad is thus a response to what has been called in a similar context "visual desperation."
James Elkins's uses the expression to represent the conditions of possibility for seeing bodies of unfamiliar creatures, arguing that it is through
analogic thinking, guided by linguistic constructions, that comprehensi-
bility can be achieved in the absence of familiar models. Elkins's field of
application is microscopy. He notes that the visualization of unfamiliar
shapes becomes translated into a vocabulary of bodies through analogies,
without which "we might see meaningless aggregates."[18]

If we adapt this insight to an examination of the desperation involved
in creating visible enemies to represent what cannot be seen, we can recognize the same strategy in the ad. It achieves a resolution of the visual
desperation through a reliance on "analogies . . . deep-rooted in our
habits of seeing."[19] The Marine Corps ad relies on "habits of seeing" that
derive from a culture that watches films that, among other things, code
the good-evil polarity with white and black. It is not surprising, therefore, that the genre from which the analogies are drawn is the Hollywood feature film. Where else can one find a domain of visual codes and
narratives shared throughout the culture?

This of course raises the issue of which films. For example, why the Arthurian legend, conveyed to the modern youth culture through such films as *Excalibur*, rather than recent military adventure films? Apart from the sensibility problem—it is difficult to fix on enemy territory and enemy identities in a world of ambiguated antagonisms—the last generation of war films in the post-Vietnam era offered visions of war that were morally ambiguous. This ambiguity created what two critics have called "dialectical disorientation," whereby what is shown is "a confrontation between two powerful, incompatible and complementary world views."[20] This has had the effect of undermining the mythologies of war that work toward recruiting warriors.

By contrast, the Arthurian analogy reasserts the mythologizing of war characteristic of films of the pre-Vietnam era without evoking the interpretive controversies that any representation of Vietnam military action would invite. And the various additional visual tropes the ad mobilizes evoke various societal myths that construct warfare as a sacred mission against an unambiguously evil adversary—a mission, moreover, that results in glory for the individuals who undertake it.

To elaborate the second domain of codes through which the ad achieves its meanings, we must consider the culture of the viewers. Perhaps the most important dimension of this culture is succinctly expressed in the observation that contemporary recruitment confronts an increasingly visual culture. More specifically, the visual forms of modernity mediate not only recruitment but also the contemporary experience of war itself. For example, the Vietnam correspondent Michael Herr and his media colleagues had trouble distinguishing experiencing the war from being media spectators: "A lot of things had to be unlearned before you could learn anything at all," Herr wrote, "and even after you knew better you couldn't avoid the ways in which things got mixed, the war itself from those parts of the war that were just like the movies."[21] The combatants had the same difficulty:

> You don't know what a media freak is until you've seen the way a few of those grunts would run around during a fight when they knew there was a television crew nearby; they were actually making war movies in their heads, doing little guts and glory Leatherneck tap dances. . . . We'd all seen

too many movies, stayed too long in Television City, years of media glut had made certain connections difficult.[22]

The recruitment ad resonates with the contemporary youth visual culture not only because it evokes a genre of adventure film—a cross between the Arthurian legend in *Excalibur* and the laser swords of Darth Vader and his young adversaries in the *Star Wars* films—but also because it resembles a Nintendo game, a participatory visual genre in which the current young generation is broadly and deeply involved. Moreover, the filmic genre articulates well with the identity appeal the Marine Corps wants to make, to invite recruits into a noble historical tradition. The various stop-action tableaux, in which individual characters are framed, are made possible by control over motion. The freeze-framing lends a timelessness or permanent validity to the heroics of the age of chivalry, while the movement of the action produces the desired narrative of the triumph of nobility and goodness over evil.

The ad therefore contains many of the visual elements necessary for it to be both intelligible and absorbing. The visual tropes translate a complex set of cultural imperatives—issues of duty, heroism, manhood, good versus evil, and alertness to the seductive dangers of women—into simple signs able to capture a visual audience whose attention span is episodic, given the architecture of the viewing venue, the multistimulus home as contrasted with the movie theater sealed off from disturbing exogenous signs.

Nevertheless, young people are not sealed off from other aspects of contemporary culture. Despite the creative energy that the Marine Corps and the J. Walter Thompson ad agency have put into this and prior recruitment ads, *Marines* magazine reported in 1993 that "young people's interest in the military is decreasing" and that the corps in response "adapts and increases its mission by 20 percent."[23]

## In Pursuit of the Real

In a situation of fragmented cultural values, the difficulty of producing marines goes beyond the recruitment stage into the training phase. However compelling the recruitment appeal might be by virtue of the readability of its forms, it must nevertheless function in the context of significant domains of cultural competition. One of these, ironically, is the culture of the Marine Corps itself. As the quintessential warrior caste, the corps has been notoriously impatient with metaphor, simulation, and symbolic antagonism. The other side of the coin of its pursuit of creating real men has been its drive to have real enemies in real combat situations against which to test these men. It has been the dominant thematic in many of the more pious and sacralizing marine stories in Hollywood films (to be discussed later), and it finds expression in official marine journalism, which in recent years has been obsessively fixated on finding and maintaining reality in parts of the Caribbean. One of the venues is Grenada and the other is Cuba.

For example, a brigadier general writing a history of the marines' Grenada assault, Operation Urgent Fury, noted with pleasure that "the near coincident Beirut deployment and Grenada intervention presented us with the problem and opportunity of collecting operational history in real time."[24] Of course, mere episodes provide less purchase on the real than an enduring enmity, and with the end of the cold war, Cuba takes on greater significance as a piece of reality, the only consistently nonsimulated enemy. For example, the lure of the "real" dominates this report on "GITMO" (the Guantánamo Bay, Cuba, marine base) by a marine journalist, reporting an interview with a rifleman at Guantánamo:

> The Marines on the front line have a respect for what's on the other side of the fence. "In the fleet (FMF), you do a lot of training but training's not real. The Marines have a real mission every single day," said SSgt. Randy Shouse, a guard chief from one of the rifle security companies. With the Cuban economy collapsing and border activity increasing every year, the defense force Marines must keep up their guard even more. But for many of them it's exciting. As Shouse described, the mission is real and for Marines fresh from boot camp and the School of Infantry, the reality of the job is motivating.[25]

In addition to the struggle that a drive for the "real" must encounter in a modern military that reproduces itself primarily through simulation strategies, there is the struggle during marine training that a warrior caste must undertake within a social and cultural context that contains both specific antimilitary attitudes and value structures that are antidisciplinary. These difficulties underlie much of the action in the

1992 film *A Few Good Men* (analyzed in the conclusion). In order to underscore both of these dimensions of marine agonism, it is appropriate to take a detour again to the actual halls of Moctezuma, the second contrastive venue I mentioned, and examine one of the more monolithic Aztec military castes and its practices before returning to examine the way the agonism has been played out for different generations of marines as represented in films.

## From the Halls of Moctezuma

"Aztec" is a term applied to a variety of Mesoamerican cultures at the time of the Spanish contact in the sixteenth century. One of these, the Mexicas (discussed in chapter 2), had for a period of about a hundred years a culture that was almost unalloyed in its support of military recruitment. The society-wide complicity stemmed from a universal commitment to a violence-inducing cosmogony, a "mystico-militaristic" story of the origin and basis for the persistence of their world.[26]

In the Mexica empire the dominant cosmogony referred to a mythical past in which its people had been "chosen by the sun" and given a supreme mission of war.[27] War was necessary in order to prevent the Mexica epoch of power from ending with the setting of their sun. According to their cosmogony, their sun would never set as long as it was nourished by the blood of human sacrifices. Accordingly, the famed Aztec flower wars (described in chapter 2) were aimed in part at acquiring sacrificial victims.

The influence of this mystico-religious narrative that impelled Mexica warfare was due primarily to the warrior-ideologue Tlacaelel, who invented the story. Although he never held an official position, he remained the power behind the throne for kings ranging from Itzcoatl in 1427 through the second Moctezuma, who reigned at the time of the Spanish invasion. Under their kingships, military recruitment proceeded without having to struggle against significant antimilitary cultural codes, as the contemporary U.S. Marine Corps has to do. The Mexica branch of Aztec culture as a whole, organized by a mystico-religious martial ideology, served military recruitment rather than placing centrifugal pressures on it.[28]

Most striking was the pervasiveness of Mexica recruiting. Under

Moctezuma II, all commoner youth ten to eleven years old went to a school that included military training.[29] Equally pervasive was the presence of military signs throughout Aztec public space. As I noted in chapter 2, when a warrior had taken two captives, he went to the palace to receive a mantle with red trim from the king. For three captives he got a richly worked garment, and for four, a special war garment as well as a complete haircut.[30] As a result, Aztec public space was dense with military signs, for "status achieved in war was marked by the honors one received, the way one's hair was worn, the jewelry one was entitled to wear, the clothing one wore in peace, and the arms, armor, and insignia one wore in war."[31]

Amplifying public recognition of the value of military engagement that these decorations conveyed were other elements of Aztec culture. For example, as one commentator has noted, rather than being a respite from the violence associated with policing the tribute economy and other operations comprising their military dominance, Aztec poetry, at least that circulating within the Mexica empire, "was deeply implicated in the carrying out of Aztec imperial policy." And the songs were "also an important part of the education of young warriors. Songs and dances were taught in the *calmecac*, houses where adolescent boys lived as they trained to become warriors, and the boys spent the evenings singing these with older warriors."[32]

Not incidental to the complicity of Aztec music with Aztec militarism was the structure of composition and performance. In contemporary industrial societies, such forms as rock music are not wholly hierarchical because class control over performance spaces such as the concert hall must vie with the airwaves and a proliferation of local performance arenas.[33] And various musical genres express the political sensibilities of countercultural segments of the society.[34]

In the case of the Mexicas, artistic genres were dominated by militarized classes. For example, there was "a professional system of composition, instruction, and performance, and with Aztec society increasingly dependent on and organized around a state of on-going warfare, it seems plausible to assume that it was in this period (and in these circles) that Aztec poetry developed into the full and elaborate forms that are found in the surviving codices."[35] There was thus a wholly complicit genre of musical poetry that reinforced the status system organized around warfare. For example, seasoned warriors were honored as "eagles" and "jaguars," as this poem celebrates:

> Nobles and kings are sprouting as eagles and jaguars in Mexico: Lord Ahuitzotl is singing arrows, singing shields. Giver of life, let your flowers not be gathered! . . . You've adorned them in blaze flowers, shield flowers.[36]

For these Aztecs, then, unlike the modern state, which has separate military institutions, war was totally imbricated within the social body, and the various cultural forms served as implicit military recruitment. In a society in which warriors are trained and reinforced by the central cultural codes, the warriors carry the realistic death-facing codes into and through battles.

One must not paint too totalizing a picture of the Aztec support of militarism, however. The Mexica militaristic theology is known to have confronted opposition from poet sages in neighboring kingdoms. These poets condemned the martial attitudes of the Mexicas, repudiated the martial-mystical version of the cosmos invented by Tlacaelel, and posed a model of the divine that presented "a less conflictive image of its relationship to mankind."[37]

Forging a more pacific version of the universe, their poetry produced an unknowable god and urged enjoyment and passivity in this life rather than obedience to the dubious command ethic of a bloodthirsty god. Their deity mocked humanity and represented the martial attitudes of Mexica kings ironically: "You are celebrated. You made divine words. But you have died."[38] And there is considerable evidence that the second Moctezuma, who was defeated by the Spaniards, had already begun to practice a less bellicose version of the Mexica mission, under the influence of these neighboring sages.[39] Nevertheless, for almost a hundred years, Mexica militarism was primarily responsive to a single grand narrative that prescribed bellicosity and dominated almost all official genres of cultural expression. In effect, social and cultural forces were largely complicit in military recruitment throughout that century.

## The Contemporary Cultural Agonism

Modern state societies generally lack single grand narratives that encourage military conquest. In state societies with separate military institutions and bureaucracies, the culture tends to code warfare not through reference to central beliefs and values, which are based on experience and are broadly learned through action (e.g., the way that most adult Norwegian men can converse knowledgeably about going to sea), but through its fictional or fantasy-type genres. As a result, military leadership must take raw amateurs and impose new and unfamiliar codes on them. Moreover, they must do so *against* the culture, even as they employ some positive and negative cultural codes in their training sessions—for example, the notorious use of misogyny and homophobia by marine drill instructors to goad new recruits by questioning their manliness. In general what trainers must do is resist various dimensions of popular culture that are distracting, fragmenting, and increasingly antidisciplinary.

In particular, if we pay attention to war films about the U.S. Marines, it is evident that since the post–World War II period and wholly celebratory examples such as *The Sands of Iwo Jima,* the tendency has been increasingly critical. This is especially the case with the post–Vietnam War genre. *Full Metal Jacket,* which departs from the traditional heroic war story not only in what it shows—the more pointless brutal aspects of both marine basic training and violent encounters on patrol in Vietnam—but also in its avoidance of traditional narrative form, is an example. It is not a heroic story in part because it resists being a story; it displays various unconnected tableaux rather than producing a narrative sequence from which one could derive a moral or political lesson.[40]

In contrast, the traditional marine story films have had an unambiguous theme: inasmuch as the marines are a separate, professionalized military agency, the training of a marine requires a struggle against aspects of the larger society and its cultural forms. As I noted, however, the portrayal of this struggle has not been the simplistic marine codes versus the other social codes model. At the same time that other cultural codes are seen as centrifugal, fragmenting, and antidisciplinary, they are opportunities as well as impediments, and marine trainers and models make positive use of them.

Because the emphasis here is on the marketing of the marines and the implicit recruitment conducted by popular culture, most of my analysis will focus on the Clint Eastwood film *Heartbreak Ridge* (1986), which was unequivocally aimed at resurrecting the Vietnam-damaged reputation of the armed services in general and the marines in particular. The Marine Corps is not ordinarily seen as an organization that makes heavy use of marketing at any level. However, despite a preference for remaining "aloof from civilian affairs, considering publicity and advertising somewhat unmilitary and undignified," the marines did establish the first military public relations bureau in Chicago in 1907[41] and have since recognized the value of feature films like *Heartbreak Ridge,* which was designed to repair their damaged reputation from the Vietnam War and the Beirut debacle.

The film had the initial logistical support of the corps, making use of its Vieques, Puerto Rico, base and following its simulated amphibious assaults with a film crew. The corps seemed to recognize that films "write history," as Anton Kaes has put it: "Along with professional historians and schools, the mass media have become the most effective and least acknowledged institutional vehicles for shaping historical consciousness."[42]

Kaes laments the vanishing of historical experience that such a mediation implies. "The past," he says, "is in danger of becoming a rapidly expanding collection of images."[43] But whatever the degradation of historical experience might be (perhaps it is just as degraded in cultures whose oral traditions or stories mediate the past), the "collection of images" is degraded history only if it makes the experience unserviceable for those who consume them. In the case of heroic marine films, the degradation has dire consequences. Filmic representations of marine history that foreground heroism and disguise the structural production of death provide a degraded account of what constitutes the experience of being a marine because they allow insufficient access to what is at stake. Heroic marine films constitute recruitment into a fantasy of male fulfillment rather than creating a frame for confronting life and death in a way that politicizes the issue and encourages reflection on struggles over who should risk death, who merits being a target of violence, and for what reasons.

In any case, despite the fact that the film followed the Department of Defense script with the full cooperation of the corps, the corps ultimately requested that credits be removed, claiming that it objected to the level of profanity in many of the scenes and to aspects of the representation of marine training and field operations.[44] "As a result," it concluded, "the film will not be used as a recruitment tool for Marines as officers had hoped it would following the air force's image gains from *Top Gun*."[45] Nevertheless, *Heartbreak Ridge* reflects the current dilemma in the implementation of marine training. And, despite its rejection by the marine command hierarchy, it is complicit with their expressed interest in historical redemption.

## Marines in Films: Cultural Recruitment

There are many ways for American political culture to reexperience the Grenada invasion. As it will be reproduced here through a film reading, the suggestion is that we can better understand ourselves if we liken the invasion to an Aztec flower war, a prestige-enhancing action rather than a territorial assertion. Indeed, Grenada, as it was produced in official discourse as well as popular culture, was experienced by many people as the resurrection of American pride in general and of the Marine Corps in particular. *Heartbreak Ridge* is a film that the American public had been long prepared to comprehend.

To supply a context for Clint Eastwood and his trainees' invasion of Grenada—the primary narrative of *Heartbreak Ridge*—a consideration of an earlier heroic marine film is essential, because it established the genre. The John Wayne version is *The Sands of Iwo Jima* (1949), a thoroughly celebratory rendition of the marines' role in World War II. Although it was released at a time when marine prestige was very high, it was preoccupied nevertheless with the struggle between marine training codes and the outer codes of the society as a whole, the theme dominating marine films ever since.

There is a remarkable parallel between John Wayne in *Iwo Jima* and Clint Eastwood in *Heartbreak Ridge*. Although both are dedicated, sober, and totally professional on duty, they are drunk and disorderly off duty. Moreover, the cause of this conduct is the same in both cases. Both of their marriages failed because their wives would not tolerate either the separations from their husbands or their proximity; they disliked being left behind but also found it difficult to live with the fierce dedication of professional marines. Dedication to codes that estrange the marine from

ordinary people is the general point to be derived from these failed marriages, and it sets up the problematic of training, for aside from preparing bodies, what Sergeants Stryker (Wayne) and Highway (Eastwood)
do is impose these codes on recruits who embrace social and cultural
codes that are at best insensitive to Marine Corps codes and at worst
anathema to them.

The representations of these diverse social and cultural codes in *Iwo
Jima* is crude and stereotypic by contemporary standards, as is the representation of the Japanese adversary, usually referred to as "Japs" or
"Nips" and once by Sergeant Stryker as "those little lemon-yellow characters." Stryker has to shape up a variety of cultural attitudes and behavioral codes that are imposed by the ethnic diversity of his unit. He must
shape a single-minded unit out of people who are portrayed as crafty
hustlers (represented by an Italian American) or mindless belligerents
(represented by two Irish brothers who keep getting into fistfights). Ethnic diversity does not produce a clash of values or identity investments;
it is a set of stereotypes that essentializes a connection between ethnicity
and character.

Wayne/Stryker acts tough and excessively authoritarian but justifies
his discipline by telling the men that unless they learn to think like
marines they will be dead. Eastwood/Highway uses the same justifica-
tion in *Heartbreak Ridge*. There is of course a very different model of
what produces dead marines—going to war and being a high-risk assault force—but the heroic marine film seems to imply that lack of discipline is what kills, and this message is reinforced in *Iwo Jima* in an
episode in which a marine stops for coffee before returning to his embattled foxhole mate with more ammunition, only to find his comrade
dead. Sergeant Stryker admonishes and ultimately assaults him for having "doped off."

But ethnic diversity and the codes it enjoins are the least of Stryker's
obstacles to producing good marines. One obstacle (also faced by Highway) is a rigid marine command that tries to do everything by the book.
And, like Highway, Stryker is threatened with court martial for his
improvisational approach to training (e.g., a fistfight with one of his
men). The other, which provides most of the dramatic tension, is the
antimilitary and antiauthoritarian civilian culture. One recruit, who is

Stryker's toughest case, is the son of a former combat comrade who has been designated by his father as "too soft" to be a good marine. The young man, Conway, represents himself as antidiscipline rather than soft and expresses disgust at the authoritarian violence of the Marine Corps. Through most of the film he remains resistant to Stryker's various uses of cultural codes (e.g., using the Mexican hat dance to train a clumsy recruit in bayonet fighting, using the expression "saddle up" every time the unit as a whole has to move somewhere) to train and goad the men, many of them from western American culture.

But Stryker's major adversary is a distrustful civilian culture, which he defeats in his struggle for Conway's heart and mind. What is ultimately successful for Stryker is his own conduct. He serves as an effective role model. His heroic deeds on the battlefield change Conway's outlook. When Stryker is killed in action, Conway takes over and uses Stryker's idiom, telling the men to "saddle up" as he leads them off into the field.

The significant influence of Wayne's portrayal of Sergeant Stryker reflected both the growing cultural authority of films in the 1950s and the relatively unchallenged prestige of military heroes in the post–World War II period. The film grossed more than five million dollars in the United States and Canada, and Wayne received a nomination for best actor for his role as well as gaining a place among the top ten most popular movie stars. When General Douglas MacArthur met Wayne, he said, "You represent the American serviceman better than the American serviceman himself."[46]

*Heartbreak Ridge* repeats most of the clichés from *The Sands of Iwo Jima*, but it is shaped by the peculiar circumstances of the military in general and the Marine Corps in particular in the post–Vietnam War era. Its narrative structure and visual tropes are all mobilized to resurrect the honor of the Marine Corps and the soldier/hero, and to do so it must create a gaping historical blind spot, the Vietnam War. The film begins with black and white footage from the Korean War and then jumps across Vietnam to a period just prior to the marine invasion of Grenada. The hero, Sergeant Highway (Eastwood), has received a Congressional Medal of Honor for his service in Korea, and very little mention is made of Vietnam except to note that he also served there.

The historical jump is visually marked. The black and white footage at the outset is a visual historical trope, for the absence of color locates the scene in the medium of documentary films of the 1950s. Marines are shown marching behind a tank, and the troop passes a sign that says 38th Parallel, leaving no doubt that we are in Korea during the war. This appears to be documentary footage from the war—mortars and heavy artillery being fired, at least one dead body lying in a street, and men in a deprived condition (e.g., stirring the broth that is cooking with their bayonets). The scene then cuts to the 1980s but stays in black and white. Highway is in a jail cell where he is regaling his cellmates with war stories. A large man with a shaved head calls him a jarhead and tells him to pipe down and, after a warning, Highway beats him into submission and resumes his storytelling as color comes in, replacing the black and white.

In the next scene, Highway is before a judge being charged with drunk and disorderly conduct; he was in a bar fight and urinated on a police vehicle. He is told by the judge that just because there is no war going on now does not give him the right to start one. Here the parallel with *Iwo Jima* is very close, for like Sergeant Stryker, Sergeant Highway can only handle perpetual war; he cannot face real life when there is no combat.

Most significant for the purposes at hand are the two kinds of struggles in which Highway is involved. One is a struggle against the marine command hierarchy. He has been reprimanded, given trivial duties, and urged to retire because of his off-duty misdemeanors. When he reports for duty at a new post, an exemplary confrontation begins between Highway and his new commander, who informs him, "This is the new Marine Corps," to which Highway responds, "I understand a lot of body bags get filled if I don't do my job." This is a repetition of the dissimulation of the hazards of combat advanced in *Sands of Iwo Jima*: only poor discipline produces dead marines. It also repeats another theme from *Iwo Jima*, a confrontation between the experienced veteran dedicated to combat duty and the bureaucrat dedicated to the rules of the command hierarchy.

The other exemplary confrontation is between Highway and a black rock and roll performer whom Highway meets before reporting to his new unit. We see the musician, Stitch (Mario Van Peebles), hustle Highway for a free lunch and take off with his gear; he is arrogant and rancorous toward social proprieties. Stitch is the Conway of *Heartbreak Ridge*—the hard nut Highway has to crack when he takes over his unit and is asked to make them combat-ready.

Here the Stitch-Highway confrontation represents the paradigmatic struggle between marine training and both general and popular culture as Highway strives to implant unfamiliar codes of conduct. At the same time, we see him using aspects of the culture, particularly masculine macho culture, as a weapon. "I'll make them life takers and heartbreakers," he says, making it clear that "real men" (i.e., marines) are not only killers but also sexual predators. And Highway makes several references to his sexual appetite (of a piece with his appetite for violent confrontation). For example, in an early scene during the training period with his unit he tells them that he has "banged more quim and kicked more ass" than they could even imagine.

Throughout the film, women are the Other to be mastered, and Highway's third task, after opposing the hostile, overrationalized marine hierarchy and opposing the cultural and social codes to win over the hearts and minds of his recruits, is to win back his wife. This ultimately follows the logic of the role of women in most Eastwood films, "which is to represent a resistance to the masculinist ethos, politics and violence of the hero . . . [and] to finally alter their relation to that ethos and give consent to its heroics."[47] But in the case of *Heartbreak Ridge*, an allegorical burden is placed on the extraction of this consent because the former Mrs. Highway represents the American public. For this third task, Eastwood uses guile rather than bluster and physical intimidation. Rather than opposing the cultural codes, he tries to adapt, and after being rebuffed in his first approaches at the bar where his ex-wife works, he is seen reading women's magazines, concentrating especially on articles that use the therapy culture's psychobabble about "meaningful relationships." It would appear that his strategy is not coherent with his approaches in his other struggles, for he is clearly posing here, and his ex-wife's first reaction upon hearing this "relationship" talk is "What have you been reading?"

As it turns out, however, posing is part of Highway's improvisational skill as a marine. A good marine is not one who blindly follows the rules but one who can improvise. This echoes an element of Stryker's canniness in *Iwo Jima*, but it also comports well with the contemporary marine recruitment ad. *Heartbreak Ridge* adds mental canniness to physical strength to create the new marine profile. Accordingly, during a crucial battle scene that mirrors an actual event during the Grenada invasion, when he and his unit are surrounded in a small building, Highway charges out into the open and then pretends to have been killed. His body serves as a marker to orient the rescue helicopter.

When he returns from the Grenada invasion, Highway walks alone across the Tarmac as various other marines are warmly greeted by lovers and spouses, and just when it appears that he will not be greeted, his ex-wife appears in the crowd, waving a small American flag. She joins him, and as they walk off together, it is unclear whether it has been his improvising with the relationship codes or his heroism that has won her back. It is clear, however, that the two are connected. And there is a good case that it is the latter, for just as the Grenada invasion has resurrected the marines' credibility with an admiring public, it seems to have restored Highway's relationship with his ex-wife. The personal narrative of Highway winning back his wife mirrors the larger story of the Marine Corps winning back its public. And by implication, the marines are cast as manly saviors protecting a feminized society in need of the disciplined violence of the "heartbreakers and life takers."

As important as Highway's winning back his wife is, however, his more central battle runs parallel with the marines' struggle to resurrect themselves in the public eye. That his most recalcitrant recruit, Stitch, is a rock musician is appropriate, for rock music has always represented the youthful, counterculture, despite the fact that it is also co-opted by economic and political structures of domination. For example, as early as the film *Blackboard Jungle* (1955) rock music was "associated with more or less delinquent teenage subcultures,"[48] and here it is represented by Stitch. That Stitch is an African American simply enhances the struggle between the marine codes and the centrifugal countercultural codes against which Highway struggles in his training sessions.

The training period itself reevokes the marine culture's impatience with simulation and longing for "the real." At one point Highway shocks both his own troops and the upper command by firing real bullets at their feet, and from time to time he fires an AK-47, "the preferred weapon of the enemy," to get "his men" familiar with the sound. Throughout training exercises, Highway violates the game and improvises to make the combat more realistic, always falling back on the idea that his men have to be prepared or they will not stay alive. He is constantly threatened with dismissal for this, as various rules are invoked (e.g., his carrying an "unauthorized weapon").

The value of the real is further invoked by the positive representation of Eastwood's character, who, like John Wayne's in *Iwo Jima*, is a battle-hardened veteran; unlike the college- and academy-trained and bureaucratically minded marines, they have experienced live battle. While Highway violates marine rules, he uses various masculinity codes to shape and goad the marine recruits. He calls them "ladies," womanizes the idea of fashion, smashes their designer sunglasses, and makes them wear the same color shirts, crushing any signs of individuality, especially its expression through apparel. In addition, like Stryker, he uses his physical superiority to crush resistance, tearing Stitch's earring out of his ear and overpowering the strongest mesomorph in the unit.

While the young men are still trying to resist, they turn again to music; at one point they invent a rap song whose lyrics speak of what a dumb "jarhead" Sergeant Highway is. When finally the day of reckoning arrives and Highway leads his unit as an "advance group" in the invasion of Grenada, two levels are on trial. The first is the Marine Corps itself, with its reputation tarnished by a general post-Vietnam resistance to military adventurism. The second is Sergeant Highway's realistic, antisimulation techniques of training—resisted by the new, academy-trained marine bureaucrats—and his drive to turn a culturally diverse group of young men whose consciousnesses have been colonized by popular culture into committed marines.

Much of the early action during the invasion is ideological at a general level rather than decisive with respect to the training of Stitch and his peers. At one point, Highway finishes off a fallen enemy soldier by firing at him at point-blank range. He then draws a cigar out of the dead man's breast pocket, sniffs it, and pronounces it to be Cuban. During the rest of the action, this cigar protrudes from Highway's mouth like a large phallus. Apart from the manhood code that the killing and cigar episode underscores, however, it stands as a legitimation of the invasion and a reinstalling of cold war cartography. Rather than an attack on a relatively defenseless Caribbean nation, it is a confrontation with Cuba, a part of the enemy East Bloc. The scene therefore reinstates what is left of the cold war cartography.

With the exception of the brief perilous period when Highway and company are pinned down by fire in a building, before the notorious helicopter rescue (obtained with a long-distance credit-card call back to a U.S. base), the rest of the operation is child's play. Garry Trudeau had it right when one of the characters in his "Doonesbury" cartoon referred to the Grenada invasion as a "Special Olympics" for the U.S. military.

What is decisive with respect to the film's resurrection narrative is the cheering of the rescued medical students when the marines break into their dormitory to free them—the nation needs them after all!—and a remark made by Stitch on the Tarmac after landing back on U.S. soil. He tells Highway that he has opted for being a marine rather than a rock star. The marine culture has triumphed over divisive popular culture.

Another important dimension to the film is the story of the achievement of manhood. Not only are the enlisted men taught to be marines through Highway's dedication and methods, but also an epicene, initially fearful ROTC officer learns to be tough. His training extends this aspect of the story. In addition, the importance of maleness is reinforced not only through the capitulation of Highway's ex-wife to his heroism but also through the way that male bonding is figured. It is toughness, not softness and caring, that survives the adventure.

At a decisive point, a worried Stitch bends over Highway after Highway has pretended to be dead. Feeling Stitch holding his hand, Highway says, "Just because we're holding hands doesn't mean we're going to be taking warm showers together in the wee hours of the morning." As Paul Smith has noted, the "amongst men" thematic, which dominates such Eastwood films, requires a foregrounding of strict heterosexualism.[49] Again ridicule of homoeroticism is employed to disparage affectionate and caring gestures among men (and to police the boundary between homosociality and homosexuality, an aspect of masculinity that I treat in chapter 5). In the last analysis, *Heartbreak Ridge* is a recruitment film par excellence, and it picks up what is novel in the television ad, for it adds to the code of toughness that of smartness. Eastwood's improvisational success adds craft to the simple sacrifice-your-body image that has long been seen as characteristic of marines.

## Conclusion

The recruitment of today's Marine Corps continues with well-targeted codes that offer the marines as an avenue for "the few and the proud" to complete themselves as men. Given that this recruitment continues through the implicit attractions in popular culture genres, we should not ignore what is perhaps the most significant of recent filmic representations from the standpoint of the corps's cultural recruitment, *A Few Good Men*. This film, like other expressions of national sentiment— official political discourse, for example—assumes that there is a crisis in the American political culture occasioned by the failure of the United States to obtain a clear victory in Vietnam. Of course this "crisis" stands as such, as Susan Jeffords has argued, especially when certain masculinity stakes are foregrounded.[50]

Films, popular culture in general, and various domains of American political discourse have tried to reply to this "crisis." And there is good reason to believe that policy decisions have also constituted a reply. It is in the context of this reply more generally that the recruitment of new marines takes place. More specifically, the crisis has had to do with, among other things, the nation's inability to regard war deaths as heroic when war itself has become an illegitimate instrument of policy. This produces at once a glitch in the mourning of war dead, a disturbance in the national memory of its recent past, and a desire for those who seek to reestablish the conditions of possibility for heroism to find new definitions and occasions. For example, on another popular culture front, Dan Rather and Norman Schwarzkopf have rehistoricized past American warfare from Vietnam backward to the Normandy invasion in World War II in television documentaries. This rehistoricization effort is central to my analysis in chapter 5.

The present is the primary focus of *A Few Good Men*. Like earlier marine films, it celebrates a version of masculinity and identifies the Marine Corps as an important site for its production, but unlike those earlier films it attempts to broaden the range of acceptable models of courage and heroism. Like *Heartbreak Ridge,* however, it is a recruitment film that is complicit with the post–Vietnam War remasculinization project.

The project is of course conveyed by the title, but much of the work is done through the misogynist treatment of Commander Galloway (Demi Moore), who fails to convince the navy brass that she can handle the defense of two marines charged with murder at the Guantánamo marine base in Cuba. That she is subsequently subjected to sexist disparagements by Colonel Jessup (Jack Nicholson), the commander of Guantánamo, reflects negatively on a particular version of masculinity; it is part of the economy of character types that the film is presenting and sorting.

Jessup is a flawed marine whose values and models of appropriate marine character are too narrow; they hark back to a now discredited epoch. The goofy softball fanatic and Harvard-trained lawyer Caffrey (Tom Cruise) is portrayed as exceeding Galloway's competence in practically all dimensions. It is ultimately *his* heroism, articulated through his risk-taking in the courtroom, that reaffirms the masculine world of protection for which the marines stand. Caffrey's bravery is, moreover, shown to be edifying to the young accused marines who had wrongly submitted their conduct to Jessup's narrow codes. You need not be a stiff-necked martinet to protect America's interests and maintain an atmosphere of justice and fairness within the warrior class. But whether Commander Galloway is disparaged uncouthly by the martinet or simply cannot compete successfully with the brave young navy lawyer, the message remains the same: manhood thrives by not needing women. Heroism is a man's job.

Ultimately, the film also affirms a model of the world that requires heroism. Apart from the collection of marine characters it portrays—some of them praise worthy, some blameworthy, and some ambiguous—what the film consistently and unambiguously maintains is the peculiarity of the marine base in Guantánamo Bay, Cuba, its proximity to danger, to a "real" enemy. Much is made of the distance between bureaucratic and combat positions in the navy. Caffrey, the young Harvard-trained lawyer selected to defend the two marines accused of killing their unit mate while trying to discipline him, is so unmilitary that he cannot even interpret the twenty-four-hour clock. His Washington venue, where he is shown playing softball, is contrasted with scenes of Guantánamo with its barbed-wire enclosures, a place referred to by Commander Jessup as a "forward position." And most telling is the surprise Caffrey registers when he is told that to be safe, he had better wear camouflage over his dress whites while he is at Guantánamo, lest he be shot at from the other side of the fence. The suggestion is that he might be mistaken for an important military or political figure.

Caffrey's ultimate acceptance of this vestige of cold war cartography reinforces this same cartography of danger. It is registered in his defense of the young marines' failure to deviate from the code that had encouraged them to "discipline" their fellow trainee. In his courtroom summation, he affirms the need for strong codes in a dangerous situation. A dangerous world is one that needs heroes (male heroes) and a menu of heroisms more inclusive than what was hitherto supplied by the Sergeant Strykers, the Gunnery Sergeant Highways, and the Colonel Jessups. And it seems that despite some tensions within the Marine Corps, it continues to supply the necessary training to produce "men" who provide that heroism.

# FIVE

# Rehistoricizing American Warfare

## Prelude: Vietnam's Resistance Continues

Ward Just's novel *American Blues* exhibits a radical entanglement between history and autobiography. The narrator, who served in the "combat zone" during the Vietnam War, has recognized that the war has also
proceeded within the mediascape. Having sought to retreat from expo-
sure to that part of the war in "warfare Washington," he is living in what
he refers to as exile in northern New England, watching television during the last week of the war, as he begins his story.[1]

He is writing a "history of the war," and he tells his wife that he "can't
end this book." She responds, "You have to let it go." "The book?" he asks.
"No," she responds, "*the war.*"[2] Unable to come to final terms with the
war, the narrator does another "tour." But his return to Vietnam provides no resolution. "What the narrator confronts in postwar Vietnam,"
as one astute reviewer has put it, "is not historical clarification but new
categories of mystery."[3] Without an American presence in Vietnam, he
recognizes his radical isolation: "I had grown comfortable inside the
American illusion and could not comprehend the Vietnamese, so it was
hopeless weighing and measuring today against yesterday."[4] The narrator learns that the Vietnamese remain radically Other; they cannot be
understood within a historical narrative in which Americans can consolidate their own collective identity, one deeply disturbed by their Vietnam War experience. Vietnam effectively resists an appropriation satis-
fying to American identity interests.

The most significant implication that can be derived from Just's playing off of biography and history is that the irresolution he experiences is precisely the opening to an ethical and political understanding of war. "History" concerned with war or with any past episode is a political problem that admits of no simple resolution. Violent confrontations with "enemy"/Others cannot be resolved by appropriating the Other to the same, by attempting to wholly resolve the enigma of otherness. The Vietnamese cannot be conceptually domesticated to provide a confirmation and validation of a narrative of American coherence and unity. Just as they resisted American "pacification" during the war, they resist symbolic pacification afterwards.

Heedless of this lesson, Norman Schwarzkopf, the American Gulf War commander, has also returned to Vietnam, in connection with his post–Gulf War media career. His endeavor, expressed both in his auto-biography, *It Doesn't Take a Hero,* and in his made-for-television docu-mentary, "Vietnam: A Soldier Returns," has been to restore an honorable American military history and to create a place for the soldier hero in it. Contrary to Just's novelistic argument, Schwarzkopf has sought to use Vietnam to achieve historical resolution. Traveling back to do a CBS documentary, along with reporter Dan Rather, who also served there during the war, he has sought to subsume the Vietnam War within a more benign narrative of the American experience than is represented in Just's novel as well as in an extensively critical literature and media representation of the United States during the Vietnam years.

Schwarzkopf's and Rather's performances in "Vietnam: A Soldier Re-turns," seek to overcode and thereby pacify the interpretive struggles that continue to locate Vietnam in a disjunctive place in narrative construc-tions of American history. While, for example, Stanley Kubrick's film *Full Metal Jacket* offers a disjunctive narrative that conveys an ambiguity as to whether "why we were in Vietnam" is a function of geopolitics or an outcome of American macho culture from the John Wayne cowboy to the culture of the Marine Corps, Schwarzkopf's scenarios attempt to im-pose coherence.[5] Schwarzkopf has therefore been involved in (re)writing history in both his autobiography, which is also aimed at reinterpreting the Vietnam War, and his television media career. Like the narrator in *American Blues,* he has entangled his autobiography with history, and the particulars of the relationship between his scripting of himself and his scripting of history help reveal aspects of the violence of representation, a continuation of war by other means. To situate Schwarzkopf's post–Gulf War media career in a critical political context, it is necessary to analyze more generally the politics of representing America's warring past.

## War Discourse in the Academy

All analyses and accounts of past wars share at least one attribute: they are performances that enter the interpretive struggles through which the history of a people is constructed. To locate a war in a people's memoryscape is, among other things, to engage in a politics of interpretation. But the grammar of this sentence is misleading because there are significant ambiguities involved in identifying a "people" for whom a collective memory can be created; there are no definitive boundaries of the "people" for whom war histories have resonance. Indeed, the process of fixing stories of past violent encounters plays a role in shaping the spaces and events that constitute the basis for being a "people." Those histories that manage to attain a level of dominance and stability create the imaginative boundaries that contain a people; they exert an influence on the self-interpretations and modes of inclusion and exclusion of the people who embrace them. They provide the contexts for valued models of subjectivity or identity, for the proprieties of various collective actions such as committing the national body to war, and for constructing a spatial imaginary—the configuration of the world—within which actions have meaning.

There are two very different kinds of history-inscribing performances, two different kinds of academic discourses on past wars that bear on the focus of this chapter. One is a strategic perspective and the other is an ethnographic perspective. The former seeks to deepen identity attachments by policing boundaries and locating dangers outside of them, while the latter seeks to attenuate identity commitments by reflecting on the boundary practices and history-making narratives through which they are shaped.

In general, those who study war from a strategic perspective tend to remain embedded in the rationales reflected in official policy discourse. Accordingly, various exemplars of the complicit, strategic approach emerged during and after the Gulf War—for example, Joseph Kruzel, who for years as a contributor to the *American Defense Annual* was among the most unambivalent enthusiasts for official policy. In the first issue after the Gulf War, he referred confidently to the unambiguous *causus belli*, which legitimated the "coalition's" attack on Iraq: "Saddam Hussein's invasion," he stated, "was an act of clear military aggression."[6]

For Kruzel, as for others in that segment of the policy analysis community infatuated with military heroics, U.S. involvement in the Gulf War provided redemption after the damage to U.S. national cohesion as a result of the defeat in Vietnam: "Defeat in Vietnam taught many powerful lessons, and military success in the Gulf was a direct consequence of failure two decades earlier."[7]

While Kruzel's approach was aimed at effacing a particular politics of memory—it was an attempt to displace political self-reflection and blame "failure" on bad logistics rather than, for example, cold war geopolitics—much of the rest of his reprise reflects an obsessive attention to the instrumentalities of violence. Euphoric about the new war technologies, he focused on the effectiveness of the various logistical moves by the U.S. Command and the future promise of the weapons. Especially sanguine about the Gulf War's implications for the future of the armaments industry, he noted that "Desert Storm should give Cruise Missile research development a great boost."[8]

Such triumphalist exclamations and war-toy obsessions aside, the centrality of one of the "lessons of Vietnam" evoked not only by Kruzel but also by many strategy-oriented scholars in political science and military history during and after the Gulf War is especially significant. The "lesson" is expressed as the need on the one hand to depoliticize the war while it is happening—avoiding politics (which Kruzel reduces to "political second guessing")[9] and suppressing information on human costs such as "body counts" (which Kruzel calls "irrelevant")[10]—and then, on the other hand, to repoliticize it afterward. The postwar move is one of representing "America" as a unified, consensual polity. Kruzel did not provide direct support for the significance of this unity during the Gulf War; he created it rhetorically and grammatically representing collective consent, for example, through such phrases as "when a nation chooses to go to war in defense of collective values."[11]

Other strategic approaches, which derived more or less the same lesson after the Gulf War, were similar to Kruzel's but functioned within a remarkably Clausewitzian discourse. Like Kruzel, the neo-Clausewitzians placed responsibility for the "victory" in the Gulf War on a lack of political ambivalence, but they were explicit in locating the Clausewitzian discursive object, the "will of the people," as a military resource. Constructing the lesson of Vietnam as a failure to summon national will, such neo-Clausewitzian strategic analysts as the military historians Michael Howard and Colonel Harry Summers reprised the Gulf War as redemptive because it involved, they argued, a reassertion of a unified national will.

More specifically, in the midst of the war, Howard evoked Clausewitz's trinity passage (discussed in chapter 2) and stated that one dimension of the trinity, the will of the people, was decisive. However, Howard's Clausewitzianisms contain the same misrecognitions within their recognitions as the original discourse penned by Clausewitz. Recognizing the fragility of that "will," and conveniently forgetting that it is supposed to have an independent and stable facticity, Howard worries that the American people's witnessing of "slaughter" might prevent a victory.[12] In short, to be a "will" it must be manipulated to remain willing.

Similarly, despite all the manifest duplicities that the Clausewitz trinity passage represents, when it gives an independent impetus to the will of the people, Colonel Summers also locates the people's will as a primary instrumentality in the successes in the war. He has no doubt that the "victory" in the Gulf War was a triumph of American will. Evoking Clausewitzian homilies at every stage of his argument, Summers locates the people "in the strategic equation"[13] and goes on to frame his discourse within the Clausewitzian grammar. His primary claim is that the victory was a function of clear objectives, where "objectives" are wholly external goals such as freeing Kuwait, destroying Saddam Hussein's "weapons of mass destruction," and so on. Relying on the official discourse, he quotes George Bush in the prologue to his chapter on objectives:

> Our objectives are clear. Saddam Hussein's forces will leave Kuwait. The legitimate government of Kuwait will be restored to its rightful place and

Kuwait will once again be free. Iraq will eventually comply with all United Nations resolutions.[14]

This position of course begs the question of why war as opposed to sanctions as the means to such objectives and, as was clear from the many statements at official levels during the war, the stakes and objectives were never unambiguously represented. However, the answer to this question is reflected in Summers's earlier remarks about Vietnam. Making clear that the Vietnam War had left the national body incomplete and irresolute, Summers persists in his redemption narrative, glossing the Gulf War as a means for domestic healing, the restoration of a unified "national will."

As I showed in my reading of Clausewitz in chapter 2, the outward-aiming gaze of strategic thinkers, who seem preoccupied with the logistics of encounter, masks the ontological impulse or inward aim of the constitution of collective coherence, their desire to represent the national body as unified and unambivalent. In marked contrast with strategic analysts, who reproduce official rationales for policy action, is the more ethnographic understanding of war (discussed in previous chapters). Rather than the "objectives" of war, treated as if they were wholly external, or the mobilization of the "people's will," the primary objects of ethnographic analyses are the identity practices that provide the conditions of possibility for war. When it is linked to a critical political concern with the present, an ethnographic sensibility, which rejects the idea that there is a privileged identity narrative, treats as essentially contentious how a given "we" is assembled and how it should understand its past, present, and future.[15] And such a sensibility functions by recognizing that insofar as there is a "national identity," it is an ongoing project rather than a fact; it emerges from an energetic cultural performance, a kind of "dream-work,"[16] which simultaneously manifests desired attachment to a people and place and fears the ambiguities in the founding stories that allow a people to cohere and consistently practice the boundaries of community.

Anthropologist Bruce Lincoln, who derives his observations from the study of tribal warfare, suggests two "social conditions" for a collectivity's sense of cohesion, a focus that has the merit of distancing the approach to war from the legitimation process involved in justifying it. Unlike that of the strategists, Lincoln's mode of analysis of war can set the stage for a critique of "what we are," for providing what Foucault has called a "critical ontology of ourselves":[17]

> First, a given group of individuals must understand themselves as a group; that is, they must be bound together in some abiding fashion by sentiments, traditions, kinship ties, institutions, residence patterns, language and the like. Second, they must understand members of some other group ("the enemy") as radically alien to them, outsiders to whom they are not connected and with reference to whom they need not refrain from violence.[18]

Lincoln adds a codicil that applies to those who are more directly involved in the violent engagements: "Warriors must be persuaded not only to risk their own lives but also to take the lives of others, and not merely random others but those whose otherness is radically marked."[19]

What bears more attention in this remark is the cultural, social, and political process by which that otherness is "marked." In the tribal societies from which Lincoln draws his conclusions, the marking is stable and relatively noncontroversial. He refers, for example, to the Anggor of New Guinea, for whom (as I noted in chapter 2) antagonisms between villages is a historical tradition with cosmological roots.[20]

The Anggor have a stable cartography of violence. The village map of friend and foe reflects a symbolic or cosmological map; the horizontal geography is locked into a stable, vertical imaginary. In contrast, the strategic analyst Kruzel operates within a wholly horizontal cartography. His map is geopolitical, and what licenses retaliatory violence is the crossing of a border on the map of nation-states. However, Kruzel's strong affirmation of this map, which permits a violent response to Iraq's boundary crossing, is accompanied by a disaffirmation of violence within boundaries.

Kruzel saw the post–Gulf War world as peaceful. His cartography of violence, which countenances only interstate antagonisms, allows no war-relevant coding for violence between peoples and states and no recognition of the domestic antagonisms that deconstruct the validity of references to and grammars of national will. When he refers to the post–Gulf War policy problem as one of securing global peace (a job for an internationalist-minded "America"),[21] he effectively dispenses non-recognition for ongoing wars involving, for example, Kurds, Miskitos, Basques, and Guatemalan peasants, among others. Unreflective acceptance of the international global imaginary led Kruzel to see a relatively peaceful, increasingly capitalist world of "liberal democracies," which do not go to war with one another. Insofar as he recognizes the struggles of peoples, he relegates them to the concept of "fragmentation."[22]

We (that "we" constructed in the discourse of interstate politics) in modern industrial societies are therefore absorbed into a geopolitical map in the way we regard "war." We are assembled as a "we" at the same time that we mark others for purposes of antagonism on the basis of spatial infractions that violate this geopolitical cartography. Nevertheless, the structures of global enforcement and the quarantining of "war" within the geopolitical map of recognized states is regarded as contentious in various academic and cultural genres. The continuous reproduction of warring organizations and warriors and the maps of enmity they produce and circulate confront continuous cultural resistances.

As a result, military establishments and their supporters—for example, strategic analysts within and outside of the academy—must continuously inscribe and adjust national and global history and construct models of the warrior's character to provide the conditions for violence that Lincoln has outlined: discourses of national unity that incorporate frames for constructing what is alien and dangerous. Warfare, as much as any of the practices of states, has been accompanied by an active history-writing impetus for those who wish to sustain the practice and make it the primary mode of national self-recognition.

Acccordingly, much of the analysis that follows is focused on the post–Gulf War struggle to reinvent the recent history of U.S. warfare and the related aims of restoring the prestige of military organizations, re-masculinizing the political frame for conceiving the significance of war, and reinstalling the prestige of the soldier hero. To provide an effective, critical context to analyze the genres within which the new historicizing of U.S. warfare is proceeding, it is important to provide a historical contrast, to once again provide an ethnography of the self by achieving significant distance from it. Our scene of writing therefore shifts to France during the Napoleonic wars to extend French hegemony throughout Europe.

## Napoleonic Propaganda I: Media and the Construction of History

Napoleon was active in the construction of a contemporary military history that would articulate well with the French nation's understanding of its past. His correspondence reflects his concern with how the academic history pursued by professors at the Collège de France would indicate properly "how the present enters history," and he actively shaped that history in a variety of ways—writing anonymous accounts of battles in the official press releases of the Grande Armée, which included commissioned engravings of battle scenes, organizing festivals to celebrate victories, and controlling the way art-historical paintings depicted battle scenes.[23] Throughout Napoleon's reign, his cultural politics accompanied his military politics, for the artifacts and art that found their way into museums were organized to reflect and legitimize military conquest, to "lend coherence to historical narrative"[24] about Napoleon's military adventures, and more generally to participate in Napoleon's assertion of French cultural superiority. Most significantly for present purposes, the commissioning, controlling, and assembling of art, along with the architecture of display, were part of his more general strategy of controlling history.[25] In the process of managing most of the historical information that circulated throughout his empire—he outlawed all press accounts of politics that did not copy the accounts in the official government press—Napoleon found painters who willingly participated in his construction of history.[26]

The media-control and history-constructing process after the famed battle of Eylau provides an exemplary case of the role of painting in shaping historical interpretation. Having determined that his primary maintenance of legitimacy would come through his ability to make sure that his "narratives of contemporary events encounter[ed] a minimum of cultural resistance,"[27] Napoleon faced a public relations problem over the battle of Eylau in 1807 because of news of significant French casualties and claims of victory by Russia. After the issue was made manifest in the press, Napoleon released additional government-controlled bulletins, organized a public festival in which the victory at Eylau was enacted, published booklets supplemented with engravings and including an eyewitness account, and created a competition for a painting showing the emperor visiting the Eylau battlefield after the victory.

The competition resulted in Gros's famous painting *Napoleon Visiting the Battlefield of Eylau*, which appeared at the Paris Salon in 1808 and is now hanging in the Louvre.[28] Then as now, visual images, as simulacra of the "real," played an important, supplementary role in determining the encoding of events as history.[29] And political and military actors since have made use of visual media to shape national support for particular policy as well as to forge a national imaginary in connection with martial values.

It is also important to note that the effect of Gros's realism owes much to the narrative quality of his canvases. Unlike, for example, the historical paintings of David, which avoided—in Norman Bryson's term, "sidestepped"[30]—narrative completion, Gros's historical paintings are realistic in a semiotic sense; they contain a continuous narrative in which story and image correspond to lead the viewer through the story the painting enacts. Thus, as a piece of progaganda, the Gros rendition of the battle of Eylau is "motivated by the need to cover up some ugly alternative versions of the events"[31]—an expensive defeat for the French, for example—and it does its work in part through its accomplishment of Napoleon's preferred narrative.

## Napoleonic Propaganda II: Personhood and Nationhood

Having analyzed the media's role as a writing vehicle in producing the history of war, we need more attention to the particular objects of such histories, to focus on what the images are about. The images constructed to legitimate a nation's identity and legitimacy in relation to warfare tend to be aimed at two related dimensions of contention. One is articulated at the level of nationhood. If we regard national solidarity as a dynamic in which the senses of attachment of the national collectivity are always in flux, we can recognize that the phenomenology of national cohesion involves an ongoing project. The national imaginary is prey to both unifying and fragmenting forces.

The other dimension of contention operates at the level of personhood. Part of every collective struggle over political self-definition involves attempts to maintain or attenuate particular imaginaries of the masculine. For example, this struggle is represented in the thought of the eighteenth-century philosopher Adam Smith, which reflects the strong relationship between the two imaginaries in European state societies. Smith's interest in economy was linked to a concern with his nation's effective governance and stability, but even though his primary preoccupation was with the nation's commerce, he lamented that an actively commercial society, which creates the possibility for and a strong interest in the consumption of luxuries, "sinks the courage of mankind." By leaving the defense of the society to specialists, others, with "their minds employed in the art of luxury," grow "effeminate and dastardly."[32]

More recently, and from a more analytic standpoint, the strong connection between the two imaginaries—the national and the masculine—has been examined by George Mosse in his historical analysis of the linkage in European states between nationalism and respectability. "Ideals of manliness," Mosse finds, are thoroughly imbricated with an impetus toward national cohesion and loyalty, and the boundaries of gender as well as the policing of "abnormal" sexualities are powerful forces affecting identity practices within the national society and creating individual and national antitypes outside.[33]

The related forces affecting constructions of both personhood and nationhood are drawn especially close together, according to Mosse, during precisely the period in which art historians are involved in either supportive or contentious responses to Napoleon's policy of policing the images of self and nation to support his imperial policy. It is a period in which the martial male body begins to constitute a representation of state power.[34]

While Gros's rendition of the battle of Eylau was designed to play into Napoleon's hands—the rhetorical force of Napoleon's figure in the center manifesting a calm, authoritative presence in the midst of the ruins of battle lends legitimacy to his imperial designs—other paintings of the period introduce resistance to both the national and manliness commitments that Napoleon's martial and cultural imperialism promoted. Exemplary in this respect is Géricault's *Charging Chasseur,* executed in 1812, precisely at the point of "the crisis in militarism provoked by the early success and eventual failure of the Napoleonic project."[35] In general, Géricault's war-theme paintings contrast significantly with the complicity of Gros's various historical canvases. For example, Gros's warriors are "coherent."[36] In his *Battle of Abouleir* (1806) he displays the French warrior Murat in a focused onslaught, prepared to slay his enemies. His sword and the posture of his horse are both coherent with his unambivalent advance.[37]

In marked contrast, Géricault's *Charging Chasseur* represents a horse and rider who have fled the battlefield. There is no clear narrative to the scene because the surrounding battle is not in evidence. The horse is twisting in confusion rather than charging in a particular direction, and the rider's sword is pointed toward the rear of the horse instead of at his enemies. Moreover, the clothing and facial expression of the rider are "disarrayed."[38]

Géricault's scene here as well as in other canvases implies a failure of masculine power and a significant "collapse of Napoleonic militarism."[39] His renditions oppose those that Napoleon specifically commissioned to celebrate his imperial designs. The painted image in early-nineteenth-century France was therefore an active participant in two related registers of militarism—patriotism (the production of a historical, national coherence) and manliness (the encouragement of a model of masculinity)—but also in displays of the crisis of masculinity in relation to the failure of national military adventures.

The effects of the power of the image on political legitimacy were not lost on subsequent French regimes, for later in the century Manet's painting of the execution of Maximilian by Mexican rebels in 1867—a disgrace for Napoleon III, who had reneged on promised military support for his puppet monarch in Mexico—was denied access to lithographic reprinting by censors at the Ministry of the Interior and was barred from display at the Paris Salon. Its first display was in Boston in 1880, and it was not viewed in France until 1884, after the deaths of both Napoleon III and Manet.[40]

## Back to the Future: Soldier Heroes as Military Historians

The kind of legitimacy crisis of the French nation in relation to both its aggressive nationhood and masculinity or aggressive personhood that was at the center of the way French painters participated in depicting history is very much at the center of post–Gulf War politics in the United States. Because the Gulf War is interpreted by some as an event that responds positively to crises of both masculinity and national cohesion produced by the U.S. failure in the Vietnam War, one of the most visible Gulf War "heroes," Norman Schwarzkopf, has been recruited into various postwar media events. His performances are aimed, it appears, at containing the damage to both martial and masculine imaginaries as a result of Vietnam. They are aimed both at restoring a positive historical narrative of the United States at war and at overcoming the crisis of masculinity by restoring one of masculinity's historical avatars, the soldier hero. And finally, his media appearances serve to reinscribe a dangerous global cartography that will continue to require an aggressive military policy.

To appreciate more fully the political implications of Norman Schwarzkopf's postwar media career—his autobiography and his participation in television documentaries—some contextual preparation is necessary. First, it is necessary to recognize that he was already cast as a media personality during the war. Based on the experience of Vietnam, the Pentagon feared that independent journalism would produce hard-to-manage representations during Desert Shield, the initial troop deployment, and Desert Storm, the attack on Iraq. Accordingly, the use of the "shield" to distance journalists and the employment of Schwarzkopf in press briefing rooms—pointing to maps, showing videos, and, in general, constructing the war as a logistical exercise—recognized a need to control representations as much as space and logistics. Eschewing details of injury and death—no "body counts"—Schwarzkopf stuck to such details as "the fine points of bombing runs."[41] Meanwhile, television networks accepted their roles as conduits rather than author/journalists.[42]

Schwarzkopf's wartime media role was remarkable in two ways. First, it participated in what Allen Feldman has called "cultural anesthesia," the "banishment of disconcerting, discordant and anarchic sensory presences,"[43] and it reflected a new temporality in the event-media relationship. Schwarzkopf's participation in the media's representation of the war was a projection of the present into the future; it anticipated the future encoding of the Gulf War as part of America's history. And the imposing of interpretations on events was aimed at a future honoring of fighting men and women and of the U.S. role in aggressively managing a new global order. "Live," in front of a national audience, Schwarzkopf used a medium that "can be said to be ahead of the historians."[44] And like Ronald Reagan's would-be assassin, John Hinckley, Schwarzkopf was always already in the future as a media personality while he was conducting the war off camera in the present.[45]

In contemporary "chronospace," where the virtual instantaneity of the delivery of images and words, like the delivery of weapons, has displaced territorial extension in the shaping of events, the events are historical *before* they happen.[46] Moments collected and narrated during the Gulf War were organized to produce the "event" of the war in a way already anticipated, so that it would produce a coherent and unifying national experience that was part of the design for the war.

Second, Schwarzkopf's appearances are aimed at a problem of legitimacy that exceeds the problematic of warfare. A nation in crisis because of various centrifugal and fragmenting forces—a growing gap between rich and poor, between ideational commitments and lived experiences, between forces seeking protection of privilege and those seeking to fulfill aspirations—often tends to look outward in order to strengthen the mythologies that substitute stories of harmony for social antagonisms. One such story evokes the idea of national character, and it has enjoyed significant professional support. The emergence of political psychology in the post–World War II United States helped encourage the view that disturbances to global peace are produced by "epidemics of irrational emotion and flawed national characters in need of containment."[47] Thus, for example, such theorists of the Third World as Lucien Pye attributed failures of democratization to national character or personality.[48] Meanwhile, those busy psychologizing political issues saw no disjunctures in the American political culture, only irrational outbursts. Looking abroad for a primary model of disorder, one American political psychologist went so far as to explain such ongoing wars as that between the Guatemalan military and the peasant guerrilla fighters in terms of the psychological frame of frustration-aggression.[49]

The complicity of the social sciences, psychology, and psychiatry in the idea that there is a natural and normal cohesive American character type served ultimately to help depoliticize issues of racism, sexism, class repression, and other forms of antagonism with a discourse on deviance and irrationality. The repression of difference at the level of institutional politics was therefore reinforced with a conceptual repression.

Nevertheless, the forces of fragmentation persist, and those that are particularly threatening to representational practices of selfhood and nationhood as coherent and undivided are, among other things, "peripheral sexualities" (hence the recent furor over gays in the military, a conflict at the level of models of individuality) and various social antagonisms (hence the recent struggle over entitlements). Adding a dimension to Herman Melville's insights about the masks of history, Slavoj Žižek has argued, within a Lacanian frame, that the drive for coherent identity at either individual or collective identity levels is necessarily always blocked. As this drive to overcome incompleteness is played out at the collective level, the imposed story of coherence is a mask that covers a void. The fact of social antagonism is displaced by a myth of undividedness. And rather than facing the disjuncture between fact and aspiration, the dissatisfaction is turned outward, becoming an "enjoyment" in the form of a disparaging model of enemy-others, dangerous character types, and outlaw nations.

As Žižek notes, it is not an external enemy that prevents one from achieving an identity with oneself; that coherence is always already impossible. But the nonacceptance of that impossibility produces fantasy in the form of "an imaginary scenario the function of which is to provide support filling out the subject's constitutive void."[50] When this kind of fantasy is elaborated at the level of the social, it serves as the counterpart to antagonism. It is an imagination of a unified and coherent society that supposedly came into being by leaving a disordered condition of struggle behind.

This mythologizing of origin, which constructs the society as a naturally bounded and consensual community, is a political story that those seeking legitimacy for a national order seek to perpetuate. But the disorder continues to haunt the order. The mythic disorder of the state of nature, supposedly supplanted by consensual association as society comes into being, continues to haunt the polity. It is displaced outside the frontiers and attributed to the Other.[51]

In short, the anarchic state of nature is attributed to relations between states. This displacement amounts to an active amnesia, a forgetting of the violence that both founds and maintains the domestic order; it amounts to a denial of the disorder within the order. This tendency to deny domestic disorder in general and to overcome more specifically the disorder and antagonisms in post–Vietnam War America—stresses between generations, between the military and civilian order, between the telling of imperialist tales and postcolonial ones—has been reflected in the media representation of post–Gulf War America. The triumphalists after the Gulf War have been attempting to write out of U.S. history the post-Vietnam agonism in which tensions within the order were acknowledged. They seek to banish a politics of intepretation and self-appraisal that was part of both official and popular culture during the post-Vietnam period. This is especially evident in the orchestration of Norman Schwarzkopf's career as a media personality.

Finally, the third and related context needed to appreciate the history-inscribing impetus of Schwarzkopf's media career in the wake of the Gulf War is the issue of personhood, particularly masculine personhood. Schwarzkopf's media career has been designed to restore the "soldier hero" to an honored place in the American political culture. And, it must be noted, to effect such a restoration is to reassert one of the "most desirable and powerful forms of idealized masculinity within western cultural traditions."[52] It must be added, moreover, in keeping with George Mosse's findings on the nationalism-masculinity relationship, that such heroes are "intimately bound up with the foundation and preservation of a national identity."[53]

Schwarzkopf's efforts therefore extend a concerted attempt at what Susan Jeffords calls "remasculinization" during the years of the Reagan and Bush presidencies, an attempt to restore an aggressive masculinity to the American polity in the face of the perceived challenge to U.S. potency in the Vietnam War. Various analysts have established connections between the disparagement of gay people and the valorization of a masculinized U.S. presence in the world of states. This obsession with masculinity is powerfully reflected in the policing of sexualities apparent in the United States' most militarized venues.

Just as other nations are the Others against whom national cohesion is to be achieved, women are the Others against whom a coherent masculinity is to be achieved. The extravagance of the reactions in such venues when there is ambiguity at either level, the national or the masculine, becomes explicable when one recognizes that the production of forms of cohesion is a performance, an ongoing masquerade. The masquerade of masculinity is rehearsed by men in front of other men. And insofar as maintaining one's male credentials requires an interminable performance, the rehearsal aspect of the masquerade must go on in a closed theater, which organizes surveillance and allows for breaks. And, because women are the Others for whom the accomplishment of masculinity is to be demonstrated—while they are to be shielded from the strenuous efforts required to achieve it—their presence during the rehearsing of the masquerade is threatening. Not surprisingly, therefore, during the recent controversy over admitting a female cadet to the last and most durable bastion of the martial male, the Citadel, one cadet explained his opposition thus: "If a girl was here, I'd be concerned not to look foolish." Another said, "You don't have to impress them here."[54]

Not unrelated to the requirement that martial masculinity be achieved in a venue without women is the policing of the boundary between the homosocial and the homosexual. At the Citadel, butt slapping, naked wrestling, and punishments with a markedly homoerotic tenor represent a bending of gender roles among the cadets. Within the cloistered confines of the Citadel, a ruthless, often feminized intimacy prevails, but outside the Citadel the cadet must act like a "man"—"a man of cold and rigid bearing."[55]

Indeed, in a variety of venues, military and otherwise, the maintenance of maleness involves a strenuous policing in which the actively homosocial, which verges on the homosexual, is not allowed to cross the boundary into the explicitly homosexual. William Friedkin's film *To Live and Die in LA* (1985) explores this policing. A group of detectives in pursuit of a counterfeiter engage in active homosocial male bonding rituals that include continual use of phallic imagery and a preoccupation with showing that they have "balls." At the same time, they maintain rigidly heterosexual personae while the object of their investigation, an artist/counterfeiter, has a relationship with a bisexual and androgynous-appearing woman and moves about in venues that are ambiguously gender coded.

The policing of counterfeit money therefore functions as a metaphor throughout the film for the policing of masculinity. To maintain the charade of an undiluted masculinity and an unambiguous sexuality, the "police" jealously protect the boundary between the homosocial and the homosexual. Eve Sedgwick, who has investigated the expression of such policing projects in the domain of English literature, has put it succinctly. She notes that there is a strong desire among men to make sure that "the diacritical opposition between the 'homosocial' and the 'homosexual'" remain "thoroughly dichotomous."[56]

Without going into an elaborate reprise of all the connections between such masculinity projects and the drive for a coherent nationhood, it should suffice to note that one of the primary venues of the national struggle over personhood has been popular culture. During the Reagan years—*To Live and Die in LA* begins rolling its credits with a voice-over from a Reagan foreign policy speech—the model of masculinity promoted, along with a specific Reagan-inspired criticism of the softness and indecisiveness of the Carter presidency, was a "tough, aggressive, strong, and domineering" one.[57] Picking up on this mentality, Hollywood decided (with notable, resistant exceptions) that this was the model audiences wanted to see and offered films with "spectacular narratives about characters who stood for individuality, liberty, militarism and a mythic heroism."[58] Although in the nineties, popular culture has begun to react against this anachronistic model, as I argued in my reading of *A Few Good Men* in chapter 4, restoring the soldier hero in some form is a major part of the relays between masculinity and national honor that inform the current media representations of prominent Gulf War figures.[59]

To set the stage for analyzing the specifics of Norman Schwarzkopf's role in the assertion of a masculinizing of American selfhood and the restoration of continuity to the military dimension of American nationhood, it is instructive to analyze an earlier military hero, Audie Murphy, whose post–World War II media career exemplifies all of the contexts related to the Schwarzkopf efforts. Because the issues were different— there were different social antagonisms, a different media-history relationship, and different perceived threats to masculinity—the comparison will help deepen the analysis.

## Inventing the Warring Body: Exemplary Biographies

Most significantly for the theoretical purposes at hand, the cultural problematic governing interpretations and meanings of World War II were very different from the interpretive struggle that has characterized both post-Vietnam and post–Gulf War America. In particular, Vietnam and its aftermath have posed an issue of masculinity very different from the forms of masculinization associated with earlier wars.

As is evident in Clausewitz's discourse, issues of maleness surround the warfare problematic for a nation, and war invariably evokes a focus on the relationship between individual warring bodies and the collective or national body. To analyze war from the point of view of a national culture, therefore, it becomes necessary to focus on what Mark Selzer has called "the relays between the male body and the national body."[60] More specifically, Susan Jeffords's argument that representations of the Vietnam War have been organized around a project of remasculinization of the American culture in response to the destabilizing of male dominance in various cultural domains is compelling.[61] The "Vietnam syndrome," whose overcoming is celebrated by Colonel Harry Summers in his reprise of the Gulf War, is a reassertion of this remasculinization project. It responds specifically to the failure of the Vietnam War to produce a valorization of warring male bodies as well as a failure to unify the national body with coherent and unambivalent public support for warring violence.

Just as the male body–national body relays in post-Vietnam and post–Gulf War America set the stage for Schwarzkopf's media career, an earlier military hero, Audie Murphy, America's "most decorated soldier," entered a context with a similar set of relays when he followed his heroics with an exemplary media career. Most significantly, anxieties about diminished masculinity also provide a background for the Audie Murphy story. These anxieties go back to the turn of the century when such significant cultural actors as Thompson Seton, a cofounder of the scouting movement, concerned themselves with the craft of making men as an "antidote to anxieties about the *depletion* of agency and virility in consumer and machine culture."[62] As the first Boy Scouts of America handbook puts it, it is necessary "to combat the system that has turned such a large proportion of our robust, manly, self-reliant boyhood into a lot of flat-chested cigarette smokers, with shaky nerves and doubtful vitality."[63]

Certainly Audie Murphy's narrative of his war experience is a story of turning boys into men, but it is also a story shaped by the social antagonisms surrounding the place of work in the national self-conception. World War II had the effect of, among other things, averting the national gaze from the struggles between workers and producers, but evidence of the struggle emerges in the idiom of Murphy's autobiography.

Murphy's account of his war experience reflects a theory of value in which the achievements of war are expressed within the discourse of work. He summons the classical legitimating political economy discourses, which link proprietorship or control over turf with labor or the expenditure of effort. His war story is expressed in large part as a story of men working, with the aid of their "tools," in this case guns, to absorb more and more real estate.

In contrast to the weapons of the Gulf War that I discussed in chapter 3, however, their "tools" do not create distance between them and their own bodies or the bodies of their antagonists. In stark contrast to the virtual realities, the dematerialized landscapes and bodies actualized in the Persian Gulf War, Audie Murphy's autobiography is a story of bodies meeting bodies and bodies meeting and penetrating the ground as the war becomes a bloody movement across foreign real estate. Suffering and dying bodies permeate Murphy's account. For example, he describes his patrol's temporary custody of three German soldiers who have been mortally wounded by his patrol compatriot Swope. They are beyond help because, as he puts it, "a battalion of doctors could not undo the work of Swope's gun." The dying and wounded bodies provide palpable evidence of the work of manly bodies and their work implements. Murphy adds several pages on the slowly dying German soldiers and the advancing morbidity of their bodies: one is "too weak to stand" and is breathing "like a terrified horse," and one has "a rattling sound in his throat."[64]

Similarly, the men from his side are described as violated bodies: "One of the scouts is caught squarely in the chest, and the upper part of his body is turned into a shower of seared, torn flesh."[65] Complementing the bodies and blood are the venues of battle: the hills, fields, rocks, ditches, and farms. The warring bodies are constantly described as being in touch with the earth—crawling into holes or ditches to escape explosions, covered with grime and mud sores.

The contrast between Murphy's descriptions of the terrain of war and those of the character Vollmer in Don DeLillo's story of World War III (which I discussed in chapter 3) is striking. Both changed their images of the earth. But while Vollmer had come to see the earth merely aesthetically, given his remote, specular vantage point in a space vehicle above the conflict, Murphy developed a reading of the earth within a semiotics of danger:

> As I plod along, I study the terrain instinctively. As a farm youngster, the land meant either hunger or bread for me. Now its shape is the difference between life and death. Every roll, depression, rock, or tree is significant.[66]

At the same time that Murphy is describing a warring venue, he is celebrating a productivist model of landscape in which labor, mixed with land, yields value. Thus, in addition to being palpably in the war, with an awareness of his own body and those of his comrades and adversaries, Murphy is also locating the value of persons and places in a political economy discourse that reflects a dominant story of the American national experience. Most of the vignettes are male bonding stories as the members of a work crew, doing violence and acquiring land, "do their jobs like men."[67]

Murphy became a war hero *during* the war. He was "a fugitive from the law of averages,"[68] having, for example, driven off scores of German troops and tanks single-handedly after they had surrounded him. The wartime *Life* magazine spread on "America's most decorated soldier," particularly the cover picture, captured the essence of Murphy's public and media appeal: "A fresh-faced second lieutenant, who looked more like one of Norman Rockwell's newspaper boys than someone you'd trust your life to, looks out at you."[69]

When James Cagney saw the picture, he helped recruit Murphy for Hollywood feature films. In *To Hell and Back* Murphy plays himself in the film version of his autobiography. In the book and film, Murphy helps to produce for the nation the story of a boy coming of age in war.

Portraying himself as someone who learns to be a hardworking and dedicated man, willing to risk his life for the nation, Murphy helped to invent himself as an exemplary American.

Murphy began a film career at precisely the time—after World War II—when the Hollywood film had managed to produce a media-created soldier hero—John Wayne in the *Sands of Iwo Jima* (discussed in chapter 4), whose character, Sergeant Stryker, allowed him to, as Lawrence Suid put it, "create a military presence that endured beyond his film portrayal." Wayne as Stryker "merged his own personality with the character" and thus "personified the ideal soldier, sailor or marine."[70]

Audie Murphy surpassed John Wayne in this respect, however, because with his entry into Hollywood films the soldier hero went beyond representation; Murphy played himself. When gossip columnist Hedda Hopper heard that Murphy would play the lead, Henry Flemming, in John Huston's 1951 film version of *The Red Badge of Courage,* she wrote, enthusiastically, "For a change we'll have a real soldier playing a real soldier on the screen. It couldn't happen at a better time."[71]

Thus Murphy emerged as a protagonist not only in films but also in the construction of public memories of war. Ours is the century, as I noted in chapter 4, in which history returns as film. As two analysts of media history put it:

> Public memory of war in the twentieth century has been created less from a remembered past than a manufactured past, one very substantially owing to assembled visual images of what was in films and television programmes ... which guide us directly to the source of widespread perceptions of war, mobilization, national identity and the nature of the enemy.[72]

There is, however, another important context for Murphy's complicity in the construction of American military history. His movie career also affects the issue of personhood, more particularly the construction of manhood. With respect to this dimension of his public persona, his role as Henry Flemming in John Huston's film version of Stephen Crane's novel *The Red Badge of Courage* is more significant than his role as Audie Murphy playing Audie Murphy in *To Hell and Back.* Like Murphy's autobiography, Crane's war story is "an anthropology of boyhood."[73] It is a story of a boy's developing character as he becomes a man. Warfare is perhaps the best arena in which the dynamic can be seen, for the process is accelerated by the intensity of the perilous confrontations.

Audie Murphy is typecast for the role, and it took little persuading when he was recommended to Huston for the lead. Crane's novel, like Murphy's World War II narrative, foregrounds the bloody clash of bodies in palpable landscapes as well as showing the movement from boyhood to manhood. Moreover, both stories operate within the same national allegory. Mark Selzer points out that an "anthropology of Boyhood" governs Crane's novel and that it is further contextualized by a "series of analogies between the individual and the national collective body." What Selzer calls the "topography of masculinity in America at the turn of the century" governs the telling in *The Red Badge of Courage* (as indeed it pervaded Jack London's "wilding stories")[74] and is still evident throughout Audie Murphy's *To Hell and Back*.

Of course Crane's novel was neither a celebration of war nor a panegyric on boys becoming male heroes. The ironic style of Crane's narrative, emphasizing the inner life of the young Henry Flemming (Crane "stages his drama of war within the mind of one man")[75] produces an impression of the futility of war and the ambiguities and confusions it engenders in its soldier protagonists. As it is put in one critical reading, Crane "tacitly exposed the youth's flimsy idealism."[76]

Although John Huston's original screenplay captured this effect, the version that was released was significantly altered by Dore Schary, MGM production head. Schary turned the story from an enactment of ambivalence and confusion, with no clear resolution, into one of a frightened boy becoming a courageous man who helped to achieve a decisive victory. The thoughts Crane gave Henry Flemming, which tend to belie this significance, are largely left out in Schary's version. And, while the original director's cut had a musical score that created disjunctions with the images and narrative, reinforcing the montage effects and therefore helping to undercut a simple heroic story (indeed, the essence of Sergei Eisenstein's filmic practice),[77] Schary cut out all aspects of the score that failed to reinforce the action and the simple narrative of success he had substituted.[78]

There is another important dimension of the construction of the meaning of war that Murphy's character helps to construct. Selzer notes that the body/landscape complex in *The Red Badge of Courage* depicts the ontological essence of wars making men. Wars that rage across landscapes and annex territories take on their meanings through a "coordination of interior states and exterior, territorial states."[79] The primary ontological ingredients are thus present in Murphy's legitimation of war; it is identity earned through valor and sanctified by the territorial/sovereignty capital it produces through territorial transgressions and consolidations.

The Audie Murphy story unfolded at a time when the nation was struggling with a particular masculinity problematic. There was a close relationship between individual male maturity and national maturity as the nation saw itself coming of age as an autonomous international actor. The coming of age of the film genre is an important co-occurrence. For the contention over models of masculinity to take place within the film genre is especially significant because the filmic apparatus, with its capacity for shot and countershot, creates an identification between male spectators and characters by dint of the formal properties of the film's visual apparatus, its construction of viewpoint. The film, in contrast to, for example, the historical portrait with which Napoleon sought to legitimate martial heroism, adds an important dimension of technology to the construction of maleness and its effects on viewers.[80]

As I have noted, the Gulf War was part of a remasculinization agenda, but it unfolded within a nation that had already come of age but was now more uncertain about the sanctity and national purpose of its warfare violence. The war was waged by a nation divided over the interpretation of its recent war experience and still involved in an active negotiation of how to locate warring bodies within the collective national body.

The Gulf War, reproduced and interpreted in the autobiograhy of Norman Schwarzkopf, functions within an ambiguous individual and national body. The book is entitled *It Doesn't Take a Hero* to distance it from the Audie Murphy type of story, but the modest disclaimer manages to include the category of hero and thereby encourage ascription of it to Schwarzkopf. The ambivalence applied to the concept of hero undoubtedly reflects an author/soldier who, chastened by the ambivalent reactions of the nation to the carnage in Vietnam, worked strenuously as a commander and public relations representative for the military both to remove bodies from the war as much as possible and to downplay his own body.

Perhaps the primary difference between Audie Murphy and Norman Schwarzkopf as heroic individual bodies that exemplify the national body is that Murphy's body was central to his account of war. He describes in detail his frequent contact with blood and dirt and the visible results of his violent confrontations with other bodies. Schwarzkopf, like Murphy, operates within a discourse of war as labor, but it is not a story of manual labor. It is work embedded in a remote, management-oriented setting, complete with statistical estimates of performance. Moreover, Schwarzkopf is explicit in his removal of bodies from performance estimates. One cannot, of course, divorce Schwarzkopf's wariness of bodies from the bad press that body counts had during the Vietnam War, which is Schwarzkopf's constant background reference for his telling of the Gulf War. And the Pentagon is implicated in helping to set Schwarzkopf's bodiless representation of the war. Its position is represented by a media admirer:

> The United States is not trying to kill people as much as it is [trying] to reduce the capacity of Iraq to prosecute an organized war effort. . . . General Schwarzkopf's main concern is that when you get into the body count business, you end up perverting the bomb damage assessment . . . you avoid talking about lives lost, and that serves both an esthetic purpose and a practical purpose.[81]

Making clear that Vietnam had taught war enthusiasts something, the commentator elaborated, "In practical terms, counting the dead invites not only mathematical errors but [also] political dangers."[82] While Murphy's bodies disappear from Schwarzkopf's narrative, there remain strong parallels. Like Murphy, Schwarzkopf characterized the impetus to his military career in terms of a boy becoming a man. Indeed, his story begins with his father going off to war and leaving him explicitly as the "man" of the house: "It was up to me to look after the girls, because men are protectors of women."[83]

But Schwarzkopf's primary narrative is not the story of boys becoming men in war. It is, rather, a long lament about the tragedy Vietnam visited on the vocation of the warrior. Audie Murphy returned from World

War II as the epitome of the hero. In contrast, Norman Schwarzkopf describes how soldiers returning from Vietnam had become invisible. After returning from Vietnam the first time, Schwarzkopf takes a taxi from the Newark airport to his mother's home, expecting the cab driver to notice his uniform and medals and say, "Hey, you're just back from Vietnam, aren't you?" But the driver says nothing, and Schwarzkopf goes on to note that "no one wanted to know about Vietnam: the public wasn't caught up in the war, not at all like the spirit I remembered from my boyhood, during World War II."[84]

Indeed Norman Schwarzkopf's story is in many ways the story of disappearing warring bodies. Apart from his politically motivated concern that body counts and other fleshly measures of performance be removed from the evaluation of military success, his own body, the body that feels and registers the horror of war, had to be canceled as well. The body as a public body must not be readable: "I had been taught at West Point that an Officer should avoid any public display of feelings."[85] Nevertheless, the need for a body and its emotions to retain significant personhood haunts Schwarzkopf's account, and it returns to haunt the proceedings in the Schwarzkopf/Rather documentary of Schwarzkopf's post–Gulf War return to Vietnam.

As one moves through Schwarzkopf's autobiography, the account lives up to his ambition to cancel bodies, particularly as it moves to his crowning achievement, the "victory in the desert." The Gulf War is a logistical phenomenon in which bodies disappear from view. It has to do with distant calculations of performance and remote ways of seeing. Paul Virilio's gloss on logistics is apropos here, for he described logistics as "the art of movement of unseen bodies."[86]

In the postmodern hyperlogistical war, violence is not flesh against flesh, or even directly visualized killing with the mediation of handheld firearms as in Audie Murphy's account. His heroics have been displaced by the verification of the efficacy of unseen bodies. Again, Virilio has anticipated the new logistical comprehension. It is, he writes, "a new idea of violence that no longer comes from direct confrontation and bloodshed, but rather from the unequal properties of bodies, evaluation of the number of movements allowed them in a chosen element, permanent verification of their dynamic efficiency."[87] This form of comprehension was already operating to some extent in World War II at some levels of command. Audie Murphy's account is delivered from ground level, the point of contact, but such points are increasingly being displaced by more remote ones.

Significantly, the U.S. public is also no longer afforded the point of view from points of violent contact—points that were still available during the Vietnam War. Today's war hero is the hero of the briefing room and the press conference, the man who organizes rather than conducts the violence. The hero, Norman Schwarzkopf, confronts maps rather than bodies and data displays rather than massed armies. The bodies he confronts more directly are all clothed and relatively civil (give or take the odd feisty news reporter).

Necessarily, this new remoteness produces a contrast in landscapes as well as bodies. While Audie Murphy confronted his adversaries in meadows, farmlands, and forests, taking real estate through bloody confrontation, Norman Schwarzkopf's venues are strategically and mythically mediated. For example, his Vietnam is a mythic geography, frustrating a man trying to do his job. The night and the jungle belong to Vietnam for the sole purpose of frustrating eager conquerors. Rather than a land of villages and farms—the kind of landscape across which Audie Murphy fought—Vietnam is a place of frustrating concealment.

Hence, by the time Schwarzkopf reaches the Gulf and engulfs it in explosives, the logistics of vision are on his side. Equipped with night-capable optical equipment and facing a sedentary, dug-in force with no foliage, only detectable bunkers, he can "see" what he wants to destroy, and his first strike is to deprive his adversary of vision: "Very early on we took out the Iraqi Airforce . . . and when we took out his airforce, we took out his ability to see what we were doing down here in Saudia Arabia."[88]

Additionally significant is the temporal structure of Schwarzkopf's war. Schwarzkopf saw himself as a media event before he acted. In contrast to Audie Murphy, who looked for danger in the landscape, Norman Schwarzkopf saw the most relevant dangers in the mediascapes of his almost immediate future. He was always already at a future press conference when he made his strategic moves. Ironically, the Civil War plays a role in Schwarzkopf's media life, as it did in Murphy's in his role as Henry Flemming in Huston's *Red Badge of Courage*.

While Audie Murphy was summoned back to the Civil War because his celebrity status showed him to be already a Henry Flemming type (if the type is oversimplified), Norman Schwarzkopf feared that the airing of the television documentary *The Civil War* was a dangerous coincidence. He reports that as a result of the showing of this series on network television, his command assumed that "the mood is changing in the U.S. and is becoming less bellicose."[89] They wanted to time the ground assault to coincide with a better mood. This reference, along with various others, makes clear that logistical calculations had the public image at least as much in view as the Iraqi adversaries. Schwarzkopf was making decisions in a way comparable to how commercial television sponsors make decisions. For example, Amtrak cancels its advertisements for taking the train during periods when a train wreck is in the news. Schwarzkopf seemed to assume that he had to aim his operations not only to surprise his adversaries but also to harmonize with media-induced public moods.

Clearly, Schwarzkopf had learned a lesson about the obtrusiveness of historical events on contemporary imaginations, for after the Gulf War his media career turned in a historical direction. Unlike Audie Murphy, who simply shifted his heroics from the battlefield to the silver screen, Schwarzkopf became a revisionist historian. His post–Gulf War trip back to Vietnam with Dan Rather was nothing less than an attempt to inscribe a different Vietnam War in the national imaginary, an opportunity afforded by his heroic status.

In "Vietnam: A Soldier Returns," Schwarzkopf tries first to remove the stigma of the slaughter in Vietnam conducted by U.S. forces.[90] The narrative, in which the carnage is largely displaced by current scenes of everyday life, is aided by Dan Rather. Speaking of contemporary Vietnam, Rather says, "It's a country now of great calm and tranquility," and the accompanying film footage shows tourist destination–type scenes in which Vietnam is an exotic, pastoral Buddhist land. Its war experiences are effaced as it is represented within the imperial eye in its prewar, preindustrial tranquility.

There are some violent scenes—U.S. soldiers torching peasant villages, for example—as Rather admits that "Vietnam brings back some dreadful memories," but he adds, to set up Schwarzkopf's theme, that "some Americans are quick to blame them on the men who fought the war." Schwarzkopf comes in on cue:

> Some people go around expecting us to be ashamed of ourselves for Vietnam. I'm not ashamed of myself. Nobody who was over here doing what their country asked them to do should be ashamed of themselves.

For Schwarzkopf, moral geography coincides with geopolitical geography. People are simply loyal citizens, and soldiers are loyal servants. Identities and spaces are exhausted by his simple cartography. Within his commentary, the interpretive struggle that has challenged the propriety of war as policy since Vietnam is swept away. To pursue the cartographic metaphor in which Schwarzkopf's "history" unfolds, we must consider the geography of the pre-Schwarzkopf intervention.

One way to construe the continuing challenges to the national imaginary produced by the self-reflective, politicized post-Vietnam cultural and artistic expressions that immediately preceded Schwarzkopf's overwriting campaign is to identify the "heterotopias"—places of otherness—within the national landscape.[91] Among these are the ones created by critical reflection on the American experience in Vietnam. As Philip Beidler has put it, "the work of Vietnam writers in their generation has . . . come to comprise nothing less than a whole vast American heterotopia."[92] It is a set of spaces of representation, produced by writers who served in Vietnam as soldiers or journalists, that oppose the spaces of certainty within which America is represented as whole rather than fragmented, certain rather than ambivalent, and resolved rather than endlessly deferred. The Schwarzkopf media career amounts to an effort to efface these heterotopias. At the same time that he attempts to restore Vietnam to an unproblematic place on an international geopolitical map, he does violence to the domestic map, opposing critical representational practices with a discourse of resolution. In place of a troubled domestic cartography, Schwarzkopf relies on a moralistic and legitimating discourse on labor and value. People who happen to be soldiers have to do their jobs. If there was a problem with the Vietnam War, it was a lack of seriousness among many of the officers and troops conducting the war.

In "A Soldier Returns," Schwarzkopf repeats the story from his autobiography about having to shape up a lax battalion he commanded when he returned to Vietnam in 1969. Ethnic slurs and stereotyping are no longer part of war literature and films. While the homosociality of fighting men unites Poles, Italians, Irish, and others in Audie Murphy's book and films, Schwarzkopf can refer only to his "men," and when he is searching for a reference group to disparage the battalion's pre-Schwarzkopf laxity, he compares their situation—after a brief, calculating hesitation—to a "gypsy camp," choosing a people that is unlikely to be able to respond.

When Schwarzkopf finally gets to places where U.S. casualties were high, he says, "I don't like it here. This is a badass place," and he gives details (which are also in his autobiography) about men stepping on mines. Again, he is angry about the concealments with which his army could not cope. The slaughter of two million Vietnamese people never seems to be part of Schwarzkopf's story of the war; it is all about the unjust criticism of U.S. troops.

Part of this "injustice" is implied in interviews with soldiers who were severely wounded while serving under Schwarzkopf. Here, the documentary, like Schwarzkopf's soldiers who stepped on land mines, is on dangerous ground. The "disabled veterans" are summoned to signify the courage, sacrifice, and continuing patriotism of heroic men, but as Sonya Mitchell has noted, "as signs of either patriotism or masculinity, war injuries are unstable," for they can be read as signs of weakness at an individual level and, at a national level, a sign that the "political system" failed to protect them.[93]

The documentary attempts to finesse this ambiguity with statements of unalloyed loyalty from the veterans and a statement by Schwarzkopf that implies unambivalent support among veterans for their roles in Vietnam. By the end of the documentary, the Gulf War arrives, and Schwarzkopf notes that while previously he didn't like to be interviewed about Vietnam, "now things have changed," and he is thrilled when Vietnam veterans throw their arms around him and say "thank you, general, somehow you made it all right."

The Norman Schwarzkopf story turns out to be a story about redemption, the redemption of the profession of soldiering as well as of the wounded, morally degraded national body. Schwarzkopf goes back to say that Vietnam is primarily about a failure of political will and not a reflection of the horrors of war or the action of those who perpetrate them. The remasculinization of America that has been the project of military and militaristic public relations continues, and Schwarzkopf's media career is at the center of it as he recreates the history of U.S. warfare. His task is nothing less than to unify the national body and make its warriors that body's uncontested representatives, even as actual fighting bodies become increasingly remote from deadly encounters.

The return to Vietnam, however, was apparently inadequate to Scharzkopf's rewriting of history. To turn the Vietnam experience into a mere speed bump in the story of America realizing itself as a unified nation destined to manage the global order and therefore always needing the soldier hero, it is necessary to get more of a historical run at it. Hence Schwarzkopf and Rather went back to Normandy as well—a propitious venue not only because the U.S. role in World War II remains less controversial than its role in Vietnam, but also because the fiftieth anniversary of the decisive invasion of Normandy, which precipitated the Allied victory in Europe, was a year away when the documentary was aired.

The Normandy invasion therefore provided an opportunity to co-opt the space of historical inscription. Hence, one year after the airing of "A Soldier Returns," in which Schwarzkopf and Rather rehistoricize Vietnam, they are seen walking along the beach at Normandy, coordinating the experience of American soldiers in the Normandy invasion with their narrative on how to locate the contemporary soldier in American political culture and American history.

It should be noted that even at the time of the Normandy invasion, its commanders were keenly aware that the battle in which they were involved would be tomorrow's history. Indeed, General Omar Bradley was appalled at what appeared to be a "competition for publicity,"[94] but his attempt to rescue war from publicity was obtuse; he failed to recognize that war is always fought in the domain of representation, in the mediascape as well as the landscape, as it exerts a force on "popular consent and memory," as Thomas Keenan notes:

> What is it to fight not for a hill or a city but for a headline or a picture? It is nothing short of war itself: that struggle not only to inscribe, represent,

to redraw the boundaries . . . and to live on, to fight in the light of another day. This violence—of battle and of publicity—is irreducible.[95]

Schwarzkopf and Rather's reinvasion of Normandy is part of a wider war of publicity. But the historical development of the mediascape within which this war is being prosecuted contains a depth of competing significations that did not exist during the first invasion of Normandy. The post–World War II vicissitudes of significance attached to the soldier hero's journeys upward and downward in public esteem form much of the background frame for the Schwarzkopf/Rather assault on cultural resistance to military heroism and honor.

## Restoring the Time Line of the Soldier Hero

The opening segments of the return to Normandy (entitled, simply, "D-Day") are devoted primarily to the U.S. soldier's peerless masculinity. In light of the ongoing controversy provoked by President Clinton's policy on gays in the military—at center stage as the documentary was being aired—it is not irrelevant that the model of masculinity presented is hyperheterosexual. Schwarzkopf and Rather are not only tying personhood to nationhood but also representing an exclusionary heterosexual masculinity as the model of the fighting soldier. They are deeply involved in "foreclosing any possibility" of imagining "alternative or oppositional masculinities."[96]

Although the contributions of women to the invasion are given some coverage, the primary significations throughout the first segment devoted to the U.S. soldier in Britain prior to the invasion are aimed at exhibiting an irrepressible and active heterosexuality of the soldier hero. Schwarzkopf had already established his heterosexual credentials in his earlier documentary—his return to Vietnam—by referring to his wife, pregnant at home during most of his tour of duty. He notes that her pregnancy resulted from a brief leave he spent with her in Japan.

Schwarzkopf does report an experience of intimate bodily contact with a man in his Vietnam reprise. One of the soldiers was injured when he stepped on a mine, and Schwarzkopf tells of lying on top of the man to keep him from moving and incurring further injury. But this intimacy is turned immediately into a legitimately masculine gesture, for

Schwarzkopf says that he "pinned him," noting that he had wrestled in college and knew how to "pin a man."

The heterosexual masculinity of the U.S. soldiers who invaded Normandy is produced within an even less subtle narrative. Much is made of their robust and irrepressible sexuality through interviews with English men and women. A former army nurse refers to them as "very brash," and an Englishman reports on how they took over the island and exhibited a sexuality with which Englishmen could not compete.

After establishing the heterosexual masculinity of the American soldier, "D-Day" evokes the code of sacrifice. Tears are shed by veterans recalling fallen comrades, and many talk about their willingness to sacrifice their bodies on behalf of the national body. Seeking to efface the more difficult issue of 58,000 U.S. casualties in Vietnam, Schwarzkopf and Rather follow up a Vietnam documentary with one on World War II, which allows them to allocate the issue of sacrifice to a less contentious war that more readily solicits a model in which the "victory" balanced the casualties.

The Normandy venue has another advantage missing during the various cold war military ventures of the U.S. armed services: throughout the footage, English and French people recall how welcome the Americans were. The welcoming code is clearly aimed at discrediting years of criticism of aggressive U.S. foreign policy throughout the cold war period, and Schwarzkopf and Rather team up to tell an official story in a venue that has been less afflicted with counterstories. Indeed, it is treated as transcendent; in his first utterance, Schwarzkopf refers to Omaha Beach as "sacred ground." Nevertheless, Schwarzkopf and Rather's reinvasion of Normandy produces domestic victims. First, it erases a history of political dissent, and second, and perhaps more significant, it undermines much of the basis for dissent; it pretends that America has responded to the world with one voice and with no significant differences in the situating of the voices that are in unison. For example, a Native American veteran who is interviewed reports that he was glad to be part of the war effort, to risk his life for "his country."

At this point, Schwarzkopf and Rather's reinvasion of Normandy constitutes a denial of the violence of an earlier invasion—the European invasion of the Americas. The fight to free Europe from Hitler's aggression and genocide becomes an occasion to deny an earlier genocidal violence. Instead of reexamining U.S. coherence and integrity and the rationale of its global violence ("defense policy"), Schwarzkopf's media career attempts to pacify domestic space, to deny other Americas within the official America as he seeks to reinstall the soldier hero. Schwarzkopf's domestic pacification also amounts to the effacement of the political action of some citizen bodies. Just as his Gulf War media strategy canceled adversarial bodies—no body counts—his postwar media career cancels domestic bodies. His repression of the spaces of dissent, particularly public spaces in which war protesters marched, denies the confrontations with protesting bodies. Demonstrators against the Vietnam War were "intervening with the body," using the body as a "physical metaphor of the reminder . . . that power and its discourse are incomplete."[97] But Schwarzkopf is focused on one particular body, that of the soldier hero, who emerges not from a troubled set of conflicting forces and peoples and spaces of political confrontation but is simply a loyal citizen responding to a summons and therefore deserving of an unambiguously honored place. The "nation" must not be divided, fragmented, or challenged; war must be sacralized rather than politicized.

In addition to restoring the soldier hero and rewriting contemporary American history against the revisions and contentions that have politicized it, Schwarzkopf's media career represents a politics of forgetting, an attempt to deny the ongoing fragmentation and identity ambiguity that characterize a nation whose career of violence can still be read at home and abroad in terms of its victims. Although "D-Day" is meant to overcome the ambiguities of America's Vietnam problem, the enigma remains.

Neither Vietnam nor the various peoples that Schwarzkopf's way of writing history seeks to domesticate and incorporate are as docile as he and Rather want to pretend (they even manage to find pro capitalist students to interview in Hanoi: Vietnamese difference is being effaced by an inevitably historical move to sameness!). Undoubtedly, the career of Ward Just's narrator is more telling. The Others with whom he seeks a reconciliation in Vietnam remain mysterious and resistant to incorporation within his "history" of the war.

Unlike the journey of Just's character to a land of enigma and resistant alterity, Schwarzkopf's pilgrimage is circular; it is an attempt to bring alterity home again and to reconcile difference with what is represented as the same, a cohesive, united America. Most essentially, it is an attempt to square a violent and disjunctive practice with a simple narrative of America as a democracy. Schwarzkopf's personal story is an allegory of the nation, an attempt to tell the official American story.

Nevertheless, as Joan Didion has made clear in her story about Vietnam—in a novel ironically entitled *Democracy*—it is impossible to subsume the experience of Vietnam, when it is read through the personal lives of people involved with that place, into such a national allegory.[98] The commitment that the American democracy has made to accepting difference is belied by both the original experience of Vietnam and later attempts, such as Schwarzkopf's, at representational violence, attempts to incorporate the Other into a self-regarding historical narrative. More generally, as Alan Nadel has noted, Didion's novel not only denies "the manifest destiny of Democracy and of the foreign policy that resembles it" but also "reveals the facts of American history to be a function of a dubious narrative convention."[99]

How might one confront difference in an ethical rather than an appropriating discursive practice? In the last chapter, I turn to a consideration of the ethics of encounter to provide an alternative not only to the violence of warfare but also to the violence of representations that seek to dissolve recalcitrant otherness into the same, that seek to deny alternative stories of identity and practices of space.

## SIX

# The Ethics of Encounter:
# Unreading, Unmapping the Imperium

He alo ā he alo
  (Face to face)

That's how you learn about what makes us weep.

He alo ā he alo
  (Face to face)

That's how you learn about what makes us bleed . . .

'A'ohe o kahi nānā o luna o ka pali;
iho mai a lalo nei
'ike i ke au nui ke au iki;
he alo ā he alo.
(The top of the cliff isn't the place to look at us; come down here
  and learn of the big and little current, face to face.)
                    PUANANI BURGESS, "Face to Face"

## Introduction: Sovereignty's Moral Cartography

Beginning with the modest statement "What I shall have to say here is
neither difficult nor contentious; the only merit I should like to claim for
it is that of being true, at least in parts," John Austin went on to disrupt
the authority of the referential view of language with an elaboration of
speech acts.[1] In fact, Austin's analysis of "performative utterances"—
what one *does* in saying something—has proven to be quite contentious,
for it reinstates two stabilities even as it destabilizes notions of the force
or meaning of utterances. In the process of showing that both performa-

tives ("I now pronounce you man and wife," for example) and descriptively oriented statements ("constatives") are equally context-dependent, Austin proceeded to make his case as if both the contexts of utterances and the identities of speaking subjects, which are essential predicates of their rhetorical force, are stable and noncontroversial.[2]

In a contentious encounter with an Austin-inspired speech-act theorist, Jacques Derrida pointed to some of the instabilities in the "system of predicates" that Austin had neglected.[3] He argued that Austin had not heeded the dependence of speech on writing, on prior "graphemic structures": the plays of difference, presence, and absence from which intelligibility emerges. Most significantly, after an inquiry into the Austinian elaboration of speech acts, Derrida showed that "the finiteness of context is never secured or simple," that there is always an "irreducible violence" involved in "the attempt to fix the context of utterances."[4]

Derrida's critique helps create the conditions of possibility for a politics and ethics of language. His analysis of intelligibility as a historically evolving practice by which meanings are institutionalized locates the significance of discursive encounters beyond the mere presence of the immediate interlocutors, displacing it to the constructed stage on which speakers perform. Recognizable speech acts draw from the archive of the already said, from what is already part of a system of meaning production from which utterances can be constructed. And, most significantly for present purposes, they rely on a normativity of space, on an implicit territoriality that tends to remain an indistinct background to focused ethical argumentation. Recognition of the extraordinary lengths to which one must go to challenge a given structure of intelligibility, to intervene in resident meanings by bringing what is silent and unglimpsed into focus, is an essential step toward opening up possibilities for a politics and ethics of discourse.

Over a decade ago, Alasdair MacIntyre achieved a similar recognition by being sensitive to a neglected temporality in ethical positions. He formulated a view of ethics with a temporally dynamic rather than a static view of the self. Acts for MacIntyre must be located within a narrative structure of performances. They take on their meanings with reference to historically evolving personae. Specifically, MacIntyre's approach to ethics is constructed around two important insights. The first is his notion of the relationship between ethics and social life, with which he seeks to overcome the estrangement between ethical thinking, history, and anthropology. For example, he shows how such contemporary ethical traditions as emotivism developed to fit particular modern "characters" such as the manager, the bureaucrat, and the therapist.[5]

The second insight derives from MacIntyre's various demonstrations that the intelligibility of action is dependent on its location within a narrative with historical depth. Using the metaphor of the theatrical character, he argues that as individual agents we are at best only coauthors of our narratives: "We enter upon a stage which we did not design ... [and] we find ourselves part of an action that was not of our making."[6] MacIntyre's recognition of the centrality of narrative goes a long way toward avoiding the empty abstractions that analytic philosophy's model of the self produces in its commitment to universal, contextless bases for judgment. However, he fails to recognize the depth and contentiousness of the narrative aspect of identity. And his spatial imaginary is too narrow, for it is focused on the immediate location of the speech act rather than the complex set of boundaries and divisions—whether consensual or contentious—that constitute the order as a whole. Seeking to restore an Aristotelian basis for virtue, MacIntyre treats narratives in terms of their forward aims, their projections toward a future world. This teleological frame obscures what is at once more basic and more contestable in the narrative context of the actor. While it is the case that, at the level of immediate public intelligibility, people's actions take on much of their significance through the temporal extension of stories, which help justify the goals of the actions, it is also the case that actions participate in other kinds of stories; they belong to people in the sense that they reaffirm who they are, where they are, and how it is that they have become part of an assemblage or a "people" in a collective sense. The identity stories that construct actors as one or another type of person (e.g., Jew versus Arab, native versus immigrant) and that territorialize identities (e.g., resident versus nomad, citizen versus foreigner) are the foundations for historical and contemporary forms of antagonism, violence, and interpretive contention over the meaning of actions.

To claim membership in a particular tribe, ethnicity, or nation—that is, to belong to a "people"—one must claim location in a particular genealogical and spatial story. Such stories precede any particular action aimed at a future result and provoke much of the contestation over claims to territory and entitlement and thus to collective recognition. To the extent that they are part of the reigning structure of intelligibility, identity stories tend to escape contentiousness within ongoing political and ethical discourses. To produce an ethics responsive to contestations over identity claims and their related spatial stories, it is necessary to intervene in the dominant practices of intelligibility.

Michel Foucault was calling for such intervention when he noted that the purpose of critical analysis is to question, not deepen, existing structures of intelligibility. Intelligibility results from aggressive, institutionalized practices that, in producing a given intelligible world, exclude alternative worlds. "We must," Foucault said, "make the intelligible appear against a background of emptiness, and deny its necessity. We must think that what exists is far from filling all possible spaces."[7]

Like Foucault, Derrida claimed that a recognition of practices of exclusion is a necessary condition for evoking an ethical sensibility. His insights into the instability and contentiousness of the context of an utterance, in his critique of Austin, provides access to what is effectively the protoethics of ethical discourse, the various contextual commitments that determine the normative implications of statements. To heed this observation, it is necessary to analyze two particular kinds of contextual commitments that have been silent and often unreflective predicates of ethical discourses. And it is important to do so in situations in which contending parties have something at stake—that is, by focusing on the ethics of encounter. Accordingly, in what follows, my approach to "the ethical" locates ethics in a respect for an-Other's identity performances with special attention to both the temporal or narrative dimension and the spatial dimension of those performances. Moreover, to produce a critical political approach to the ethics of the present, it is necessary to oppose the dominant stories of modernity and the institutionalized, geopolitical versions of space, which support existing forms of global proprietary control, for both participate unreflectively in a violence of representation.

The ethical sensibility offered in the thought of Emmanuel Levinas provides an important contribution to the ethics-as-nonviolent-encounter thematized in my analysis. Levinas regarded war, the ultimate form of violence, as the suspension of morality; "it renders morality derisory," he said. Moreover, Levinas's thought fits the more general anti-Clausewitzian/antirationalist approach to war thematized in prior chapters, for Levinas regarded a strategically oriented politics—"the art of foreseeing war and of winning it by every means," which is "enjoined as the very essence of reason"—as "opposed to morality."[8]

In order to oppose war and promote peace, Levinas enacted a linguistic war on the governing assumptions of Western philosophy. He argued that philosophy from Plato through Heidegger constructed persons and peoples within totalizing conceptions of humanity. The ethical regard, he insisted, is one that resists encompassing the Other as part of the same, that resists recognizing the Other solely within the already spoken codes of a universalizing vision of humankind. However problematic Levinas's notion of infinite respect for an alterity that always evades complete comprehension may be (an issue I discuss later), it nevertheless makes possible a concern with the violence of representation, with discursive control over narratives of space and identity, which is central to my analysis. Edward Said emphasized the ethicopolitical significance of systems of discursive control, locating the violence of imperialism in the control over stories: "The power to narrate, or to block other narratives from forming and emerging, is very important to culture and imperialism, and constitutes one of the main connections between them."[9]

Indeed, contemporary neoimperialism resides in part in the dominance of a spatial story that inhibits the recognition of alternatives. A geopolitical imaginary, the map of nation-states, dominates ethical discourse at a global level. Despite an increasing instability in the geopolitical map of states, the more general discourses of "international affairs" and "international relations" continue to dominate both ethical and political problematics. Accordingly, analyses of global violence are most often constructed within a statecentric, geostrategic cartography, which organizes the interpretation of enmities on the basis of an individual and collective national subject and on cross-boundary antagonisms. And ethical theories aimed at a normative inhibition of these antagonisms continue to presume this same geopolitical cartography.[10]

To resist this discursive/representational monopoly, we must challenge the geopolitical map. Although the interpretation of maps is usually subsumed within a scientific imagination, it is nevertheless the case that "the cartographer's categories," as J. B. Harley has put it, "are the basis of the morality of the map."[11] "Morality" here emerges most significantly from the boundary and naming practices that construct the map. The nominations and territorialities that maps endorse constitute, among other things, a "topographical amnesia."[12] Effacements of older maps in contemporary namings and configurations amount to a non-recognition of older, often violently displaced practices of identity and space. Among the consequences of this neglected dimension of cartography, which include a morality-delegating spatial unconscious and a historical amnesia with respect to alternatives, has been a radical circumspection of the kinds of persons and groups recognized as worthy subjects of moral solicitude. State citizenship has tended to remain the primary basis for the identities recognized in discourses such as the "ethics of international affairs."[13]

The dominance and persistence of this discursive genre, an "ethics" predicated on absolute state sovereignty, is evident in a recent analysis that has attempted to be both critical of the ethical limitations of the sovereignty system and aware that "conflict has increasingly moved away from interstate territorial disputes."[14] Despite these acknowledged sensitivities, the analysis proceeds within a discourse that reinstalls the dominance of geopolitical thinking, for it remains within its cartography and conceptual legacy. Arguing for a humanitarianism that avoids interstate partisanship, the writers go on to reproduce the geopolitical discourse on war, which grants recognition only to state subjects. Even as they criticize the language of "intervention" as a reaffirmation of a sovereignty discourse, they refer to the "Persian Gulf War" on the one hand and "insurgencies" on the other.

As I noted in chapter 1, Bernard Nietschmann has shown that the map of global warfare changes dramatically when one departs from the language of sovereignty. Challenging the state-oriented language of war and unmapping the geostrategic cartography of "international relations," Nietschmann refers to the "Third World War," which is "hidden from view because the fighting is against peoples and countries that are often not even on the map"—a war in which "only one side of the fighting has a name." Focusing on struggles involving indigenous peoples, Nietschmann proceeds to map 120 armed struggles as part of the "war." In his mapping, only 4 of the struggles involve confrontations between states, while 77 involve states against nations.[15]

In order to think beyond the confines of the state sovereignty orientation, it is therefore necessary to turn to ethical orientations that challenge the spatial predicates of traditional moral thinking and thereby grant recognition outside of modernity's dominant political identities. This must necessarily also take us outside the primary approach that contemporary philosophy has lent to (Anglo-American) ethical theory. As applied at any level of human interaction, the familiar neo-Kantian ethical injunction is to seek transcendent values. Applied to the interstate or sovereignty model of global space more specifically, this approach seeks to achieve a set of universal moral imperatives based on shared values and regulative norms.

This dominant tradition has not yielded guidance for specific global encounters because it fails to acknowledge the historical depth of the identity claims involved in confrontations or collisions of difference— difference that includes incommensurate practices of space and conflicting narratives of identity. The tradition depends instead on two highly abstract assumptions. The first is that morality springs from what humanity holds in common, which is thought to yield the possibility of a shared intuition of what is good. The second is that the values to be apprehended are instantiated in the world and are capable of being grasped by human consciousness, wherever it exists. As Hegel pointed out in one of his earliest remarks on Kantian moral reasoning, Kant's system involves "a conversion of the absoluteness of pure identity . . . into the absoluteness of content."[16] Because, for Kant, the form of a concept is what determines its rightness, there remains in his perspective no way to treat "conflicts among specific matters."[17]

A brief account of an encounter between alternative spatial imaginaries helps to situate the alternative ethical frame to be elaborated later. It is provided by the reflections of the writer Carlos Fuentes after an unanticipated encounter with a Mexican peasant. Lost while driving with friends in the state of Morelos, Mexico, Fuentes stopped in a village and asked an old peasant the name of the village. "Well, that depends," answered the peasant. "We call it the Village Santa Maria in times of peace. We call it Zapata in times of war." Fuentes's meditation on this response reveals the historical depth of forms of otherness that exist relatively unrecognized within modernity. He notes that the peasant has existed within a narrative trace that tends to be uncoded in the contemporary institutionalized discourses on space:

> That old campesino knew what most people in the West have ignored since the seventeenth century: that there is more than one time in the world, that there is another time existing alongside, above, underneath the linear time calendars of the West. This man who could live in the time of Zapata or the time of Santa Maria, depending, was a living heir to a complex culture of many strata in creative tension.[18]

Fuentes's reaction constitutes an ethical moment. Provoked by an Other, he engages in an ethnographic self-reflection rather than reasserting modernity's dominant temporal and spatial imaginaries; he recognizes an Other who cannot be absorbed into the same. His reaction cannot therefore be contained solely within what constitutes the ethical life of his community. By encountering an alterity that is at once inside and wholly outside of the particular narrative within which his social and cultural self-construction has been elaborated, he is able to step back from the story of modernity that is continually recycled within the West's reigning discourses on time and space: "What we call 'modernity' is more often than not this process whereby the rising industrial and mercantile classes of Europe gave unto themselves the role of universal protagonists of history."[19]

Face to face with an otherness that these "protagonists," those who have managed to perform the dominant structures of meaning, have suppressed, Fuentes is able to recover the historical trace of that otherness and, on reflection, to recognize that the encounter must yield more than mere affirmation for his practices of self. Most significantly, the encounter produces a disruption of the totalizing conceptions that have governed contemporary societies—for example, the illusion that they are unproblematically consolidated and that they have quelled recalcitrant subjectivities. Therefore, in order to elaborate the ethical possibilities toward which Fuentes's story points, we can consider an approach that assails such totalizations with the aim of providing an ethics of encounter.

## Levinas and the Ethics of the Face to Face

Fuentes's experience and the conclusions he draws from it are elaborately prescripted in the ethical writings of Levinas, for whom the face-to-face encounter and the experience of the Other as a historical trace are crucial dimensions of an ethical responsibility. To confront Levinas is to be faced with an ethical tradition quite different from those traditionally applied to issues of global encounter. In Levinas's ethical thinking and writing, morality is not an experience of value, as it is for both the Kantian tradition and Alasdair MacIntyre's post-Kantian concern with an anthropology of ethics, but a recognition of and vulnerability to alterity.

This conception of vulnerability to alterity is not a moral psychology, as is the case with, for example, Adam Smith's notion of interpersonal sympathy.[20] It is a fundamentally ethical condition attached to human subjectivity; it is an acceptance of the Other's absolute exteriority, a recognition that "the other is in no way another myself, participating with me in a common existence."[21] According to Levinas, we are responsible to alterity as absolute alterity, as a difference that cannot be subsumed into the same, into a totalizing conceptual system that comprehends self and Other. For relations with Others to be ethical they must therefore be nontotalizing. Rejecting ontologies that homogenize humanity, so that self-recognition is sufficient to constitute the significance of Others, Levinas locates the ethical regard as a recognition of Others as enigmatically and irreducibly other, as prior to any ontological aim of locating oneself at home in the world: "The relations with the other . . . [do] not arise within a totality nor does it establish a totality, integrating me and the other.[22]

Ontologies of integration are egoistically aimed at domesticating alterity to a frame of understanding that allows for the violent appropriation of the space of the Other:

> My being in the world or my 'place in the sun,' my being at home, have
> not also been the usurpation of spaces belonging to the other man whom
> I have already oppressed or starved, or driven out into a third world; are
> they not acts of repulsing, excluding, exiling, stripping, killing? [23]

To be regarded ethically, the Other must remain a stranger "who disturbs the being at home with oneself."[24] The ethical for Levinas is, in sum, "a non-violent relationship to the other as infinitely other."[25] If we recall the problematic presented in chapter 5, it should be evident that within a Levinasian ethical perspective, one would, for example, accept Ward Just's perpetually enigmatic Vietnam rather than endorse Norman Schwarzkopf's domesticated version.

However, the story of the ethical is not a simple tale of rejecting comprehension and embracing enigma. Indeed, as one follows Levinas's argumentation, a number of problems and inconsistencies present themselves (I treat them later). Before considering Levinas's contributions and deficiencies, it is important to recognize that Levinas's ethical practice is not a matter of mere injunction, not something he simply writes about; it emerges as well in his struggle to distance himself, in his writing practices, from the very philosophical tradition of the West that, at the same time, has enabled his ethical thinking. An ethics of responsibility for Levinas takes the form of agonistic relationships with key figures in his philosophical patrimony, most significantly Hegel and Heidegger, whose influences Levinas tries to overcome by rescripting the linguistic structure of philosophical discourse.

The primary contention is conducted within Heideggerian language, for the philosophical depth of Levinas's ethics of infinite responsibility to alterity is revealed in both his debts *to* and his departures *from* Heidegger. Indeed, prepositions are crucial here, for while Levinas accepts Heidegger's notion of the individual's indissoluble connection to alterity, he rejects the Heideggerian grammar of the self-Other relationship. The rejection takes the form of two grammatical shifts enacted in Levinas's writing. First, Levinas changes the preposition from *with* to *in front of.* Whereas for Heidegger the relationship to the Other "appears in the essential situation of *Miteinandersein,* reciprocally being with another," Levinas expresses resistance to the "association of side-by-side" that Heidegger's *Mit* suggests: "It is not the preposition *mit* that should describe the original relationship with the other."[26] It is instead the in front of, the face to face that locates the ethical relation to the Other. This grammatical shift to the face to face acknowledges the fundamental separation of the self from the Other. To maintain an ethical bond with the Other, to maintain the infinity of the Other, is to see the self in its relation to something "it cannot absorb."[27]

The second important grammatical shift expresses Levinas's rejection of the Heideggerian ontology of Being and being with. Having swung the Other around to a position of face to face, and having recognized that instead of self-confirmation the Other provides a disruption of the self's abiding, leaving one never at home, Levinas adds a grammatical change at the level of discursive interaction; he shifts the case of enunciation. Standing in front of the Other, in a conversation with which one greets the Other, the conversational summons to alterity is in the vocative, not the nominative:

> To speak, at the same time as knowing the Other, is making onself known to him. The Other is not merely known, he is *greeted* [salué]. He is not only named, but also invoked. To put it in grammatical terms, the Other does not appear in the nominative, but in the vocative.[28]

This vocative summons, or unqualified greeting, is an important part of the nonviolence that Levinas ascribes to authentic conversation, a speaking that performs a "moral relationship of equality."[29]

Levinas's struggle against philosophy within the language of philosophy is also manifested in his debts to and departures from Hegel. His indebtedness to Hegel is reflected in the dialectical frame with which he locates selves in a relationship with alterity. But, rejecting Hegel's narrative of overcoming contradiction and achieving reconciliation, the mechanisms with which the Hegelian dialect moves toward resolution, Levinas states, "It is not a matter of traversing a series of contradictions, or of reconciling them while stopping History. On the contrary, it is toward a pluralism that does not merge into a unity that I should like to make my way."[30]

While Levinas's struggle with Heideggerian language was effected grammatically, his linguistic encounter with Hegel involves attention to narrative structure. In order to represent the self's journey toward alterity, Levinas juxtaposes an Abrahamic journey to the Odyssean one that drives Hegel's narrative of the self's enounters with alterity: "To the myth of Odysseus returning to Ithaca, we wish to oppose the story of Abraham, leaving his fatherland forever for a land yet unknown."[31] The biblical Abraham's journey, in response to Jehovah's summons, represents an infinite responsibility to God. In Levinas's version, however, the journey is treated as an allegory of a more general responsibility to alterity. Alterity must remain infinitely Other; hence the encounter with alterity is not to be domesticated or brought home. The narrative of the *Odyssey*, in which Odysseus returns home, is a Hegelian dialectical journey in which alterity simply serves the enhancement of the self.

Levinas's struggle with Hegel represents more than a philosopher-to-philosopher confrontation. In rejecting the circular journey of Odysseus as an allegory of the self's encounters with alterity, Levinas is rejecting philosophy (in the Hegelian sense of self-reflection) in favor of religion. The novelist Lars Gustafsson seems to affirm this Levinasian insight in the meditation of one of his male characters on the difference between homo- and heterosexual encounters:

> I was amused by the funny mirror effect that appears when you go to bed with someone of the same sex. You return to your own world so to speak, although from a different direction; you see the world you just left in a new light. Women always retain their mystery. I can understand why philosophers have always been more interested in boys than girls. Girls are theology, boys are philosophy.[32]

We arrive at Levinas's position by replacing sexuality with ethics and Gustafsson's "girls" with Others more generally (indeed, Levinas seems to wholly subordinate gender and sexuality to ethical relations—a point I take up later). What is important at this juncture is to note that Levinas represents "the ethical relation as a religious relation" and rejects, for example, Plotinus's proto-Hegelian conception that "the soul will not go toward any other thing, but towards itself."[33] He sees the relationship with the Other as being like a consciousness of God as irremissibly Other, as a being one has a duty to recognize as separate.

Levinas's textual practice reveals his dependence on those whose positions he rejects. His efforts to extract himself from those traditions are an important part of his ethics of language; they constitute much of the performative aspect of his attempt to use the "saying" to avoid the traps of the already "said." Indeed, Levinas's notion of the way the ethical is performed in conversation, in "saying," which disrupts the "said," is central to his ethical sensibility as well as the performative aspect of his writing. This accords with his more general opposition to philosophical systems as totalizing structures that reduce to the same—for example, those like Hegel's that posit a universalizing consciousness, which reconciles difference and overcomes opposition, as the essence of human subjectivity.

The primary "said" for Levinas is the reigning philosophical discourse within which interpersonal encounters are conceptually contained. It is the domain of obtuse consciousness, a consciousness that elides the past and present and thereby closes off history. Consciousness thematizes the past, depluralizing it and inhibiting the effects of encounters.[34] In contrast, the proximity of the Other in conversation is a saying that disrupts the incorporation of the Other's past into a thematized said. The said allows the Other to be face to face as a "trace," which is a mark of the Other's being there in a way that disturbs preconceived orders of the world.[35]

This Levinasian notion of the trace—"a face signifies as a trace . . . a face is in the trace of the utterly bygone, utterly past absent"[36]—accords with the impact on Carlos Fuentes of the encounter with the peasant; as though for the first time, Fuentes became attuned to a bygone order of temporality and space in this face-to-face conversation.

But Levinas's linguistic war has been carried on primarily against the violence of the conceptual apparatus of philosophy. As a result, his ways of speaking and writing have attempted to enact his commitment to saying, to resist allowing his discourse to reify a conceptually "frozen" world of "documents":

> Words are disfigured or 'frozen' when language is transformed into documents and vestiges. The living word struggles against this transfer of thought into vestige, it struggles with the letter that appears when there is no one there to hear.[37]

Levinas's resistance to the already inscribed discourses of the "said" is, of necessity, only partially successful. While he manages to twist and turn Heideggerian and Hegelian language with his grammatical innovations and alternative narrative structures, ultimately, as Derrida has effectively shown, Levinas's attempt to, for example, draw himself out of

Heideggerian ontology with an ethicometaphysical transcendence pre-supposes Heideggerian ontological transcendence.[38]

That Levinas's language is profoundly Heideggerian is not so much a fatal flaw as it is the reflection of a more general dilemma. Any war against a form of language must come from within. While speech can counter the violence of language by disrupting language's pretension to conceptual mastery, it must inevitably do some violence and thereby affirm aspects of what it resists if it is to remain intelligible. Even a recognition of difference presupposes a prior conceptual practice. It is for this reason that Derrida argues that an ethical regard requires one to acknowledge this dilemma. By avowing the continuing violence of one's own discourse, one commits the least possible violence. The most violent position, he asserts, is precisely the commitment to total nonviolence.[39]

Levinas's linguistic struggle was aimed at minimizing that violence, at resisting the anticipatory conceptualizations through which alterity is denied an independent existence and thereby a worthiness of ethical solicitude. For Levinas, the encounter with the Other must be resistant to all conceptualizations because "concepts suppose an anticipation, a horizon within which alterity is amortized as soon as it is announced precisely because it has let itself be foreseen."[40]

As many recent analyses of the European voyages of "discovery" have shown (and as I emphasized in chapter 1), it was in part the conceptually proleptic construction of the alterity of the "New World" that encouraged a violent rather than an ethical apprehension of the Native American Other. In the case of Christopher Columbus, the anticipatory regard with which he constructed the indigenous peoples of the Americas as "Indians" derived in part from a fantastic medieval cartography, various "mappemondes" (world maps mentioned in Columbus's journal from his first voyage), which owed more to biblically inspired fantasy than to geographic hypothesizing.[41]

The violent encounters associated with the initial European contacts with the "New World" were therefore not merely the result of philosophical conceptualizations. They emerged from a "said" that already existed in narratives on peoples (e.g., the discourse on savagery) and world-constructing cartographies, which preempted an ethical form of encounter.

To approach this supplement to the history of philosophical discourse it is useful to consider two of Levinas's more egregious blind spots, ways in which he gives in wholly to the already "said." The first of these emerges in his understanding of Israel's relationship with Palestinians. When the question of Palestinians as Other was posed bluntly to Levinas—"isn't the 'other' above all the Palestinian?"—Levinas's response was to refer to Palestinians as aggressors and enemies and to conclude that "there are people who are wrong."[42]

What makes Palestinians wrong? It becomes evident in Levinas's understanding of what "Israel" is, a "coincidence of the political and spiritual."[43] Israel provides the "opportunity to carry out the social law of Judaism."[44] This is an astounding partisanship from one committed to wholly nonanticipatory ethics of encounter, one who grants rights to the "neighbor" that are "prior to all entitlement," rights based on "absolute identity."[45]

Ironically, the partisanship is entailed precisely in Levinas's attempts to take Israel beyond partisanship by interpreting "Jewish life," as it is represented through Israel past and present, as a model for all humanity. Jewish doctrine—that of the rabbinic tradition as Levinas reads it—is "a doctrine that is none the less offered to everyone . . . This is the sovereignty of Israel."[46] Thus, the same thinker who has charged ontological commitments to space with a "usurpation of spaces belonging to the Other,"[47] who has argued that "the defense of the rights of man corresponds to a vocation outside the state,"[48] can say that the "sovereignty of the state incorporates the universe," that "in the sovereign state, the citizen will finally exercise a will," and that "man recognizes his spiritual nature in the agency he achieves as a citizen, or even more so, when acting in the service of the state."[49]

Evidently, Levinas's attachment to the venerable story of state sovereignty, and even to a Hegelian spiritualization of states as instruments of spiritual reconciliation, collides with his commitment to an unqualified respect for alterity and makes him veer away from his commitment to an ethical bond that precedes all such ontological and spatial attachments. In his perspective on Israel, his model of alterity seems ultimately not to heed the Other's stories of self and space.

This neglect of competing narratives is even more evident when one examines Levinas's second blind spot, his neglect of the feminine aspect of alterity. Apart from his use of pronouns—in evidence in his statements about sovereignty, which seem to construct the ethical subject as masculine—and apart from his more general indifference to sexual difference,[50] Levinas's discussion of Jewish women in the Old Testament is wholly inattentive both to women's effective public roles and to their victimization.

In the case of Jewish women, Levinas, the talmudic scholar and exemplar of the close reader, offers a bleary-eyed celebration of women as "charming" and woman as "genius of the hearth": "the house is woman the Talmud tells us"; "Jewish women are mothers, wives and daughters" whose "silent footsteps in the depths and opacity of reality" make "the world precisely inhabitable."[51]

How could such an assiduous, hermeneutically oriented reader miss, for example, what Mieke Bal has called to our attention, the home of the Old Testament as a place of danger for women? Focusing on the murder of women in the Book of Judges, Bal notes, for example, that "the house is a place where daughters [who are murdered by fathers] meet their undoing."[52]

Levinas's Old Testament takes on its coherence in what Bal refers to as a "political coherence" concerned with "the geography of the land to be conquered": "Stories about women have been subordinated," she asserts, "to the major historiographical project, which is nationalistic and religious."[53] This is certainly Levinas's project, which both directs his reading of Israel and is implicated in his failure to politicize "Jewish women" in the Old Testament.[54]

What does Levinas's project necessarily miss, aside from the murder of women (by heroic "judges," among others)? Among other possible stories, it misses the way in which women are active in the public sphere. They are not simply, as in his characterization, acting as keepers of the hearth. Delilah, Yael, and Deborah, for example, kill men on behalf of their tribal factions and thereby create significant political results.[55]

By producing a reading that constitutes what she calls a "counter coherence," Bal resists the pious religious nationalism that Levinas's reading recirculates. For purposes of this analysis, what is especially significant about Bal's reading is that the identities of Jewish women in the Old

Testament are wholly different when one heeds a different narrative and is more attentive to spatial imagery. "Daughters who live in their father's houses are the least safe," she notes, and, most importantly, this recognition arises from a different kind of spatial story that she discerns in the Old Testament. Instead of the land of Israel to be conquered, the story of space "becomes meaningful on a smaller scale of individual houses to be conquered."[56]

Despite Levinas's lack of sensitivity to such other stories and spaces, his more general position, centered on the self in its performativity of a respectful relationship with alterity, provides an important basis for thinking an ethics of encounter. Ultimately, Levinas's reading of the Talmud, as contrasted with his legitimation of the State of Israel and his casual treatment of Jewish women in the Old Testament, is not aimed at recovering a genealogical claim to specific territory. In his talmudic readings, Levinas enacts, rather than a narrative of identity, an encounter between Jewish thought and the philosophy of ethics. To be Jewish, for Levinas, is to accept what he calls "a difficult freedom."[57] He sees the significance of Judaism as a performance of the ethical, as a doing before hearing or knowing; it is an acceptance of the Torah as something prior to the choice between good and evil, a "consent prior to freedom and non-freedom."[58] For Levinas, this aspect of Judaism migrates out of its containment in the Old Testament and becomes an allegory of the ethical in general. Acceptance of the Torah (of God and the law of God) is the condition of possibility for beginning the history of the Jewish people, and, more generally, doing before hearing translates as an injunction to regard ethical responsibility as prior to conceptualization. [59]

Levinas's reversal of the sequence as the essence of Jewish thought is thus his enactment of a rejection of ontological thinking in which a universalizing concept of being precedes the significance of action. For Levinas, one makes a pact with the good; one rejects violence before one seeks to understand good and evil. Responsibility to alterity as infinite simply is.[60] The talmudic Levinas is thus complementary to the philosophical Levinas. This is not the Levinas seeking a fixed narrative to legitimate Israeli nationalism but the Levinas seeking a permanent disengagement of the self from conceptualization, from what he calls "the temptation of knowledge,"[61] which appropriates the Other to a preexisting understanding and thereby negates the possibility of an ethical encounter.

It is important nevertheless to explore further the trap to which Levinas (in two instances) and others have fallen prey in their failure to practice an ethics of encounter, expressed in their lack of attention to others' stories and practices of space. Such an exploration necessitates a greater degree of specificity, a focus on the narratives through which specific kinds of persons and locations have emerged and achieved levels of institutionalized recognition. To descend from the level of abstraction offered by Levinas and seek to avoid the contradictions produced by his adherence to a male-dominated story of national emergence, we can return to his most important text, the Old Testament, and engage yet another reading of it, one that bears not only on the fates and roles of Jewish women but also on the ambiguities of their identities as "Jews."

## Narrative Encounters

"And I will give unto thee, to thy seed after thee the land wherein thou art a stranger, all the land of Canaan, for an everlasting possession" (Genesis 17:8). In addition to the historical and contemporary violence that has sprung from the consequences of this divine land grant, the biblical promise by Jehovah to Abraham resulted in a paradox in the midst of the primary identity story of the Jewish people. This paradox is at the center of an Old Testament reading by Edmund Leach, an elaborate exercise of Lévi-Strauss's method of structural interpretation.[62]

Resisting the ordinary, theological/hermeneutic model for reading, Leach's analysis is anthropological; it is focused on "a patterning of arguments about endogamy and exogamy."[63] He begins with a contradiction that has plagued Jewish history "from the earliest times right down to the present day":

> On the one hand the practice of sectarian endogamy is essential to maintain the purity of the faith, on the other hand exogamous marriages may be politically expedient if peaceful relations are to be maintained with hostile neighbors.[64]

This tension is revealed in the biblical texts, which "consistently affirm the righteousness of endogamy and the sinfulness of exogamy" but nev-

ertheless have those in the main genealogical line, from Judah onward,
taking foreign wives. Because of the political pressure on the texts to
conform to "the doctrine of the unique legitimacy of the royal house of
Judah and the unitary ascendency of Solomon and Jerusalem," however,
the marriages are regarded as legitimate, within-tribe ones. Thus, for example, although neither Tamar nor Ruth is an Israelite, and indeed their
approaches to members of the Israelite lineage (Judah and Boaz, respectively) are those of harlots (the former explicitly and the latter implicitly), the descendants are represented as pure-blooded.[65]

What emerges from Leach's reading is a treatise on land and politics.
The Old Testament is cast as a story that has been arranged both to legitimate Jewish title to the "land of Canaan" and to affirm the historical coherence of the Jewish people. By paying close attention to the paradoxes
brought about by the contradictions between the rules of endogamy and
exogamy, Leach shows how the text has turned the arbitrary into the coherent and unitary. The most significant implications for the discussion
here derive from the interconnections among narrative, space, and collective identity exemplified in Leach's analysis. What constitutes Jewish
identity through the centuries is commitment to a continuous genealogical and spatial story.

This, of course, does not distinguish the Jewish collective identity
from many others; collective identities are almost always a combination
of narrative depth and spatial extention. A "people" maintains and reproduces its unity and coherence by continually performing its identity,
by telling and retelling a story that legitimates its model of who is inside
and who is outside as well as by territorializing that exclusiveness. But
ironically, the drive toward exclusivity draws a people ever closer to its
Other(s), to those who serve to help the "people" recognize itself as a
separate whole.

Thus, in the modern period, the Israeli Jewish society "has been connected with the Arab as if he were its Siamese Twin."[66] As Nurith Gertz
has noted, the Arab, "the figure expelled from the camp," has held "the
key to the identity" of the Jew."[67] Despite this paradox, however, Israel is
a paradigmatic case of identity stability, for its Other has remained the
same. Israel's Arab has been like the United States' Soviet threat during
the cold war; it has consistently been the Other. In the case of Israel,

however, there is a crucial difference. Arabs remain within, no matter how much they are expelled to the outside, because of the shared cultural histories and texts of Jews and Arabs. The identity economy of sameness and difference with which Israeli nationalism has tried to produce claims for exclusivity contains irresolvable ambiguities. Although the Israeli national identity has been stable, its basis has required a denial of otherness within.[68]

Nevertheless, while the identity dependence of the Jew on the Arab has been denied at the level of official discourse, various forms of cultural expression in contemporary Israel have challenged a model that asserts an unproblematic exclusivity for Israeli Jewish identity.[69] The problematic that Leach discloses in the Old Testament has therefore persisted. The production of identity coherence and exclusivity continues to be a matter of how a people's story is told. For this reason, it is propitious to return again to a controversy over a reading of the Old Testament, one that produced a lively exchange between scholars speaking for Jews and Arabs. This exemplary exchange is between Michael Walzer and Edward Said over Walzer's contribution to the Jewish people's historical identity assertion in his *Exodus and Revolution*.[70]

Unlike Leach's reading, Walzer's is identified as hermeneutic; he sought not to look at the repetitive structure of the various fragments but rather to assemble them in order "to grasp the deepest meaning of the interpretations."[71] Walzer's reading bridges his roles as a "connected critic" and political theorist. As a connected critic he reads as a Jew who is sympathetic to Israeli nationalism but critical of some Israeli domestic policy. As a political theorist, he constructs Exodus as an exemplary liberation story that has been influential in inspiring subsequent liberationist radicals.

Apart from his concern with political theory and despite his recognition that "every reading is a construction, a reinvention of the past for the sake of the present," Walzer's *Exodus and Revolution* stands as a reaffirmation both of the coherence of the Jewish people and of Israeli nationalism. Unlike Leach, Walzer represents the narrative as untroubled and noncontradictory; for him, it is a linear story, "a journey forward—not only in time and space. It is a march toward a goal, a moral progress, a transformation." While this is how Walzer represents the view of the

authors of the Old Testament, his characterization displays no ambiva-
lences about the coherence of the people in the story—it is the march of
the "people of Israel"—and how they have territorialized their identity.
It is for Walzer, as for the Old Testament scribes, "the promised land,"
and similarly the conquest of Canaan—both during the time of the exodus and now, in terms of the institutionalized conquest that the State of
Israel represents—is not a mere land grab, not a merely "territoralist"
story, but a moral tale. The land can be held only in righteousness—in
obedience to the law (as interpreted within the Jewish tradition) and in
juxtaposition to the practices, such as idolatry, of non-Jewish Others.[72]

Moving from Leach's story to Walzer's, one finds a dramatic reversal
of the identity economy of ancient and modern Israel. In both stories,
what is taken by force of arms is overcoded by a story of legitimate title,
but here the similarity ends. Leach is clear about the administration of
silences and the management of contradiction. He shows that ancient
Israelite identity required the suppression of alterity within, a set of stories that denied the tribal hybridization of the "children of Israel." And
he shows how the domesticated otherness within is expunged so that it
can be expelled as otherness without. The "other tribes" remain in the
story only as territorial and moral adversaries.

By contrast, Walzer's reading operates from this foundation based on
erasure. He assumes an unproblematic identity coherence and tells a
simple boundary story. Presuming a singularity of identity for the Jewish people, he must at once exclude the Other (Canaanite), recognize
its simultaneous necessity for constituting the same (the Jew as non-
Canaanite), and its disruption (its claim to the same territorial identity).
A Jew as an individual is not a Canaanite, and Israel, which Walzer identifies unproblematically as a "Jewish State," must expel disruptive elements, or, in his more benign imagery, "help people to leave."[73] In short,
Walzer employs a representational economy to do violence. He allows
the Jews an unmediated presence by denying their debts to alterity, but
this labor of preservation or maintenance, begun in ancient texts and
repeated in his retelling, requires a negation of otherness.

In his review of *Exodus and Revolution*, Edward Said reminds us of
this violence by providing what he calls a "Canaanite view" of Exodus.
Said's representational economy is also debt-denying, for his "Canaan-

ites" are represented as just as consolidated and autonomous a historical emergence as Walzer's "Jews." Nevertheless, Said effectively identifies the scarcity of the moral solicitude in Walzer's story, which is not only a moral tale—specifically, a redemption story—but also a nationalist one. Canaanites cannot ultimately be objects of moral concern because Walzer's affirmation of a nationalist political geography is also a moral geography. Jewish control over the State of Israel is part of the redemption story, and Walzer "minimizes ... a sense of responsibility for what a people undergoing redemption does to other less fortunate people, unredeemed, strange, displaced and outside moral concern."[74]

In effect, "Canaanites" are not legitimately on the map of Israel in Walzer's story. One could tell more ambiguous and contentious stories that reveal the narrative twists and turns by which peoples and their identities are gathered and dispersed and boundaries are drawn. But Walzer is an advocate of unambiguous identity and spatial boundaries. In his response to Said, as elsewhere, he draws them tightly around identities for persons and peoples, and he wants spatial separations between peoples rigorously policed: "Good borders make good neighbors. And a good border, in time of growing national antagonisms, is a line so drawn that different people are on different sides."[75] At the level of explicit policy, Walzer is opting, as Said notes, for partition, but much of the spatial contribution to his rigorous identity economy is textual. Because Walzer identifies Israel as a Jewish state, state violence is merely "policy" (some of which he condemns as overly messianic), while Palestinian violence is "terrorism." This is of course the category of all nonstate violence in discourses, which sacralize and otherwise fail to represent as contentious existing state boundaries.

The Walzer-Said encounter therefore replays an ancient one. Two incompatible identity narratives are involved; two different identity performances collide as "Jew" and "Canaanite" contest both the past and the present with incommensurate claims to space and practices of identity. Here, as in the past, the antagonists question each other's moral eligibility. Their clash is textual, and a violence of representation is involved, for there is, particularly on Walzer's part, a strong "heading,"[76] a forward motion, which Walzer ascribes to the Exodus story and is also exemplified in his legitimation of the "Jewish State."[77] The forward motion

Walzer ascribes to the historic spatial and moral destiny of the Jewish people is reproduced in his narrative.

## Other Headings

In order to locate the Walzer-Said confrontation, and the historical Israeli-Palestinian confrontation, in the context of the Levinasian ethical sensibility, it is necessary to supplement Levinas's idea of the face to face on the basis of some critical reflections that suggest modifications to his model. In his critical yet sympathetic reading of Levinas, Derrida has pointed to a dilemma intrinsic to the imperative of an aconceptual and infinite recognition of an Other. He notes that one cannot recognize an Other in any way without a prior economy of sameness and difference. A discursive economy of identification necessarily precedes the apprehension of an Other. Sharing Levinas's concern to avoid the violence or at least the reductive forces inherent in representations, Derrida holds, nevertheless, that some violence is unavoidable and suggests a model for minimizing that violence, for doing "the least possible violence."[78]

Derrida's injunction to minimize violence is not elaborately thematized in his critical reading of Levinas, but he hints that an appreciation of the discursive and practical conditions of initial encounter can open up the possibility for a rethinking by reflecting on and attenuating the conceptions in which the self is aimed toward the Other as part of a history of both material and representational domination. In arguing that "language can only indefinitely tend toward justice by acknowledging and practicing the violence within it," Derrida goes on to suggest a vigilance against the violence of language by "taking history, that is finitude, seriously."[79] Having thus pointed to the latent violence of any economy of discourse, Derrida has subsequently practiced this vigilance by turning to a more historically informed reading of representational violence, focusing specifically on what he has called the European advance on the rest of the globe.

To return to what I characterized earlier as Walzer's endorsement of the "forward motion" and the "historic spatial and moral destiny of the Jewish people" in his reading of Exodus, Derrida has an implicit rejoinder in his cautions about the European advance, which has failed to take cognizance of "the heading of the other." Insofar as the aims (headings)

of the Other as well as of the otherness of one's own heading (contradictions, ambiguities, paradoxes) are ignored, an encounter with an Other
cannot avoid the egocentrism or moral exclusivity that exemplifies
Walzer's exodus story.

More generally, with respect to encounters with alterity, Derrida cautions that "there is another heading, the heading not being only ours."
Before embarking, then, "we must remember . . . we must *remind ourselves,* the heading of the other being perhaps the first condition of an
identity or identification that is not an egocentrism destructive of oneself and the other."[80]

Apart from his cautions about the irreducible violence of representation that necessarily precedes encounters, the supplement that Derrida
provides to Levinas's ethics of encounter is a historically framed model
of subjectivity. The encounter between two subjects is not between two
I's but two we's, and each "we" is a narrative construction, a textually
bounded "we" whose boundaries can be attenuated with an acceptance
of the ambiguities and paradoxes imminent in the stories through which
the collective self is lent coherence.

Accordingly, analyzing identity politics in contemporary Europe,
Derrida discerns a paradox (a "double injunction") not unlike the one
Leach discloses in the Old Testament:

> *On the one hand,* European cultural identity cannot (. . . "must not") . . .
> be dispersed . . . into a myriad of provinces, into a multiplicity of self-
> enclosed idioms or petty little nationalisms. . . . It cannot and must not
> renounce places of great circulation or heavy traffic, the great avenues
> or thoroughfares of translation and communication and thus of mediati-
> zation. But, *on the other hand,* it cannot and must not accept the capital
> of a centralizing authority that, by means of trans-European cultural
> mechanisms . . . would control and standardize, subjecting artistic dis-
> courses and practices to a grid of intelligibility.[81]

Most pertinent for the discussion here is the ethical sensibility that
Derrida derives from this aporia in the midst of the European identity.
He asserts that the lack of a clear "path" in the encounter with alterity
(within and without) is precisely what opens the way to an ethics and
politics: "When the path is clear, when a certain knowledge opens the
way in advance . . . one simply applies or implements a program,"

whereas "ethics, politics, and responsibility, *if there are any,* will only ever have begun with the experience and experiment of the aporia."[82]

Derrida goes on to elaborate the senses in which the dominant European self-understanding has led to a failure in ethical discernment, precipitated by its moral geography. Having taken itself "to be a promontory, an advance—the avant-garde of geography and history," it has (and "will have") "never ceased to make advances on the other."[83]

The European advance on the Americas provides an exemplary case in which to appreciate Derrida's arguments. By the nineteenth century, when European self-understanding had fully adopted a geopolitical cartography, John Stuart Mill helped to formulate and consolidate the new, state-oriented moral geography within which nonstate peoples were regarded. While, for example, the Jesuits of the seventeenth century had universalized a model of sacred space to deny the significance of indigenous spirituality in the Americas,[84] Mill universalized the European state model of space to deny them significant presence in general and nationhood in particular.

As I noted in chapter 1, Mill employed the venerable discourse of savagery but gave it a new spatial spin; he located Native Americans as a thinly scattered, disordered people. Unable to perceive their structures of sociability in that they were markedly un-European, he regarded their asocial character as a sufficient pretext to disqualify them from significant claims to being either a coherent collectivity or eligible for recognition on the basis of their land use, which did not comport with the idea of "property" familiar to one whose model was European proprietary relations. Inasmuch as Mill's reading of Native American practices was not disinterested, occurring as it did in an essay justifying intervention, he was, in Derrida's terms, underwriting the "advance" of the European, which took no heed of "other headings."[85]

Apart from its immediate legitimation for colonization, Mill's interpretive complicity with the European "advance" exemplifies more generally the interrelationship of spatial practices and ethical sensibility. To be an object of moral solicitude, one must occupy space and have an identity that commands recognition of that occupation. Mill's disparagement of American peoples is simply the modern, state-oriented cartography of violence. It is a moral complacency based on the universalization of a particular spatial imaginary and mode of dwelling within it, a failure to allow one's particularities the instability and contingency that an ethical regard would suggest they deserve when confronted by alternatives.

To disclose the structure of this spatial complacency and ethical insensitivity, Gilles Deleuze and Félix Guattari have represented the confrontation between the emerging state system and various tribal peoples with a geometric metaphor. The coming of the state, they suggest, created a disturbance in a system of "itinerant *territoriality*."[86] While the normative geometry of these itinerantly oriented societies takes the form of a set of nonconcentric segments, a heterogeneous set of lineage-based power centers integrated through structures of communication, the state is concentric in structure, an immobilized pattern of relations controlled from a single center. The state-oriented geometry produces a univocal code, a sovereignty model of the human subject that overcodes all segmental affiliations. For this reason, those, like Mill, schooled in the geometry of the state cannot discern a significant social and political normativity in segmentally organized groups. They see no collective coherence in peoples with a set of polyvocal codes based on lineage. In short, having changed the existing geometry, linear reason of state dominates, privileging what is sedentary and disparaging and arresting what moves or flows across boundaries. It makes labor sedentary and counteracts vagabondage, and it gives the nomad no space for legitimate existence (in various senses of the word *space*).[87]

This lack of legitimacy continues to be reflected in the inattention to spatial practices and marginalized identities in contemporary political and ethical discourses. Specifically, among what is silenced within state-oriented societies are nomadic stories, the narratives through which nonstate peoples have maintained their identities and spatial coherence. In the context of what Deleuze and Guattari call the state geometry, they are not able to perform their identities, to be part of modern conversations. Such cartographic and, by implication, ethnographic violence forecloses conversation. This violence of state cartography is elaborately described and powerfully conceptualized in Paul Carter's account of the European encounter with Australian Aboriginal peoples.[88]

The European state system's model of space involved boundaries and frontiers, and its advance during its colonizing period pushed frontiers outward. During the "stating" of Australia,[89] when the European spatial imaginary was imposed, those on the other side of the frontier, the Aborigines, were given no place in a conversation about boundaries. Carter suggests what amounts to a Levinasian ethical frame for treating boundaries. The boundary could be seen as "a corridor of legitimate communication, a place of dialogue, where differences could be negotiated." Indeed, by regarding a boundary as "the place of communicated difference" instead of proprietary appropriation (the European model), the Europeans would have summoned a familiar practice from the Aborigines. For Aborigines, boundaries are "*debatable* places," which they regarded as zones for intertribal communication.[90]

As we know, however, Australia was ultimately "settled," and the boundaries served not to acknowledge a cultural encounter but to establish the presence of the Europeans, practically and symbolically. This violence, which substituted for conversation, is already institutionalized in the form of what is represented as "Australia" just as other names and boundaries on the dominant geopolitical world map are rigidified and thus removed from the possibility of encounter. To the extent that community, society, and nation fail to reflect the otherness within, we have a cartographic unconscious, an ethics of ethics that establishes a set of exclusionary practices that are represented in the seemingly innocent designations of people and place. The various discourses springing from this unconscious are legion; for example, as I noted earlier, "the ethics of international affairs" reaffirms the violences, the nonencounters and nonconversations, that the state system perpetuates. It is time to unread the old map and begin the process of writing another one, a process without limit.

## Writing an Ethics of Community

Thus far, I have dwelled on the performative aspect of an ethical regard. As understood by Levinas, the ethical is the enactment of a response to the summons of alterity beyond or prior to any institutionalized normativity; for Derrida it is an attempt to minimize the violence of that prior normativity. For both, the responsibility to alterity precedes all conceptions, however persistent and irreducible they may be. At a minimum,

what is required to heed this summons of the Other is a distancing from
the prolepses through which Others are already inscribed—for example,
the cartographies and discourses through which J. S. Mill constructed
North American peoples as asocial and nonnational.

The required distance comes in part through modes of writing that
are open to encounter with difference. The ethical apprehension or regard of alterity outside of institutionalized inscriptions, as practiced by
Levinas and Derrida, for example, is achieved with performances intrinsic to their writing practices. Because the obverse of the ethical regard,
a violent one, consists in appropriating alterity to an already inscribed
set of conceptualizations, ethical practices, realized as writing performances, require a degree of unreading, unmapping, and rewriting. This
requirement of undoing was evident in Levinas's struggle to extract an
ethics from a philosophical tradition in which it had been suppressed.
He had not only to struggle within the language of philosophy by redi-
recting many of its dominant tropes (twisting and turning that which already twists and turns) but also to confront a philosophy suffused with
Greek conceptualizations with an even more venerable tradition, Jewish
thought as he understands it. Inasmuch as "Jewish thought" is also available to contemporaries in a form that is mediated by the Greek philosophical tradition, however, Levinas's talmudic readings involve an unreading of a long tradition of Greek-influenced commentary.[91]

To the extent that Levinas has failed to heed his own ethical injunctions, it has been a result of insensitivity to the complex self-Other inter-
relations repressed in the construction of the stories that have assembled
such entities as "Jews" and "Jewish thought." For example, Ammiel Alcalay has shown how contemporary "Jewish discourse" represses its
historic Arab influences and notes how the Hebrew language itself—and
consequently much contemporary Hebrew literature—has arisen from a
dissociative impulse in which a shared Jewish-Arab cultural tradition
has been erased. Recalling what he refers to as a "Levantine culture," Alcalay discloses a historical narrative of Arab-Jewish hybridity expressed
in Arab and Jewish literatures prior to the establishment of the State of
Israel.[92]

Restoration of Levantine cultural sensibilities, according to Alcalay,
would attenuate the radical othering that characterizes the identity prac-

tices of contemporary Israeli Jews and Palestinians. Instead of narrations of Israeli and Palestinian nationalism, Arab and Jew could be Other to each other within a tradition of interactive identity creation instead of a geopolitically based antagonism. They could tell themselves a story in which they recognize a positive association based on shared traditions. Alcalay's rereading of the Arab-Israeli relationship remaps cultural difference and comports well with the general strategy of Levinas, whose enactments of the ethical have demanded a strenuous unreading, a resistance, expressed ultimately as a form of writing, to the institutionalized "said" of philosophy.

Therefore, despite its blind spots, the Levinasian model should be heeded. Focusing on its fundamental resistance to essentialized and forgetful readings of identities and spaces, Derrida, in his reading of Levinas, has emphasized that *an* ethics cannot be explicated precisely because the institutionalized said, resident in discourse, reproduces a violence toward alterity; it can only be enacted through "the perpetual undoing of the said."[93] Significantly, Derrida prefers the imagery of writing to "saying," suggesting that it is perhaps a better mode for "escaping empirical urgencies" and that "the writer more effectively renounces violence."[94]

Recognizing the limits of Levinas's struggle, Derrida challenges the confinements of the already said and attempts to think what has been unthinkable. Accordingly, his deconstructive writing points toward a remainder, that which is excluded or unrecognized in the established system of intelligibility. Its ethical force therefore consists in its challenge to prevailing conditions of possibility for recognition. Inasmuch as any system of thought will always produce its remainder, any final recovery of what is remaindered is impossible. Yet an ethics, embodied in Derrida's deconstructive practice, recognizes the necessity of pursuing that remainder nevertheless.[95] It accepts both the impossibility and the necessity to pursue it at the same time. Derrida's practice therefore recognizes that the responsibility to alterity amounts to a permanent excursion; it takes the form of writing practices that disrupt the totalities within which identity spaces and domains are shaped and confined.

Before pursuing more specifically an ethics of writing, it is necessary to address how what may seem like a solitary struggle participates in an ethics in the more familiar sense of being communitarian in its implications. Not surprisingly, to do this it is necessary to unread the traditional way that the individual-community relationship has been inscribed in contemporary social theory.

Jürgen Habermas, for whom both encounters and the communitarian pull in discourse are paramount, provides a convenient point of departure for this purpose. Habermas constructs the individual as an independent mode of consciousness and then asserts that an ethical orientation requires that individual to engage in self-reflection when confronted with an Other who pursues a different "interest." Habermas therefore reverses the Levinasian order of ethical understanding by starting the individual off with a reflection on the question "What should I do?" understood in the context of that individual's "strong preferences."[96] In the next step, that individual's "preferences" are forced into a reflective encounter, undergoing a "transformation" with the recognition that one's preferences affect the interests of others.

Alterity thus enters Habermas's picture rather late, in the context of Levinasian time. Alterity becomes significant for Habermas well after conceptualizations are brought to the public market. But apart from the way that Habermas's temporal ordering produces a mediated rather than an absolute responsibility to alterity, his perspective effectively denies the dimension of alterity that is always already there in the mobilization of the discourses of action and preference, in the "said" within which individuals construe who they are, what they might do, and who else is out there with conflicting preferences. To build community, in short, Habermas begins by denying it in favor of a scattering of isolated, independent forms of consciousness.[97] In effect, Habermas divorces individuals from collective relations in order to effect a marriage ceremony—one that was already consummated in the linguistic resources mobilized by individuals in their reflective consciousness—later. He seeks to build an intersubjectivity after having removed an intersubjectivity that is always already there in intelligible modes of subjectivity.

Denying the subject's preexisting debts to alterity, Habermas constructs a community of impartial communication that is precisely one that cannot become ethical.[98] Because it exists only in the public discourses mobilized in confrontations of preferences, it supplies no mechanism to push beyond the limits of the already inscribed normativities. Habermasian consensuality is limited, in short, to the domain of the "said." In stark contrast, the force of Levinasian and Derridean thought-as-writing is disruptive rather than consensual. It is aimed toward overcoming the limits of the possible resident in the "said."

Where, then, is community in this project of disrupting the institutionalized "said"? Derrida sees community as precisely the aim of his deconstructive questioning of philosophical and other discourses' pretensions to totality or mastery. Community for Derrida is that which is constituted by questioning of the possibility of community in the face of its ultimate impossibility, the impossibility of a definitive answer.

Derrida's community is thus based on the ethical injunction to continually question the limits of conceptions of community. It is "a community of the question about the possibility of the question."[99] This view of community makes possible an ethics of encounter, for it seeks to go beyond community as already enclosed within the conceptual practices of a given collectivity. It is community always open to unforeseeable encounter.

Jean-Luc Nancy has produced a similar view, which also mounts an implicit challenge to the Habermasian view of community as communicative. Recognizing that the practice of an ethics of encounter must confront the closures of community within the already said, he has characterized the move toward an ethical community as the "unworking of communication," a resistance to everything that would bring community to completion." Locating this unworking in the domain of writing, Nancy advocates what he calls a "literary communism" in which "no one is assured of their identity."[100] Rather than accepting the violence of identity politics, which seeks to make names stick, the ethical sensibility therefore takes the form of loosening and attenuating what has already been named, thereby allowing various forms of alterity with contending modes of denotation and meaning to enter into the negotiation of space and identity.[101] What remains is a need to explore exemplars.

## Conclusion: Two Exemplary Writing Performances

There are two specific writing performances that, in different ways, have practiced an ethics of openness to encounters with alterity while at the same time recognizing the radical contingencies of space and identity. One is located in an ethnographic investigation by Michael Taussig and the other in a novel by Peter Handke. Ethnographic and literary discourses suggest themselves as ways into the ethical because both, in their more critical modes, achieve distance from reigning structures of representation, but they do so with radically different strategies.

In the case of ethnography, we find a practice that is close to a constituent element in Levinas's idea of ethics, the need for a proximity beyond distancing modes of representation. Investigators who have combined a philosophical and an ethnographic interest have noted that in contrast to modern industrialized societies, various tribal peoples have practiced a radically nonrepresentational mode of encounter with alterity. For example, speaking of the Hurons of the seventeenth century as represented in the writings of the French Jesuits, Michael Pomedli discerned what he calls an excursive rather than a discursive approach to Others.[102] As I noted in chapter 2, instead of appropriating alterity to a preexisting discursive system, the Hurons closed the distance through practices of incorporation—adopting, consuming/eating, and so on.

While the Hurons certainly practiced extreme violence—cruel tortures and killings of enemy/Others—at the same time they resisted a certain violence of representation, thereby perhaps avoiding the more totalizing or genocidal forms of violence that more representationally oriented cultures have practiced on Others whom they have identified, within their cartographic and narrative frames, as less worthy of moral solicitude.

Taussig also focuses more on the excursive than the discursive dimension of encounter. In a provocative analysis of the role of the nonrepresentational practice of mimesis, he offers some very particular instances of a nonappropriating mode of relation to alterity. In his version of Levinasian "proximity," Taussig's aim is to resist "context-free reason" and to reinstate what he deems crucial to the way thought can arrive at its object, through "its sensuousness, its mimetricity."[103]

Like Levinas, Taussig is engaged in a war with language. In his case, however, it is not the discourse of philosophy but of ethnographic modes of representation. He favors an ethnography that does what various mimetically oriented peoples do: it moves toward objects, embodying alterity through mimicry or replication. Pursuing this mode of approaching alterity, Taussig explores how various usages of magic—an Embera shaman's making of a model of a gringo spirit ship, for example—might have an influence on the writing practice of the ethnographer. His suggestion is that a mimesis practiced by the ethnographer will have an estranging effect on writing, distancing it from its traditions of representation in order to allow it to approach alterity rather than appropriate it.[104]

Thus, in addition to providing an approach to alterity, mimesis allows Taussig to recognize the appropriating nature of his own representational practices. By paying attention to how alterity has mimed the West or "first world," he seeks a mimetic vertigo that will disrupt the Western narrative of encounter with the peoples of the non-West. To the extent that one can see the West as "mirrored in the eyes and handiwork of its others" it might undermine the ethnographic project of "intellectual mastery" that has characterized Western knowing.[105]

As Taussig notes, this ethnographic project of intellectual mastery has not been confined to academic or intellectual space; it has articulated with projects of political domination, as for example in its construction of "good savages" and "bad savages," with the good as a "presentation of unsullied origin" and the bad a sign of "waste, degeneracy, and thwarted narrative."[106] These signs, which "fell on the Indian," have been part of a practice of both appropriation and erasure of "Indianness" in Western narratives of political evolution.

Taussig's struggle against such representations is an attempt to restage the encounter with "Indians," to allow their stories and practices to migrate into ethnographic writing practices. This will, among other things, aim the Western stories back on themselves, allowing those who have lived by them to reassess their practices of self. For example, noting a mimetic practice of the women of the Cuna tribe of Panama, Taussig refers to their use of the RCA Victor listening-dog logo on the appliquéd blouses they make.[107] From the point of view of the Western intellectual project, the recording device played a significant role in the discovery and recording of "primitive peoples."

In contrast, Taussig allows the mimetic practice of Cuna women, who copy the dog as a magical emblem, to influence his rethinking of the power of the RCA logo in the Western commercial sphere. While RCA had thought of the power of the logo in terms of its symbolism of fidelity—making use of the old Western allegory that produces the dog as a symbol of faithfulness—Taussig, heeding the practice of Cuna women, emphasizes "the way it exploits the alleged primitivism of the mimetic faculty." On this reading, the logo "can be thought of as display-ing a mimetic superpower in action, the mimetically capacious dog straining itself pleasureably to distinquish copy from original as it comes through the ear trumpet of the phonograph."[108] Here Taussig allows a mimetic practice to help him disclose a suppressed magical practice in a West that has attributed such practices wholly to the Other.

Most striking, however, is the way Taussig's writing mimes the disrup-tive effects of mimetic practices that are his subject. In a section on the spiritual geography of Cuna cosmology, a series of non-Euclidean land-scapes, Taussig discloses the irony of Western ethnography as it attempts to contain conceptually a mimetic practice within a representational one.[109] He allows Cuna mimetic geography, a play of visual translations between women's bodies and spirited landscapes, to create the mimetic vertigo in his own writing, which plays metaphorically with images of mimesis:

> Thus the joker in the mimetic pack is smartly dealt. We are lost, yet per-haps not uncomfortably between so-called levels of reference, cross refer-ence, and . . . all-of-a-sudden altering landscapes in which the Great Mother's house *is* another woman's body, more specifically, spirit copies of her womb genitalia.[110]

In the Western world of names, the myths of propagation, procreation, and rebirth as well as constructions of female sexuality and male domina-tion, which were undoubtedly deeply influential in the proprietary im-pulses and practices with which landscapes are now controlled and in-vested, have been largely erased from a commercially and geopolitically oriented cartography. Nevertheless, there is striking evidence in the West's fictional literatures of the way geographic imaginaries reflect an imbrica-tion of femininity, sexuality, and political/economic predation.

Anne McClintock has disclosed this interrelationship between sexual-ity and cartography in Henry Rider Haggard's *King Solomon's Mine,* a novel "far from innocent of the tensions of empire"[111] that emerged out of the Western colonial mentality in the late nineteenth century. Haggard, a British colonial administrator in South Africa, produced a bestseller in which, quite near the beginning, a map displays an entanglement of geopolitical domination, the search for wealth, and a Western view of the sexuality of the black woman.

Haggard's map, attributed in the story to a sixteenth-century Portuguese trader and used to guide English gentleman treasure seekers, is organized in the form of a woman's body. The map is dominated by two mounds denoted as "Sheba's breasts": an inverted view of it reveals that it is "the diagram of a female body." Moreover, "the body is spread eagled and truncated—only those parts are drawn which explicity denote female sexuality."[112] As McClintock puts it, the map

> assembles in miniature the three narrative themes which govern the most widely read and influential late victorian novels: cartography as a form of military appropriation, the transmission of white male power through control of the black female body, and the plundering of the land's riches.[113]

Two implications derive from this mimetic dimension of Haggard's map. First, we are able to recognize that the mimetic practice, now largely suppressed within contemporary cartography, has nevertheless been part of an otherness *within* Western practices of producing the Other. Second, while in Haggard's case mimesis was complicit with a colonial imperialist project—producing a "conflation of the themes of colonial space and sexuality"[114]—in Taussig's it belongs to an ethics of writing.

In contrast to Haggard's reinscription of a dominance structure of representation, a conceptual vertigo is manifested in Taussig's writing. *His* incorporation of a mimetic influence constitutes a moment of unmapping of contemporary, forgetful cartographic practices. Rather than resisting the mimetic practices of an-Other, Taussig allows himself to be affected by them, and to register the impact in his writing.[115]

In his novel *Slow Homecoming*, Peter Handke has practiced a similar unmapping. In effect, he performs an ethical relation to alterity through a writing that is an unreading of the dominant discourse of place. Like Taussig's, Handke's writing struggles to free itself from a violent patrimony. While Taussig has seen himself as heir to an appropriating ethnographic practice of representation, Handke, an Austrian by birth, has seen himself as heir to a European vocabulary of space and identity that has bred violence. Concerned, like Levinas, with the Holocaust as a paradigmatic event—although he is descended from victimizers rather than being a survivor—Handke attempts through his literary performance to escape his patrimony. His protagonist and alter ego, Sorger, an Austrian geoscientist, ultimately is able to speak outside of the already established discourses on space as he travels through various landscapes. He is freed from being "the faithful replica of death-cult masters." Finding that he must "hate himself for having been possessed by dead monsters, as though they were kinsmen," he wants to say "I no longer have a father."[116]

To appreciate Sorger's struggle it is necessary to glimpse the narrative as a whole, in which, like Levinas, Handke favors the saying over the said. Handke's writing is performative as Sorger enacts an ethical relationship with places and peoples. Sorger's "slow homecoming" begins in "the Far North," designated as such because Handke is avoiding the violence of names, pointing significantly at the outset to a contrast between conceptual and proximity practices respectively as Sorger's abode is described as both a laboratory and a dwelling.[117]

At work on an essay titled "On Spatial Configurations," Sorger finds that he cannot rely on "the conventions of his science," finding instead that landscapes become accessible to him only when "the mind has time to find ties with it." In keeping with the Derridean/Levinasian recognition of the violence of representation, Sorger "at times felt that his study of landscape was a science of peace."[118] And it is soon evident that the peace or nonviolence can be achieved through Sorger's ability to contact or speak directly to alterity rather than accepting the already inscribed designations of persons and places.

In a moment that evokes Taussig's use of mimesis to unmap representational practices, Sorger is sketching a tract of land that has been turned upside down by an earthquake. It was only "as he sketched" that he could "sense the overpowering force of the tremor."[119] His mimetic encounter with this piece of landscape affords him a hitherto prohibited appreciation of the mimetic practices of the Indians of the region (with whom he has had only one intimate contact, a sexual relationship with someone referred to only as "the Indian woman").[120]

As he sketched, "he observed how the formless mound of clay transformed itself into a grimace, and then he knew he had seen that grimace before—at the Indian woman's house, on the dance mask that was supposed to imitate an earthquake." Sorger's epiphany is then generalized, for at that moment "he gained a sudden understanding of masks in general," and "this led to the idea of a series of dance steps, and in a single moment Sorger experienced the earthquake and the human earthquake dance."[121] In short, through a mimetic rather than representational practice, Sorger/Handke moves toward appreciation and respect for both places and peoples who dwell in them.

Able finally to dwell in this ethical sense—resisting the violence of inherited and distancing conceptualizations and naming practices—Sorger leaves "the Far North" and travels through what Handke's text renders as "places of names." Having appreciated an ability to know a landscape and its people by minimizing the mediations of language, Sorger is struck with how his travels to "places of names" disorient his sense of space. He feels excluded, as if his voice has been lost or as if it belongs to someone else.

This is what leads to Sorger's recognition that he must cast off dead monsters and develop his own mode of saying, his "science of peace." The "said"—the history of inscription of place names—can be cast aside, for Sorger has learned "that history is not a mere sequence of evils, which someone like me can do nothing but despise—but has also, from time immemorial, been a peace-fostering *form* that can be perpetuated by anyone (including me)."[122]

Handke's story *about* Sorger's rejection of the violence of names—as he travels through such places as "Mile High City," "The Big City," and so on—is reflected not only in the narrative of Sorger's various experiences and thoughts but also in his grammatical choices. Throughout the early part of the narrative, the story is told in the third person. After Sorger's epiphany, his recognition that he can cast off the already said, "he" becomes an "I," and by the end of the narrative, Sorger addresses himself from the vantage point of an-Other as "you."[123]

Through his grammatical play, narrating while shifting narrative standpoints, Handke enacts an ethics of nonviolence as his Sorger changes to a mode of proximity with alterity through his rejection of preconceived scripts. Also, the ironic play in the text, as Sorger discovers the violence of naming and achieves an ability to extract his recognitions from imposed meanings, constitutes an "ethical irony,"[124] a mode of linguistic practice that undermines fixities and coherences attached to named places and subjectivities.

For example, when Sorger hears "He's just an animal—an animal gone mad, and there's only one way to deal with mad animals, exterminate them," he is able to achieve an ironic distance by situating the remark in an unexpected way. In this case, a night clerk turns out to be reading from a newspaper.

More generally, shedding the structure of past, violent inscriptions, Sorger is finally able to live in the present, to achieve a "presence of mind" in his reaching out to the world, to become "capable of penetrating to the depths of space and of participating in the peaceful beauty of his present."[125] Sorger's ability to find peace in his present by finding a voice that struggled to free itself from what Samuel Beckett has called, in a work with the same insight, "their vociferations"[126] is exemplary. And, more generally, the writing and insights of both Taussig and Handke are exemplary; they reflect an ethical practice that is continuous with the approach to ethics elaborated throughout this chapter, which seeks to oppose an ethics of writing to a violence of representation and by analogy a commitment to respect for alterity to the impulse toward war. There are no definitive answers to the issues of identity and space that either bring people together peacefully and respectfully or drive them toward violent confrontation. An ethics and politics that accepts uncertainty would encourage encounter rather than conceptual mastery. It would transform the spaces of inclusion and exclusion that constitute peoples and their Others into domains in which place and person must be endlessly negotiated. It would regard the stories that have produced various consolidations of place and peoples as practices subject to that same negotiation. When various stories or versions of the present promote an end to ethics and politics—for example, those that proclaim the end of history—those who are interested in keeping ethics and politics alive must work on more promising stories. More specifically to the point of the genre in which I am presently functioning, those of us who write on global matters can only facilitate perpetual encounters by practicing a writing that is resistant to all static maps and all fixed identity stories.

The ethical regard toward which Levinas and Derrida have pointed and its enactment in the exemplary writing practices of those who, like Taussig and Handke, resist representational violence can be approached if we allow those examples, along with others to which I have referred throughout this investigation, to migrate into our various practices of space and identity. Finally, apart from the impetus to write against conceptual closures, their injunctions and enactments amount to a call to unread the global histories and unmap the moral geographies that fix the violence of representation one simply reproduces when one remains unreflectively within the already said.

# Notes

## Preface

1. Randolph M. Siverson and Harvey Starr, *The Diffusion of War: A Study of Opportunity and Willingness* (Ann Arbor: University of Michigan Press, 1991), p. 31.

2. See Etienne Balibar, "The Nation Form: History and Ideology," trans. Chris Turner, in Etienne Balibar and Immanuel Wallerstein, *Race, Nation, Class: Ambiguous Identities* (London: Verso, 1991), pp. 86–106. Balibar states: "*Every social community reproduced by the functioning of institutions is imaginary,* that is to say, it is based on the projection of individual existence into the weft of a collective narrative, on the recognition of a common name and on the traditions lived as the trace of an immemorial past (even when they have been fabricated and inculcated in the recent past). But this comes down to accepting that under certain conditions, *only* imaginary communities are real" (emphasis in the original).

3. Paul Veyne, "The Inventory of Differences," trans. Elizabeth Kingdom, *Economy and Society* 11, no. 2 (1982): 76.

4. Ibid.

5. C. R. Whittaker, *Frontiers of the Roman Empire* (Baltimore: Johns Hopkins University Press, 1994), p. 6.

6. Ibid., p. 11.

7. Ibid., p. 14.

8. Ibid., p. 19.

## 1. Violence in the American Imaginaries

Portions of this chapter originally appeared in "Moral Geographies and the Ethics of Post Sovereignty," *Public Culture* 7 (Spring 1964).

1. As a rule, the names of individual tribes are applied by other tribes. Hence, Niantic is translated as "those who live at the point," and the Pequots, the major focus of this discussion, are "the destroyers." The Pequots had moved down to the region from northwest of what is now Connecticut, and as Isaac de Rasieres of the

Dutch West India Company observed in 1626, the other tribes in the region were "held in subjection by the Pyquans"; quoted in J. Franklin Jameson, ed., *Narratives of the New Netherlands 1609–1664* (Bowie, Md.: Heritage, 1990). The translations of Niantic/Nehantic and Pequot are from John C. Huden, *Indian Place Names of New England* vol. 18 (New York: Museum of the American Indian, 1962).

2. Richard Drinnon, *Facing West: The Metaphysics of Indian-Hating and Empire-Building* (New York: New American Library, 1980).

3. Ibid., p. 55.

4. See Barry O'Connell, ed., *On Our Own Ground: The Complete Writings of William Apess, a Pequot* (Amherst: University of Massachuesetts Press, 1992). Already, since publication of this book, political theorist William Connolly has moved Apess into the American political theory canon by confronting Tocqueville's acceptance of the violence of European territorial practices with Apess's words on behalf of the Native American victims. See William Connolly, "Tocqueville, Territory, and Violence," chapter 3 in *The Ethos of Pluralization* (Minneapolis: University of Minnesota Press, 1995).

5. O'Connell, ed., *On Our Own Ground*, p. xxi.

6. Ibid.

7. This account is taken from Neil Asher Silberman, "The Pequot Massacres," *Military History Quarterly* 1 (Spring 1989): 74.

8. Drinnon, *Facing West*, p. 43.

9. Ibid.

10. Ibid., p. 44.

11. Ibid., p. 42

12. Mather makes this connection on the title page of his "history," *Magnalia Christi Americana* (London, 1702).

13. Ibid., p. 36.

14. Quoted in John Peacock, "Writing and Speech after Derrida: Application and Criticism," in Francis Barker et al., *Europe and Its Others,* vol. 2 (Colchester: University of Essex, 1985), p. 83.

15. Drinnon, *Facing West*, p. 41.

16. Ibid.

17. Immanuel Wallerstein, *The Modern World System: Capitalist Agriculture and the European World Economy in the Sixteenth Century* (New York: Academic Press, 1976), pp. 199–200.

18. The quotations are from David Harvey's "The Production of Spatial Configurations: The Geographical Mobilities of Capital and Labour," in his *The Limits to Capital* (Oxford: Basil Blackwell, 1982), p. 373. However, the emphasis on space as a product of capitalism, which inspired Harvey, was developed by Henri Lefebvre. See in particular his *The Production of Space,* trans. Donald Nicholson-Smith (Oxford: Basil Blackwell, 1991).

19. Gilbert W. Haggerty, *Wampum, War and Trade Goods West of the Hudson* (Interlaken, N.Y.: Heart of the Lakes Publishing, 1985), p. 103.

20. Ibid., p. 110.

21. J. S. Slotkin and Karl Schmitt, "Studies of Wampum," *American Anthropologist* 51 (April 1949): 234.

22. This point is elaborated by Lynn Ceci, "Native Wampum as a Peripheral Resource in the Seventeenth-Century World System," in Laurence M. Hauptman and James D. Wherry, eds., *The Pequots in Southern New England* (Norman: University of Oklahoma Press, 1990), pp. 48–63.

23. Ibid., p. 55.

24. This part of the account is provided in William A. Starna, "The Pequots in the Early Seventeenth Century," in Hauptman and Wherry, eds., *The Pequots in Southern New England*, pp. 33–47.

25. Matthew Dennis points out that the similarity of the mythologies of the various tribes in the region is cited as evidence for the early founding of the Iroquois league, well before the European invasion. See his *Cultivating a Landscape of Peace* (Ithaca, N.Y.: Cornell University Press, 1993), pp. 76–115.

26. Peacock, "Writing and Speech after Derrida," p. 84.

27. Marcel Mauss, *The Gift*, trans. Ian Cunnison (London: Cohen and West, 1970), p. 93.

28. Ibid., p. 94.

29. Ceci, "Native Wampum," p. 61.

30. Francis Jennings, *The Ambiguous Empire* (New York: Norton, 1984), p. 85.

31. Reported in Nicholas K. Blomley, *Law, Space, and the Geographies of Power* (New York: Guilford, 1994), pp. 101–2.

32. Frank G. Speck, "The Functions of Wampum among the Eastern Algonkian," *Memoires of the American Anthropological Association* 6 (January–March 1919), 53.

33. Stephen C. Saraydar, "No Longer Shall You Kill: Peace, Power, and the Iroquois *Great Law*," *Anthropology and Human Quarterly* 15, no. 1 (February 1990): 22. For an extended analysis of Iroquois condolence rituals, see Dennis, *Cultivating a Landscape of Peace*.

34. Jennings, *Ambiguous Empire*, p. 71.

35. The quotation is from Renata Saleci, "The Fantasy Structure of Nationalist Discourse," *Praxis International* 13, no. 3 (October 1993): 217, but the point originates in Elaine Scarry, *The Body in Pain: The Making and Unmaking of the World* (Oxford: Oxford University Press, 1985).

36. See John D. Cushing, ed., *The Earliest Laws of the New Haven and Connecticut Colonies 1639–1673* (Wilmington, Del.: Michael Glazier, 1977), p. 34.

37. Kirk Johnson, "Pequots Invest Casino Wealth in New Game: Party Politics," *New York Times*, August 30, 1994, pp. 1, 9.

38. Ibid.

39. Ibid.

40. As James Clifford discovered in an analysis of a dispute over the Mashpee people's claims on tribal lands, contemporary "Indian" identity has contentious predicates. A contemporary Native American group assembles tribal identity out of a complex history of conflict and negotiation. Indiannness therefore involves a way of looking at one's historical antecedents. There is no unambiguous facticity. See

James Clifford, "Identity in Mashpee," in *The Predicament of Culture* (Cambridge, Mass.: Harvard University Press, 1988), pp. 275–346.

41. See Michel Foucault's conversation with geographers in "Questions on Geography," in Colin Gordon, ed., *Power/Knowledge* (New York: Pantheon, 1980), p. 68.

42. This later injunction is elaborated in Gilles Deleuze and Félix Guattari, *Anti-Oedipus,* trans. Robert Hurley, Mark Seem, and Helen R. Lane (New York: Viking, 1977), pp. 139–272.

43. Henri Lefebvre, "Reflections on the Politics of Space," *Antipode* 8 (May 1976): 3.

44. Arjun Appadurai, "Patriotism and Its Futures," *Public Culture* 5, no. 3 (1993): 417.

45. "Honecker Trial Starts Nov. 12," *New York Times,* October 21, 1992, p. A-4.

46. *New Yorker,* September 28, 1992, p. 111.

47. Don DeLillo, *White Noise* (New York: Viking-Penguin, 1985).

48. Michel Foucault, "Governmentality," in Graham Burchell, Colin Gordon, and Peter Miller, eds., *The Foucault Effect* (Chicago: University of Chicago Press, 1991): pp. 87–104.

49. Ibid., p. 100.

50. Michel Foucault, *The History of Sexuality,* trans. Robert Hurley (New York: Pantheon, 1978), p. 25.

51. Foucault, "Governmentality," p. 100.

52. Ibid., p. 102.

53. Paul Virilio, *Pure War* (New York: Semiotext[e], 1983), p. 47.

54. Ibid., p. 54.

55. Michel Foucault, "Of Other Spaces," trans. Jay Miscowiec, *Diacritics* 16 (Spring 1986): 22.

56. Ibid.

57. A. J. Gurevich, *Categories of Medieval Culture,* trans. G. L. Campbell (London: Routledge & Kegan Paul, 1985), p. 295.

58. Fernand Braudel, *Afterthoughts on Material Civilization,* trans. Patricia M. Ranum (Baltimore: Johns Hopkins University Press, 1977), p. 26.

59. See Bruce Kapferer, *Legends of People Myths of State* (Washington, D.C.: Smithsonian Institution Press, 1988), pp. 49–84.

60. William Connolly, *Identity\Difference* (Ithaca, N.Y.: Cornell University Press, 1991), p. 207.

61. Peter Hulme, *Colonial Encounters: Europe and the Native Caribbean 1492–1797* (New York: Methuen, 1986), p. 21.

62. This story is well told by Gordon Brotherston at the outset of his *Book of the Fourth World* (New York: Cambridge University Press, 1992), p. 1.

63. Ibid., p. 4.

64. Quoted in Graham Huggan, "Decolonizing the Map: Post Colonialism, Post-Structuralism and the Cartographic Connection," *Ariel* 20, no. 4 (October 1989), 118. For an elaboration that treats the various ideational contexts of the Mercador maps, see the source of the quote: José Rabasa, "Allegories of the *Atlas,*" in Francis Barker et al., *Europe and Its Others,* vol. 2 (Colchester: University of Essex, 1985): 1–16.

65. For a treatment of this dimension, see Sneja Gunew, "Denaturalizing Cultural

Nationalisms: Multicultural Readings of 'Australia,'" in Homi Bhabha, ed., *Nation and Narration* (New York: Routledge, 1991): 99–120.

66. J. S. Fontaine, "Public or Private? The Constitution of the Family in Anthropological Perspective," *International Journal of Moral and Social Studies* 3, no. 3 (1988): 280.

67. See, for example, Julian V. Minghi, "Recent Developments in Political Geographic Research," in Alan D. Burnett and Peter J. Taylor, eds., *Political Studies from Spatial Perspectives* (New York: John Wiley, 1981): 33–42.

68. Emmanuel Wallerstein, *The Modern World System* II: *Mercantilism and the Consolidation of the European World-Economy 1600–1750* (New York: Academic Press, 1980), p. 51.

69. Ibid.

70. Isaac de Rasieres in Jameson, ed., *Narratives of the New Netherlands*, p. 103.

71. Joseph Conrad, "Geography and Some Explorers," in *Last Essays* (New York: Doubleday, Page, 1926), p. 6. Conrad's chronology of the stages of imperial geography (pp. 1–21) runs from "geography fabulous," based on myths of the new world, through "geography militant, coinciding with the invasions," to "geography triumphant," providing representations of the settlements and nationalizations.

72. Lesley B. Cormack, "Geography and the State in Elizabethan England," in Anne Godlewska and Neil Smith, eds., *Geography and Empire* (Cambridge, Mass.: Blackwell, 1994), p. 13. Cormack makes the point that early modern geography helped to affirm and perpetuate an English tendency, expressed in political theories, to see the world as theirs by right of conquest. A key writer in this genre of geographic writing was Richard Hakluyt, a "travel geographer." See pp. 13–30.

73. Raymond J. Larson, "An Analysis of the Racial Views of Adam Smith as Expressed in *The Wealth of Nations*," *Wisconsin Academy Review* 40, no. 4 (Fall 1994): 9–12.

74. Smith's remarks lamenting the cruelty toward Native Americans can be found in book IV, chapter ix, paragraph 77 of *An Inquiry into the Nature and Causes of the Wealth of Nations* (Indianapolis, Ind.: Liberty Classics, 1981).

75. John Stuart Mill, *Essays on Politics and Culture,* ed. Gertrude Himmelfarb (New York: Doubleday, 1962), p. 52.

76. Ibid.

77. Ibid., p. 406.

78. James Axtell, "The Invasion Within: The Contest of Cultures in Colonial North America," in Howard Lamas and Leonard Thompson, eds., *The Frontier in History: North America and Southern Africa Compared* (New Haven, Conn.: Yale University Press, 1981), pp. 241–42.

79. Paul Carter, *The Road to Botany Bay* (Chicago: University of Chicago Press, 1991), p. 221.

80. Ibid., p. 321.

81. Ibid., p. 120. See also William Cronon, George Miles, and Jay Gitlin, "Becoming West: Toward a New Meaning for Western History," in Cronon, and Gitlin, *Under an Open Sky: Rethinking America's Western Past* (New York: Norton, 1992), pp. 3–17. The authors note the way that what was once a "frontier," a domain in which inter-

cultural relations were negotiated in the American West, became a "region," a domain in which the dominant norms of the settlers had become nonnegotiable.

82. Ibid., p. 136. For more on the imperialistic cartography associated with the European settling of Australia and a highly politicized treatment of European and American geographic imaginaries, historical and contemporary, in general, see Derek Gregory, *Geographic Imaginations* (Cambridge, Mass.: Blackwell, 1994).

83. The map is at the beginning of Mather's history of the New England church, *Magnalia Christi Americana*. Much of this discussion is based on William Boelhower's commentary on the work, "Stories of Foundation, Scenes of Origin," *American Literary History* 5, no. 3 (Fall 1993): 391–428.

84. Boelhower, "Stories of Foundation," p. 392.

85. Ibid.

86. Carter, *Road to Botany Bay*, p. xxi.

87. Boelhower, "Stories of Foundation," p. 393.

88. Keith H. Basso, "'Speaking with Names': Language and Landscape among the Western Apache," in *Language and Culture: Essays in Linguistic Anthropology* (Tucson: University of Arizona Press, 1990): 138–61 .

89. Ibid., p. 159.

90. Ibid., p. 160.

91. Grace A. Turkington, Mary A. S. Mugan, and Myron T. Pritchard, *Lessons in Citizenship* (Boston: Ginn, 1928), p. 84.

92. This emptiness model of the Americas has played an important role in the history of the Euro-American identity in the United States. As Myra Jehlen notes, "The prior vacancy of the continent was their crucial founding fiction, both asserted directly and implicitly in the self-conscious narrativity with which the story of America 'began.'" See Myra Jehlen, *American Incarnation: The Individual, The Nation, and The Continent* (Cambridge, Mass.: Harvard University Press, 1986), p. 9.

93. Turkington, Mugan, and Pritchard, *Lessons in Citizenship*, pp. 86–87.

94. Noted in Hauptman and Wherry, eds., *The Pequots in Southern New England*, p. 12.

95. Bernard Nietschmann, "The Third World War," *Cultural Survival Quarterly* 11, no. 3 (1987): 1-16.

96. Ibid., p. 1.

97. Charles Tilly, *Coercion, Capital, and European States* (Cambridge, Mass.: Blackwell, 1990), p. 69.

98. Ibid.

99. Samuel Huntington, "The Clash of Civilizations?" *Foreign Affairs*, Summer 1993, pp. 22–49.

100. This point is made in a critique of Huntington's essay. See Fuad Ajami, "The Summoning," *Foreign Affairs*, September/October 1993, pp. 2-9.

101. Homi Bhabha, "DissemiNation: Time, Narrative, and the Margins of the Modern Nation," in Bhabha, ed., *Nation and Narration* (New York: Routledge, 1991), p. 301.

102. Aimé Césaire, *Discourse on Colonialism,* trans. Joan Pinkham (New York: Monthly Review Press, 1972), p. 11.

103. Ibid., p. 23.

104. Father Le Jeune, *The Jesuit Relations and Allied Documents* vol. 6. (Cleveland: Burrows Brothers, 1898), p. 153.

105. Brian Moore, *Black Robe* (New York: Dutton, 1985), p. ix.

106. For a treatment of "reverse ethnology," see Martin Fuchs, "The Reversal of the Ethnographic Perspective: Attempts at Objectifying One's Own Cultural Horizon: Dumont, Foucault, Bourdieu," *Thesis Eleven*, no. 34 (1993): 104–23.

107. See especially Clifford Geertz, *Negara: The Theater State in Nineteenth Century Bali* (Princeton, N.J.: Princeton University Press, 1980).

108. From Paolo Caruso, ed., *Conversazioni con Lévi-Strauss, Foucault, Lacan* (Milan: 1969); a translation appears in Martin Fuchs, "Reversal of the Ethnographic Perspective," p. 120.

109. David Wellbery, introduction to Friedrich Kittler, *Discourse Networks 1800–1900* (Stanford, Calif.: Stanford University Press, 1990), p. ix.

110. The expression is taken from the title of Myra Jehlen's treatment of the literary agonistics surrounding this narrative in her *American Incarnation*.

111. Shane Moran, "Melville, Frontiers, and the Metaphysics of Indian-Hating: A Note Toward a Reading of *The Confidence-Man*," *Oxford Literary Review* 14, no. 1–2 1992: 133. A similar insight into the text's tendency to destabilize reading is expressed by Michael Paul Rogin, who makes the point that the reader as much as the various characters in Melville's story falls victim to the confidence games. See his *Subversive Genealogy: The Politics and Art of Herman Melville* (New York: Knopf, 1983), p. 242.

112. Herman Melville, *The Confidence-Man: His Masquerade* (New York: Norton, 1971), p. 5.

113. Ibid., p. 34.

114. Ibid., p. 121.

115. This part of my argument is influenced by Moran's "Melville, Frontiers, and the Metaphysics of Indian-Hating."

## 2. Warring Bodies and Bodies Politic

Portions of this chapter originally appeared in "Warring Bodies and Bodies Politic," *Body and Society* 1 (Fall 1994), and in a chapter by the same name in Michael J. Shapiro and Hayward R. Alker, eds., *Challenging Boundaries: Global Flows, Territorial Identities* (Minneapolis: University of Minnesota Press, 1996).

1. For an elaboration of a neo-Hegelian approach to war and an explicit focus on the concept of the "ontological rift," see Janine Chanteur, *From War to Peace*, trans. Shirley Ann Weisz (Boulder, Colo.: Westview, 1992), pp. 195–211.

2. *Hegel's Philosophy of Right*, trans. T. M Know (Oxford: Oxford University Press, 1962), #324, p. 209.

3. Ibid.

4. G. W. F. Hegel, *Natural Law*, trans. T. M. Knox (Philadelphia: University of Pennsylvania Press, 1975), pp. 94–95.

5. For various treatments of Hegel on war, see H. G. ten Bruggencate, "Hegel's Views on War," *Philosophical Quarterly* 1, no. 1 (October 1950): 58–60; Shlomo

Avineri, "The Problem of War in Hegel's Thought," *Journal of the History of Ideas* 22, no. 4 (October–December 1961): 463–74; D. P. Verene, "Hegel's Account of War," in Z. A. Pelcynski, ed., *Hegel's Political Philosophy: Problems and Perspectives* (Cambridge: Cambridge University Press, 1971); and Steven Walt, "Hegel on War: Another Look," *History of Political Thought* 10, no. 1 (Spring 1989): 113–24.

6. *Hegel's Philosophy of Right*, addition #188 (to #324 in text), p. 295.

7. *Hegel's Phenomenology of Spirit*, trans. Arnold Miller (Oxford: Oxford University Press, 1977), #455, p. 272.

8. Ibid.

9. Ibid.

10. *Hegel's Philosophy of Right*, addition #188 (to #324 in text), p. 295.

11. Ibid.

12. Ibid., #338, p. 215.

13. Alexandre Kojève, *Introduction to the Reading of Hegel*, trans. James H. Nichols Jr. (Ithaca, N.Y.: Cornell University Press, 1969), p. 3.

14. Ibid., p. 38.

15. Ibid., p. 39.

16. Ibid., p. 40.

17. Edward Said, "East Isn't East: The Impending End of the Age of Orientalism," *Times Literary Supplement,* February 3, 1995, p. 3.

18. Brian Moore, *Black Robe* (New York: Dutton, 1985).

19. Ibid., p. ix.

20. Kojève, *Introduction to the Reading of Hegel*, p. 40.

21. Ibid., p. 41; emphasis in the original.

22. For a review of the controversy and the follow-up treatment in the same magazine, see John T. Correll, "The Last Act at Air and Space," *Air Force Magazine,* September 1994, pp. 58–64. The same writer makes the distinction between a political versus an aeronautical view in "The Three Doctors and the *Enola Gay*," *Air Force Magazine,* November 1994, p. 8.

23. See Miguel Leon Portilla, *The Aztec Image of Self and Society,* trans. Charles Brown and J. Jorge Klor de Alva (Salt Lake City: University of Utah Press, 1992), p. 36.

24. Ross Hassig, *Aztec Warfare* (Norman: University of Oklahoma Press, 1988), p. 39.

25. Ibid.

26. Ibid., p. 41.

27. Ibid., p. 128.

28. John Ingham, "Human Sacrifice at Tenochtitlan," *Comparative Studies in Society and History* 26 (1984): 379.

29. Hassig, *Aztec Warfare,* p. 10.

30. Carl von Clausewitz, *On War,* ed. and trans. Michael Howard and Peter Paret (Princeton, N. J.: Princeton University Press, 1976), p. 69.

31. See in particular Peter Paret's discussion of this Clausewitzian attitude in *Clausewitz and the State* (New York: Oxford University Press, 1976).

32. Carl von Clausewitz, "Our Military Institutions," in Peter Paret and Daniel

Moran, eds., *Historical and Political Writings* (Princeton, N.J.: Princeton University Press, 1992), p. 317.

33. Ibid., p. 318.

34. Ibid., p. 334.

35. E.g. Clausewitz, *On War,* p. 80.

36. Ibid., p. 75.

37. Ibid., p. 86.

38. Ibid., p. 113.

39. Ibid., p. 127.

40. See ibid., pp. 187ff.

41. Ibid., p. 89.

42. Ibid., p. 138.

43. See Jacques Lacan, "The Mirror Stage as Formative of the Function of the I as revealed in Psychoanalytic Experience," in *Ecrits,* trans. Alan Sheridan (New York: Norton, 1977), pp. 1–7.

44. Lacan, "Function and Field of Speech and Language," in *Ecrits,* p. 80.

45. Lacan, "Aggressivity in Psychoanalysis," in *Ecrits,* p. 20.

46. This thesis is elaborated throughout David Campbell, *Writing Security* (Minneapolis: University of Minnesota Press, 1992), but the neo-Lacanian view that is expressed bears a resemblance to the discussion in Slavoj Žižek's essay on nationalism, "Enjoy Your Nation as Yourself," in *Tarrying with the Negative* (Durham, N.C.: Duke University Press, 1993), pp. 200–237.

47. Peter Birkett Huber, "Violence and Social Order among the Anggor of New Guinea," in Martin A. Nettleship, R. Dale Givens, and Anderson Nettleship, eds., *War, Its Causes and Correlates* (The Hague: Mouton, 1975), p. 619.

48. Ibid., p. 620.

49. Ibid., p. 626. For an account of similarly structured cosmologies practiced by various tribal peoples, see Mary W. Helms, *Ulysses' Sail: An Ethnographic Odyssey of Power, Knowledge, and Geographic Distance* (Princeton, N.J.: Princeton University Press, 1988).

50. Ibid., p. 630.

51. Campbell, *Writing Security,* pp. 186–87.

52. *The Jesuit Relations and Allied Documents* vol. 6 (Cleveland: Burrows Brothers, 1898), p. 153.

53. The expression is in Jochen Schulte-Sasse and Linda Schulte-Sasse, "War, Otherness, and Illusionary Identifications with the State," *Cultural Critique,* no. 19 (fall 1991): 68.

54. Ibid., p. 70.

55. Ibid., p. 79.

56. Michael M. Pomedli, *Ethnophilosophical and Ethnolinguistic Perspectives on the Huron Indian Soul* (Lewiston, N.Y.: Edwin Mellen, 1991), p. 70.

57. *Jesuit Relations and Allied Documents* vol. 13, pp. 171–73.

58. Ibid.

59. Charles Tilly, *Coercion, Capital, and European States, AD 990–1990* (Cambridge, Mass.: Basil Blackwell), p. 67.

60. Ibid., p. 69

61. Aimé Césaire, *Discourse on Colonialism*, trans. Joan Pinkham (New York: Monthly Review Press, 1972), p. 23.

62. This commentary on the Huron souls is taken from Pomedli, *Ethnophilosophical and Ethnolinguistic Perspectives*, p. 59.

63. Ibid., p. 62.

64. Michel Foucault, *The History of Sexuality*, trans. Robert Hurley (New York: Pantheon, 1978), p. 137.

65. Pomedli, *Ethnophilosophical and Ethnolinguistic Perspectives*, p. 64.

66. Ibid., p. 68.

67. Schulte-Sasse and Schulte-Sasse, "War, Otherness," p. 79.

68. Colin L. Powell, "U.S. Forces: Challenges Ahead," *Foreign Affairs* 71 (Winter 1992/1993): 32–45.

69. Ibid., p. 32.

70. Butler's remarks are reported in Eric Schmitt, "Head of U.S. Nuclear Forces Plans for World of New Foes," *New York Times*, February 25, 1993, p. A1.

71. *Honolulu Advertiser*, February 3, 1993, p. D1.

72. Charles Krauthammer, "The New Evil Empire," *Washington Post*, January 1, 1993, p. A19.

## 3. That Obscure Object of Violence

Portions of this chapter originally appeared in "That Obscure Object of Violence: Desire and Logistics in the Gulf War," *Alternatives* 17 (1992), and in David Campbell and C. Michael Dillon, eds., *The Subject of Violence* (Manchester: University of Manchester Press, 1993).

1. Don DeLillo, "Human Moments in World War III," *Esquire*, July 1983, p. 122.

2. See McKenzie Wark's *Virtual Geography* (Bloomington: Indiana University Press, 1994) for a treatment of this kind of geography and its implications for the media representation of warfare.

3. The citations are from Frederic Miyayrou, "*Le corps etendu: Chronique d'un jour sans histoire*/The Extended Body: Chronicle of a Day with No History," Diller and Scofidio, *Visite aux armées: Tourismes de guerre/Back to the Front: Tourisms of War* (Basse-Normandie: F.R.A.C., 1994), p. 182.

4. Paul Virilio, *The Vision Machine* (Bloomington: Indiana University Press, 1994), p. 11.

5. Ibid., p. 12.

6. The details of the Red Line Agreement and the subsequent history of oil exploitation in the region are treated extensively in Edward Peter Fitzgerald, "The Iraq Petroleum Company, Standard Oil of California and the Contest for Eastern Arabia, 1930–1933," *International History Review* 13, no. 3 (August 1991): 441–65.

7. George Will, "Saddam: Hitler of the Arab Map," *Honolulu Advertiser*, August 8, 1990, p. A14.

8. Matthew Dennis, *Cultivating a Landscape of Peace: Iroquois-European Encounters in Seventeenth Century America* (Ithaca, N.Y.: Cornell University Press, 1993),

p. 71. The section of the passage in quotations is from Champlain's account of his voyages.

9. Ibid.

10. Dennis's account is influenced here by Joseph-François Lafitau's *Customs of the American Indians Compared with the Customs of Ancient Times*, Publications of the Champlain Society 48, 2 vols. (Toronto, 1974).

11. *New York Times*, December 9, 1991, p. 6.

12. Ibid.

13. Theodore A. Postal, "Lessons of the Gulf War Experience with Patriot," *International Security* 16, no. 3 (1991/1992): 119.

14. Ibid.

15. John Ellis, *The Machine Gun* (New York: Arno, 1981), p. 175.

16. For the civility narrative, see Norbert Elias, *The Civilizing Process: The Development of Manners*, trans. Edmund Jephcott (New York: Urizen, 1978).

17. Wark, *Virtual Geography*, p. 43.

18. Max Weber, "The Meaning of Discipline," in Hans Gerth and C. Wright Mills, eds., *From Max Weber: Essays in Sociology* (New York: Oxford University Press, 1946), p. 261.

19. Ibid., pp. 261–62.

20. The advertisement appears in *Britain's Gulf War* (London: Harrington Killbride, 1991), p. 2.

21. This part of my analysis is based on the observations and rhetoric of Chris Hables Gray, "The Cyborg Soldier: The US Military and the Post-modern Warrior," in Les Levidow and Kevin Robbins, eds., *Cyborg Worlds: The Military Information Society* (London: Free Association Books, 1989), pp. 43–72.

22. Perhaps the closest approximation to this version of the story is in Karl Mannheim, *Man and Society in an Age of Reconstruction* (New York: Harcourt Brace, 1940).

23. *Britain's Gulf War*, p. 31.

24. Thucydides, *The Peloponnesian War* (Chicago: University of Chicago Press, 1989), p. 50.

25. Ibid., p. 44.

26. Ibid., p. 45.

27. Paul Virilio and Syvère Lotringer, *Pure War*, trans. Mark Polizotti (New York: Semiotext[e], 1983), p. 18.

28. Avital Ronell, "Support Our Tropes," in Nancy Peters, ed., *War after War* (San Francisco: City Lights Books, 1992), pp. 48–49.

29. See Martha D. Pollak, "Art and War: Renaissance and Baroque Treatises in Military Architecture," in Pollak, ed., *Military Architecture, Cartography and the Representation of the Early Modern European City* (Chicago: Newberry Library, 1991), pp. xi–xxxvi.

30. Ibid., p. xxviii.

31. Ibid., p. xxii.

32. For a discussion of this shift, see Manuel De Landa, *War in the Age of Intelligent Machines* (New York: Zone, 1991), p. 77.

33. Alexander Koyre, *From the Closed World to the Infinite Universe* (New York: Harper & Brothers, 1958), p. vi.

34. Pollak, "Art and War," p. xxxv.

35. Ibid., p. xxxvi.

36. De Landa, *War in the Age of Intelligent Machines,* p. 77.

37. Ibid., p. 28.

38. Virilio in *Pure War* (p. 16) quotes a statement from the Pentagon c. 1945–50: "Logistics is the procedure following which a nation's potential is transfered to its armed forces, in times of peace as in times of war."

39. "A300 Downing Clouds Aegis Capabilities," *Aviation Week & Space Technology* 29 (July 11, 1988): 19.

40. Peter Grier, "Aegis to Put Swagger in the Navy's Step," *Christian Science Monitor,* August 21, 1988.

41. *Time* , July 18, 1988.

42. "A3000 Downing," p. 19.

43. Don DeLillo, *Libra* (New York: Viking, 1988), p. 77.

44. Paul Virilio, *War and Cinema,* trans. Patrick Camiller (New York: Verso, 1989), p. 11.

45. Alan Sekula, "The Instrumental Image: Steichen at War," in *Photography against the Grain: Essays and Photoworks 1973–1983* (Halifax, Nova Scotia: Press of the Nova Scotia College of Art and Design, 1984), p. 35.

46. Paul Virilio, *The Vision Machine,* p. 6.

47. Jay L. Larson and George A. Pelletiere, *Earth Data and New Weapons* (Washington, D.C.: National Defense University, 1989).

48. Ibid., p. 7.

49. Ibid., p. 28.

50. Television interview with Kenneth Adelman on "The Secret War," Arts and Entertainment Channel, September 1991.

51. Karl Marx, *Capital* vol. 1, trans. Ben Fowkes (New York: Vintage, 1977), p. 155.

52. Jean Joseph Goux, *Symbolic Economies,* trans. Jennifer Curtiss Gage (Ithaca, N.Y.: Cornell University Press, 1990), p. 123.

53. This discussion is based on Goux's summary in *Symbolic Economies,* pp. 69ff.

54. Jack Goody, *The Logic of Writing and the Organization of Society* (New York: Cambridge University Press, 1986), pp. 12, 13.

55. Ibid., p. 22.

56. Ibid.

57. Friedrich Kittler, *Discourse Networks 1800–1900,* trans. Michael Metteer with Chris Cullens (Stanford, Calif.: Stanford University Press, 1990), pp. 177–78.

58. Ibid., pp. 195, 214.

59. "The Secret War."

60. This scenario is developed in Jacques Lacan, "The Mirror Stage as Formative of the Function of the I as Revealed in Psychoanalytic Experience," in *Ecrits,* trans. Alan Sheridan (New York: Norton, 1977), pp. 1–7.

61. Jacques Lacan, "Agency of the Letter in the Unconscious; or, Reason Since Freud," in *Ecrits,* p. 175.

62. Jacques Lacan, *Four Fundamental Concepts of Psychoanalysis*, trans. Alan Sheridan (London: Hogarth, 1977), p. 189.

63. See Slavoj Žižek's explication of this point in *The Sublime Object of Ideology* (London: Verso, 1989), p. 194. Žižek also uses Buñuel's films, *Cet Obscure Objet* among others, to illustrate the implications of a Lacanian approach to the object of consciousness.

64. This point is made in James Der Derian, "Videographic War [II]," *Alphabet City*, Summer 1991, pp. 4–12.

65. David Tomas has stated that what is required to oppose such speed and information channeling in "the age of the smart bomb" is that "individuals and groups must also be able to mobilize, organize, and express themselves so as to create new spaces for political consciousness, and they must do so by way of collective technologies of observation and modes of representation that are capable of matching the media's speed of articulation and thus its ability to electronically link and create new interest groups while escaping prohibitive economic costs and technological complexity." David Tomas, "Polytechnical Observation: An Artistic and Popular Response to Political Events in the 'Age of the Smart Bomb,'" *Public*, no. 6 (1992): 9.

66. Elaine Scarry, *The Body in Pain: The Making and Unmaking of the World* (New York: Oxford University Press, 1985), p. 67.

67. Ibid.

68. All references and quotations in this paragraph are from "The Secret War."

69. Now, a few years after the Gulf War, what was once a current event dominated by the military's point of view is becoming a more ambiguous "history." The television series *Frontline* created a two-part documentary, shown January 9 and 19, 1996, that displayed some of the struggles within the U.S. military over Gulf War strategy, and, increasingly, what was once interpreted as an unambiguous victory is being interpreted as "less complete now than in 1991, when a ticker tape parade rolled through Manhattan." See R. W. Apple Jr., "The Latest History of the Gulf War," *New York Times*, February 4, 1996, Section 4, p. 3.

70. General Peroot on "The Secret War."

71. *New York Times*, February 14, 1991, p. A16.

72. Charles Krauthammer, "The Unipolar Moment," *Foreign Affairs* 70 (1990–91).

73. Ibid., p. 30.

74. William Pfaff, "Redefining World Power," *Foreign Affairs* 70 (1990–91): 34.

75. Ibid., p. 48.

## 4. From the Halls of Moctezuma to the Tube and Silver Screen

1. Keith Hopkins, *Conquerors and Slaves* (New York: Cambridge University Press, 1978), p. 36.

2. Michael McKernan, *The Australian People and the Great War* (Melbourne: Thomas Nelson, 1980), p. 13.

3. Ibid., pp. 17, 15, 43, 15.

4. For the influential treatment of the role of the print media in creating the

phenomenon of nationalism and national identification, see Benedict Anderson, *Imagined Communities,* rev. ed. (London: Verso, 1991).

5. Ibid., p. 62.

6. These data are from *Department of Defense, Selected Manpower Statistics, Fiscal Year 1991* (Washington, D.C., 1992), p. 113.

7. *Dixie Digest,* March 1991, p. 13.

8. This reading of the ad in terms of codes is inspired by Roland Barthes's later kind of semiotic reading, in which a text is broken up into various "lexia." This approach is exemplified in his *S/Z,* trans. Richard Miller (New York: Hill and Wang, 1974), and in "Textual Analysis of Poe's 'Valdemar,'" in Robert Young, ed., *Untying the Text* (Boston: Routledge & Kegan Paul, 1981), pp. 133–61.

9. See Jean Pierre Vernant, *The Origins of Greek Thought* (Ithaca, N.Y.: Cornell University Press, 1982), pp. 62–63.

10. Georges Vigarello, "The Upward Training of the Body from the Age of Chivalry to Courtly Civility," in Jonathan Crary et al., eds., *Fragments for a History of the Human Body* part two (New York: Zone, 1989), pp. 149–99.

11. Michel Foucault, *Discipline and Punish: The Birth of the Prison,* trans. Alan Sheridan (New York: Pantheon, 1977), p. 135.

12. Vigarello, "The Upward Training of the Body," p. 152.

13. Ibid., p. 149.

14. Ibid., p. 151.

15. Ibid., p. 153.

16. For a treatment of the theme of the evil, beguiling woman in the Old Testament, see Mieke Bal's *Lethal Love: Literary Feminist Readings of Biblical Love Stories* (Bloomington: Indiana University Press, 1987).

17. Barbara Ehrenreich, foreword to Klaus Theweleit, *Male Fantasies* vol. 1, trans. Stephen Conway (Minneapolis: University of Minnesota Press, 1987), p. xiii.

18. James Elkins, "On Visual Desperation and the Bodies of Protozoa," *Representations*, no. 40 (1992): 33–34.

19. Ibid.

20. Karen Rasmussen and Sharon Downey, "Dialectical Disorientation in Vietnam War Films: Subversion of the Mythology of War," *Quarterly Journal of Speech* 77 (1991): 77.

21. Michael Herr, *Dispatches* (New York: Avon, 1977), p. 226.

22. Ibid., p. 225.

23. *Marines* 22, no. 4 (May 1, 1993): 13.

24. E. H. Simmons, foreword to Ronald H. Spector, *U.S. Marines in Grenada 1983* (Washington, D.C.: History and Museums Division Headquarters, 1987), p. iii.

25. Lance corporal Anthony G. Souza, "Gitmo: Marine Forces at Guantanamo Bay, Cuba Defend Front Line in Communist Country," *Marines* 21 (1992): 11.

26. Miguel Leon Portilla, *The Aztec Image of Self and Society,* trans. Charles Brown and J. Jorge Klor de Alva (Salt Lake City: University of Utah Press, 1992), p. 36.

27. Ibid., p. 79.

28. Ibid., chapter 3.

29. Inga Clendinnen, "The Cost of Courage in Aztec Society," *Past and Present,* no. 107 (1985): 47.

30. Ross Hassig, *Aztec Warfare* (Norman: University of Oklahoma Press, 1988), p. 39.

31. Ibid., p. 41.

32. David Damrosch, "The Aesthetics of Conquest: Aztec Poetry before and after Cortez," *Representations,* no. 33 (1991): 101.

33. This process is covered in Jacques Attali, *Noise: The Political Economy of Music* (Minneapolis: University of Minnesota Press, 1985).

34. See, for example, the sections on music in Paul Gilroy's *Black Atlantic* (New York: Routledge, 1991).

35. Damrosch, "Aesthetics of Conquest," p. 105.

36. Ibid.

37. Leon Portilla, *Aztec Image of Self and Society,* p. 163.

38. Ibid., p. 167.

39. Ibid.

40. This interpretation of *Full Metal Jacket* is influenced by Bill Krohn's "*Full Metal Jacket,*" in Jonathan Crary and Sanford Kwinter, eds., *Incorporations* (New York: Zone, 1992), pp. 428–35.

41. James A. Donovan Jr., *The United States Marine Corps* (New York: Praeger, 1967), pp. 184–85, 181.

42. Anton Kaes, *From Hitler to Heimat: The Return of History as Film* (Cambridge, Mass.: Harvard University Press, 1989), p. 196.

43. Ibid., p. 198.

44. *Variety,* November 26, 1986, p. 3.

45. Ibid., p. 29.

46. See Emanuel Levy, *John Wayne: Prophet of the American Way of Life* (Metuchen, N.J.: Scarecrow, 1988), p. 40.

47. Paul Smith, *Clint Eastwood: A Cultural Production* (Minneapolis: University of Minnesota Press, 1993), p. 113.

48. David James, "Rock and Roll in Representations of the Invasion of Vietnam," *Representations,* no. 29 (1990): 89.

49. Smith, *Clint Eastwood,* p. 143.

50. Susan Jeffords, *The Remasculinization of America: Gender and the Vietnam War* (Bloomington: Indiana University Press, 1989).

## 5. Rehistoricizing American Warfare

1. Ward Just, *American Blues* (New York: Viking, 1984), p. 9.

2. Ibid., p. 15.

3. Thomas Myers, *Walking Point* (New York: Oxford University Press, 1988), p. 219.

4. Just, *American Blues,* p. 201.

5. This reading of *Full Metal Jacket* is encouraged by Rich Schweitzer's treatment in "Born to Kill: S. Kubrick's *Full Metal Jacket* as Historical Representation of Amer-

ica's Experience in Vietnam," *Film & History* 20, no. 3 (September 1990): 67. Although some (e.g., Susan Jeffords in *The Remasculinization of America: Gender and the Vietnam War* [Bloomington: Indiana University Press, 1989]) have argued that *Full Metal Jacket* endorses a masculinist ideology, I endorse the view that Kubrick's film is critical of the masculinity codes that help perpetuate violence. For this kind of reading, see, for example, Paula Willoquet-Maricondi, "Full-Metal-Jacketing; or, Masculinity in the Making," *Cinema Journal* 33, no. 2 (Winter 1994): 5–21.

6. Joseph Kruzel, "After the Storm: Perspectives on the Gulf War," *American Defense Annual 1991–1992* (New York: Macmillan, 1992), p. 1. Perhaps, like the Hurons described in chapter 2, Joseph Kruzel had both a war and a peace soul. As a deputy assistant secretary of defense and an envoy pursuing a peace accord in Bosnia, he died in August 1995 when the armored vehicle in which he was traveling plunged off a cliff. He deserves to be honored for his commitment to peace as much as criticized for his fascination with war.

7. Ibid., p. 2.

8. Ibid., p. 13.

9. Ibid., p. 16.

10. Ibid., p. 2.

11. Ibid.

12. Michael Howard, "Clausewitz: Man of the Year," *New York Times,* January 28, 1991.

13. Colonel Harry G. Summers Jr., *On Strategy II: A Critical Analysis of the Gulf War,* p. 19.

14. Ibid., p. 162.

15. A similar perspective is suggested by William Reddy, "Postmodernism and the Public Sphere: Implications for an Historical Ethnography," *Cultural Anthropology* 7, no. 2 (May 1992): 135–68.

16. This mapping of the Freudian idea of dream-work onto nationalism's form of attachment is elaborated in Stathis Gourgouris, "Notes on the Nation's Dreamwork," *Qui Parle* 7, no. 1 (Fall/Winter 1993): 81–101.

17. Michel Foucault, "What Is Enlightenment?" trans. Catherine Porter, in Paul Rabinow, ed., *The Foucault Reader* (New York: Pantheon, 1984), p. 50.

18. Bruce Lincoln, "War and Warriors: An Overview," in *Death, War, and Sacrifice* (Chicago: University of Chicago press, 1991), p. 141.

19. Ibid.

20. Peter Birkett Huber, "Violence and Social Order among the Anggor of New Guinea," in Martin A. Nettleship, R. Dale Givens, and Anderson Nettleship, eds., *War, Its Causes and Correlates* (The Hague: Mouton, 1975), p. 619.

21. Kruzel, "After the Storm," p. 13.

22. Ibid., p. 25.

23. The discussion and quotation here are drawn from Michael Marrinan, "Literal/Literary/'Lexie': History, Text, and Authority in Napoleonic Painting," *Word & Image* 7, no. 3 (July–September 1991): 177.

24. Constance Sherak, "*Ouvert au public:* The Musée Napoleon and the Politics of Appropriation," *Stanford Literary Review* 6, no. 1 (Spring 1989): 16.

25. For other accounts of this process that implicate the museum, see Lynn Hunt, *Politics, Culture, and Class in the French Revolution* (Berkeley: University of California Press, 1984), and Martin Rosenberg, "Raphael's *Transfiguration* and Napoleon's Cultural Politics," *Eighteenth-Century Studies* 19, no. 2 (Winter 1985–86): 180–205.

26. Marrinan, "Literal/Literary/'Lexie,'" p. 186.

27. Ibid.

28. Ibid.

29. It is important to recognize, however, that because modern visual media are increasingly recognized for their capacity to construct images, the epistemological status of the image is no longer unambiguously on the side of the real. For a dicussion of this, see Paul Virilio, *War and Cinema: The Logistics of Perception*, trans. Patrick Camiller (New York: Verso, 1989).

30. Norman Bryson, "Representing the Real: Gros' Paintings of Napoleon," *History of the Human Sciences* 1, no. 1 (May 1988): 87.

31. Ibid., p. 99.

32. Adam Smith, *Lectures on Jurisprudence*, ed. and trans. R. L. Meek, D. D. Rafael, and P. G. Stein (Indianapolis: Liberty Classics, 1982), p. 540.

33. George Mosse, *Nationalism and Sexuality: Respectability and Abnormal Sexuality in Modern Europe* (New York: Howard Fertig, 1985), pp. 1–22.

34. For a discussion of this, see Norman Bryson, "Gericault and 'Masculinity,'" in Norman Bryson, Michael Ann Holly, and Keith Moxey, *Visual Culture* (Hanover, N.H.: University Press of New England, 1994), pp. 228–57.

35. Ibid., p. 236.

36. Ibid., p. 238.

37. Ibid.

38. Ibid.

39. Ibid., p. 243.

40. Otto Friedrich, *Olympia: Paris in the Age of Manet* (New York: HarperCollins, 1992), pp. 73–76.

41. Ernest Larsen, "Gulf War TV," *Jump Cut*, no. 36 (May 1991): 5.

42. Ibid., p. 4.

43. Allen Feldman, "On Cultural Anesthesia: From Desert Storm to Rodney King," *American Ethnologist* 21, no. 1 (May 1994): 405.

44. P. W. Taylor, "Back to the Future? Integrating the Press and Media into the History of International Relations," *Historical Journal of Film, Radio, and Television* 14, no. 3 (1994): 322.

45. Don DeLillo suggests that contemporary media have changed the temporal significance of assassinations. Hinckley, he argues, saw himself as a future media event before he shot at Reagan. See his "American Blood: A Journey through the Labyrinth of Texas and JFK," *Rolling Stone*, December 8, 1983.

46. This insight is owed to Paul Virilio, especially as expressed in Paul Virilio and Sylvère Lotringer, *Pure War*, trans. Mark Polizotti (New York: Semiotext[e], 1983).

47. Ellen Herman, *The Romance of American Psychology: Political Culture in the Age of Experts* (Berkeley: University of California Press, 1995), p. 305.

228 Notes to Chapter 5

48. Lucien Pye, *Politics, Personality, and Nation Building* (New Haven, Conn.: Yale University Press, 1962).

49. Ted Robert Gurr, "Urban Disorder: Perspective from the Comparative Study of Civil Strife," *American Behavioral Scientist* 11 (March–April 1968): 50–55.

50. Slavoj Žižek, "Beyond Discourse Analysis," in Ernesto Laclau, ed., *New Reflections on the Revolution of Our Time* (London: Verso, 1990), p. 252.

51. This insight is drawn from Geoffrey Bennington, "The Frontier: Between Kant and Hegel," in *Legislations: The Politics of Deconstruction* (New York: Verso, 1994), p. 265.

52. Graham Dawson, *Soldier Heroes: British Adventure, Empire and the Imagining of Masculinities* (New York: Routledge, 1994), p. 1.

53. Ibid.

54. Susan Faludi, "The Naked Citadel," *New Yorker,* September 5, 1994, p. 65. The Citadel's mentality is a vestige of, among other things, the territorial version of masculinity promoted by Theodore Roosevelt. As one commentator has noted, in his autobiographical writings, Roosevelt, an advocate of aggressive masculinity, "fought to defend and create separate male territories where boys, male adolescents, and adult men could freely interact" ("Theodore Roosevelt and the Culture of Masculinity," *The Journal of American History* 8 (March 1995): 152.

55. Ibid., pp. 80, 81.

56. Eve Kosofsky Sedgwick, *Between Men: English Literature and Male Homosocial Desire* (New York: Columbia University Press, 1985), p. 2.

57. Susan Jeffords, *Hard Bodies: Hollywood Masculinity in the Reagan Era* (New Brunswick, N.J.: Rutgers University Press, 1994), p. 10.

58. Ibid., p. 11.

59. See, for example, the ad for the book by General Khaled Bib Sultan, whose *Desert Warrior,* published in 1995 by HarperCollins in the United States, continues the production of Gulf War "heroes." The ads says, among other things: "He held together a coalition of forces from 37 nations to help defeat Saddam Hussein" (*New York Times Book Review,* May 21, 1995, p. 18).

60. Mark Selzer, *Bodies and Machines* (New York: Routledge, 1992), p. 63.

61. Jeffords, *Remasculinization of America.*

62. Selzer, *Bodies and Machines,* p. 149.

63. Quoted in ibid., p. 149.

64. Audie Murphy, *To Hell and Back* (New York: Henry Holt, 1949), pp. 42, 44.

65. Ibid., p. 99.

66. Ibid., p. 84.

67. Ibid., p. 142.

68. Roger J. Spiller, "The Price of Valor," *Military History Quarterly* 5, no. 3 (Spring 1993): 100.

69. *Life,* July 16, 1945.

70. Lawrence Suid, *Guts & Glory* (Reading, Mass.: Addison-Wesley, 1978), p. 92.

71. Quoted in Lillian Ross, *Picture* (New York: Rinehart, 1952), p. 27.

72. John Whiteclay Chambers II and David Culbert, introduction to *Historical Journal of Film, Radio and Television* 14, no. 4 (1994): 355.

73. Selzer, *Bodies and Machines,* p. 49.

74. Ibid., pp. 149, 151–52.

75. The statement is from a review by George Wyndham published shortly after the book was published; it is quoted in Clark Mitchell, introduction to *New Essays on the Red Badge of Courage* (New York: Cambridge University Press, 1986), p. 6.

76. Ibid., p. 12.

77. See Sergei Eisenstein (with Vselovod Pudovkin and Sergei Alexandrov), "Statement," *Zhizn Isskusstva*, no. 32 (August 5, 1928): 15.

78. These details are provided in Ross, *Picture*.

79. Selzer, *Bodies and Machines*, p. 164.

80. This observation is influenced by Norman Bryson's discussion in "Gericault and Masculinity."

81. *New York Times*, February 3, 1991, Section L, p. 14.

82. Ibid.

83. Norman Schwarzkopf with Peter Petre, *It Doesn't Take a Hero* (New York: Bantam, 1992), p. 1.

84. Ibid., pp. 153–54.

85. Ibid., p. 135.

86. Paul Virilio, *Speed and Politics,* trans. Mark Polizzotti (New York: Semiotext[e], 1986), p. 38.

87. Ibid.

88. Norman Schwarzkopf, "The Strategy behind Desert Storm," in Summers, *On Strategy II,* p. 271.

89. Schwarzkopf, *It Doesn't Take a Hero,* p. 401.

90. *CBS Reports with Dan Rather,* June 30, 1993.

91. For a provocative rendering of the spatial practices of modernity in terms of the proliferation of heterotopias, places of otherness, see Michel Foucault, "Of Other Spaces," trans. Jay Miscowiec, *Diacritics* 16 (Spring 1986): 22–29.

92. Philip D. Biedler, *Re-Writing America: Vietnam Authors in Their Generation* (Athens: University of Georgia Press, 1991), p. 6.

93. Sonya Mitchell, "Danger on the Home Front: Motherhood, Sexuality, and Disabled Veterans in American Postwar Films," *Journal of the History of Sexuality* 3, no. 1 (July 1992): 110.

94. Quoted in Thomas Keenan, "Live from/En Direct de," in Elizabeth Diller and Ricardo Scofidio, *Visite aux armées: Tourismes de guerre/Back to the Front: Tourisms of War* (New York: Princeton Architecture Press, 1994), p. 132.

95. Ibid., p. 133.

96. The expression belongs to Graham Dawson; see his critique of the view of essentialist feminism in *Soldier Heroes* (New York: Routledge, 1994), p. 17.

97. The quote is from William Chaloupka's masterful essay on the Gulf War: "Suppose Kuwait's Main Product Was Broccoli: The Street Demonstration in U.S. Politics," in Frederick M. Dolan and Thomas L. Dumm, eds., *Rhetorical Republic: Governing Representations in American Politics* (Amherst: University of Massachusetts Press, 1993), p. 155. The conceptions on which the remarks are based are from Peter Sloterdijk's *Critique of Cynical Reason,* trans. Michael Eldred (Minneapolis: University of Minnesota Press, 1988).

98. See Joan Didion, *Democracy* (New York: Simon and Schuster, 1984). And, for an excellent discussion of the way the novel erodes one's "ability to believe in personal and national allegories," see Alan Nadel, "Failed Cultural Narratives: America in the Postwar Era and the Story of *Democracy*," *Boundary 2* 19, no. 1 (Spring 1992): 95–120.

99. Ibid., p. 117.

## 6. The Ethics of Encounter: Unreading, Unmapping the Imperium

1. John Austin, *How to Do Things with Words* (Cambridge, Mass.: Harvard University Press, 1962).

2. Austin did not make a sharp distinction between kinds of utterances. He argued that the descriptive (locutionary) and performative (illocutionary and perlocutionary) aspects of utterances are levels of force within a given speech act, not ways of characterizing different speech acts.

3. Jacques Derrida, *Limited Inc.* (Evanston, Ill.: Northwestern University Press, 1988), p. 14.

4. Ibid., p. 137.

5. Alasdair MacIntyre, *After Virtue* 2d ed. (Notre Dame, Ind.: University of Notre Dame Press, 1984), p. 73.

6. Ibid., p. 213.

7. Michel Foucault, "Friendship as a Way of Life," in *Foucault Live,* ed. Sylvère Lotringer, trans. John Johnson (New York: Semiotext[e], 1989), p. 209.

8. Emmanuel Levinas, *Totality and Infinity,* trans. Alphonso Lingus (Pittsburgh: Duquesne University Press, 1969), p. 21.

9. Edward Said, *Culture and Imperialism* (New York: Knopf, 1993), p. xiii.

10. For a significant challenge to the "ethics of international affairs" tradition, see the recent work of David Campbell: *Sovereignty, Ethics, and Narratives of the Gulf War* (Boulder, Colo.: Lynne Rienner, 1993) and "The Deterritorialization of Responsibility: Levinas, Derrida, and Ethics after the End of Philosophy," *Alternatives* 19, no. 4 (December 1994).

11. J. B. Harley, "Cartographic Ethics and Social Theory," *Cartographica* 27, no. 2 (Summer 1990): 1–23. It must be added that "morality" as a problem has been too much absorbed into a temporal rather than a spatial model, one that privileges individual consciousness, which implies an intrinsic temporality rather than discourse. For this reason, Foucault has suggested that recognition of the ethicopolitical implications of discourse requires "the use of spatial, strategic metaphors." See the interview "Questions on Geography" in Colin Gordon, ed., *Power/Knowledge* (New York: Pantheon, 1980), p. 71.

12. The expression belongs to Paul Virilio, *The Vision Machine* (Bloomington: Indiana University Press, 1994), chapter 1.

13. This tradition in ethics is most clearly represented in the essays, written mostly by academics, found in the journal *Ethics & International Affairs,* published by the Carnegie Council on Ethics and International Affairs.

14. Jarat Chopra and Thomas G. Weiss, "Sovereignty Is No Longer Sacrosanct: Codifying Humanitarian Intervention," *Ethics & International Affairs* 6 (1992): 98.

15. Bernard Nietschmann, "The Third World War," *Cultural Survival Quarterly* 11, no. 3 (1987): 1, 7.

16. G. W. F. Hegel, *Natural Law,* trans. T. M. Knox (Philadelphia: University of Pennsylvania Press, 1975), pp. 60–61.

17. Ibid., p. 77. Indeed, Kant himself displayed a recognition of the inadequacy of mere formalism. His use of examples undercuts his commitment to the "absoluteness of content" to which Hegel referred. As David Lloyd has shown, the specific historical referents of Kant's discourses on judgment are necessitated by his transcendental interests. See David Lloyd, "Kant's Examples," *Representations,* no. 28 (Fall 1989): 34–54.

18. Carlos Fuentes, "Writing in Time," *Democracy* 2, no. 1 (January 1982): 61.

19. Ibid., p. 64.

20. The relevant work is Adam Smith's *Theory of Moral Sentiments.* I treat the problems associated with constructing ethics around a moral psychology such as Smith's in my *Reading "Adam Smith": Desire, History and Value* (Newbury Park, Calif.: Sage, 1993).

21. Emmanuel Levinas, *Time and the Other,* trans. Richard Cohen (Pittsburgh: Duquesne University Press, 1987), p. 75.

22. Levinas, *Totality and Infinity,* p. 251.

23. Sean Hand, *The Levinas Reader* (London: Basil Blackwell, 1989), p. 82.

24. Levinas, *Totality and Infinity,* p. 39.

25. Jacques Derrida, "Violence and Metaphysics," in *Writing and Difference,* trans. Alan Bass (Chicago: University of Chicago Press, 1978), p. 38.

26. Levinas, *Time and the Other,* pp. 40, 41.

27. Levinas, *Totality and Infinity,* p. 80. It is not clear how starkly opposed Heidegger's position is to Levinas's, because his *with* is meant to disclose a hermeneutic of shared involvement. Certainly there is a strong suggestion of hermeneutic closure in Heidegger's notion of a "co-state-of mind" and a "co-understanding," which he attributes to self-other communication (*Being and Time,* trans. J. Macquarrie and E. Robinson [New York: Harper and Row, 1962], p. 205). And, further, the condition of possibility for communication inheres in Heiddeger's *with,* which reflects an ontology that precedes communication. One's "being-towards-oneself" already contains the relationship-of-Being that one has toward Others. But Heidegger does recognize a face to face in the self-Other relationship. It is a mediated one, however; it follows the individual's confrontation with anxiety, which discloses the coinvolvement in the world with Others. Here Heidegger evokes the face to face with the Other, which follows from a recognition that one is not ultimately alone with anxiety (*Being and Time,* p. 233). Nevertheless, the *with* is the dominant hermeneutic and ethical preposition. It reflects what Heidegger sees as an intrinsic sharedness that every "I" contains. Self-recognition involves at the same time a recognition of one's witness. Ultimately, then, Heidegger's *with* is aimed at disclosing the relationship of ontology to interpretation, the way that self-interpretation requires a recognition of

coinvolvement. Levinas's face to face is aimed at providing an ethics that must precede both ontology and communication.

While Levinas has good reason to distinquish his position from an ideal of communication or a prior being-in-common, it is less clear that Heidegger meant to suggest a frame in which one must recognize the Other as the same as oneself. What is common for Heidegger is that the self is with others in the world, in terms of how one has the world. And, as Derrida has shown, it is difficult to posit a condition of recognition of Others without a prior conceptuality that allows for an economy of sameness and difference (see Derrida's *Violence and Metaphysics,* which treats the aporias of a conceptless recognition of alterity). Heidegger references are from *Being and Time.* For a nuanced treatment of Heidegger's ideas of the location of the Other, see Peg E. Birmingham, "Logos and the Place of the Other," *Research in Phenomenology* 20 (1990): 34-54.

28. Emmanuel Levinas, *Difficult Freedom,* trans. Sean Hand (Baltimore: Johns Hopkins University Press, 1990), p. 7.

29. Ibid., p. 8.

30. Levinas, *Time and the Other,* p. 42.

31. Emmanuel Levinas, "The Trace of the Other," trans. Alphonso Lingus, in Mark C. Taylor, ed., *Deconstruction in Context* (Chicago: University of Chicago Press, 1986), p. 348.

32. Lars Gustafsson, *Funeral Music for Freemasons,* trans. Yvonne L. Sandstroem (New York: New Directions, 1983), p. 122.

33. Levinas, *Difficult Freedom,* p. 16.

34. Emmanuel Levinas, *Otherwise than Being; or, Beyond Essence,* trans. Alphonso Lingus (The Hague: Matinus Nijhoff, 1981), p. 37.

35. See Emmanuel Levinas, "Meaning and Sense," in *Collected Philosophical Papers,* trans. Alphonso Lingus (Dordrecht: Martinus Nijhoff, 1987), pp. 102ff.

36. Ibid., p. 103.

37. Hand, *Levinas Reader,* p. 148. Much of the talmudic tradition is resistant to fixing texts; it is oriented toward effacing rather than deepening received textual interpretations. This spirit of talmudic reading is treated, with a variety of historical exemplars, in Marc-Alain Ouaknin, *The Burnt Book: Reading the Talmud,* trans. Llewellyn Brown (Princeton, N.J.: Princeton University Press, 1995).

38. Derrida, "Violence and Metaphysics," p. 141.

39. Ibid., p. 130.

40. Ibid., p. 95.

41. This is treated in many places, but for a succinct and focused account, see Valerie I. J. Flint, *The Imaginative Landscape of Christopher Columbus* (Princeton, N.J.: Princeton University Press, 1992), pp. 3-41.

42. Hand, *Levinas Reader,* p. 294.

43. Levinas, *Difficult Freedom,* p. 216.

44. Ibid., p. 217.

45. Emmanuel Levinas, *Outside the Subject,* trans. Michael B. Smith (Stanford, Calif.: Stanford University Press, 1994), p. 117.

46. Levinas, *Difficult Freedom,* p. 217.

47. Hand, *Levinas Reader*, p. 82.

48. Levinas, *Outside the Subject*, p. 123.

49. Levinas, *Difficult Freedom*, p. 216.

50. Simon Critchley has an excellent discussion of Levinas's difficulties with "the feminine"; see Simon Critchley, "'Bois': Derrida's Final Word on Levinas," in Robert Bernasconi and Simon Critchley, eds., *Re-Reading Levinas* (Bloomington: Indiana University Press, 1991).

51. Levinas, *Difficult Freedom*, p. 31.

52. Mieke Bal, *Death and Dissymmetry* (Chicago: University of Chicago Press, 1988), p. 170.

53. Ibid., p. 169.

54. For a reading that focuses on Levinas's treatment of Israel as an "ethical nation," which, it is argued, displaces his ethics, see George Salemohamed, "Levinas: From Ethics to Political Theology," *Economy and Society* 21, no. 2 (May 1992): 192–206.

55. Bal, *Death and Dissymmetry*, p. 14.

56. Ibid., pp. 171, 169.

57. Emmanuel Levinas, *Nine Talmudic Readings*, trans. Annette Aronowicz (Bloomington: Indiana University Press, 1990), p. 37.

58. Ibid., p. 39.

59. My discussion of Levinas's reading of the Talmud has benefited from the excellent treatment of Jill Robbins, *Prodigal Son/Elder Brother* (Chicago: University of Chicago Press, 1991), pp. 100–132.

60. Influenced in part by Levinas, John Caputo has a provocative treatment of responsibility as something that simply is—that is, as a fact with which to begin rather than a problem to be worked out. See John Caputo, *Against Ethics* (Bloomington: Indiana University Press, 1993).

61. Levinas, *Nine Talmudic Readings*, p. 34.

62. Edmund Leach, "The Legitimacy of Solomon," in Michael Lane, ed., *Structuralism: A Reader* (London: Jonathan Cape, 1970), pp. 248–92.

63. Ibid., p. 248.

64. Ibid., p. 257.

65. Ibid., pp. 258, 266, 271–74.

66. Nurith Gertz, "A World without Boundaries: Israeli National Identity in the Eighties as Expressed in Cinema and Literature," *Discours social/Social Discourse* 4, no. 3 (Summer–Autumn 1992): 156.

67. Ibid. Gertz treats the way that this paradox is explored differently in contemporary Israeli film and literature.

68. See Ammiel Alcalay's *After Jews and Arabs: Remaking Levantine Culture* (Minneapolis: University of Minnesota Press, 1993) for a treatment of the historical imbrication of Jewish and Arab culture.

69. See Gertz, "World without Boundaries," for examples.

70. Michael Walzer, *Exodus and Revolution* (New York: Basic Books, 1985).

71. Michael Walzer, "Exodus and Revolution," *Jewish Spectator* 54, no. 1 (Spring–Summer 1989): 29–30.

72. Walzer, *Exodus and Revolution,* pp. x, 12, 102.

73. Michael Walzer, "An Exchange: 'Exodus and Revolution,'" *Grand Street* 5, no. 4 (Summer 1986): 247.

74. Edward Said, "Michael Walzer's 'Exodus and Revolution': A Canaanite Reading," *Grand Street* 5, no. 2 (Winter 1986): 104–5.

75. Walzer, "An Exchange," p. 247.

76. The term belongs to Jacques Derrida, *The Other Heading: Reflections on Today's Europe,* trans. Pascale-Anne Brault and Michael B. Naas (Bloomington: Indiana University Press, 1992).

77. There is also, of course, a heading or aim to Said's discourse. It is produced on behalf of Palestinian entitlements, seeking to head off the forward motion of Israeli national consolidation. But in this particular exchange, the primary force of Said's writing is deconstructive—that is, it is aimed at displacing closure with aporia.

78. Derrida, *Violence and Metaphysics,* p. 130.

79. Ibid., p. 117.

80. Derrida, *The Other Heading,* p. 15; emphasis in the original.

81. Ibid., pp. 38–39; emphasis in the original.

82. Ibid., p. 41.

83. Ibid., p. 49.

84. See my treatment of the Jesuit-Huron encounters in chapters 1 and 2.

85. See John Stuart Mill, "On Intervention," in *Essays on Politics and Culture,* ed. Gertrude Himmelfarb (Garden City, N.Y.: Doubleday, 1962), p. 52.

86. Gilles Deleuze and Félix Guattari, *A Thousand Plateaus,* trans. Brian Massumi (Minneapolis: University of Minnesota Press, 1987), p. 209; emphasis in the original.

87. The conceptual language of this section derives from Deleuze and Guattari's discussion.

88. Paul Carter, *The Road to Botany Bay: An Essay on Landscape and History* (Chicago: University of Chicago Press, 1989).

89. G. M. Dillon and Jerry Everard, "Stat(e)ing Australia: Squid Jigging and the Masque of State," *Alternatives* 17, no. 3 (Summer 1992): 218–312.

90. Carter, *Road to Botany Bay,* pp. 165, 163.

91. This dilemma faced by Levinas is treated by Derrida in *Violence and Metaphysics,* by Robbins in *Prodigal Son/Elder Brother,* and by Critchley in *The Ethics of Deconstruction* (Cambridge, Mass.: Blackwell, 1992).

92. Alcalay, *After Jews and Arabs.*

93. This expression is Critchley's; see *The Ethics of Deconstruction,* p. 43.

94. Derrida, *Violence and Metaphysics,* p. 102.

95. Some of the ideas in this section are also expressed in Drucilla Cornell, *The Philosophy of the Limit* (New York: Routledge, 1992), pp. 71–72. My discussion here has been edified by her insights.

96. Jürgen Habermas, *Justification and Application: Remarks on Discourse Ethics,* trans. Ciaran Cronin (Cambridge, Mass.: MIT Press, 1993), p. 5.

97. Sylviane Agacinski has offered a similar critique, noting that Habermas's notion of communicative rationality contains a theory of the subject that posits an "initial atomism"; see Sylviane Agacinski, "Another Experience of the Question; or,

Experiencing the Question Other-Wise," in Eduardo Cadava, Peter Connor, and Jean-Luc Nancy, eds., *Who Comes after Subject* (New York: Routledge, 1991), p. 13.

98. The Lacanian idea of the denial of debts to alterity is elaborated by Samuel Weber in *Institution and Interpretation* (Minneapolis: University of Minnesota Press, 1987).

99. Derrida, *Violence and Metaphysics*, p. 80.

100. Jean-Luc Nancy, *The Inoperative Community*, trans. Peter Connor et al. (Minneapolis: University of Minnesota Press, 1991), pp. 40, 77.

101. William Connolly provides a similar injunction in his elaboration of an "ethics of critical responsiveness." Turning to the language of Deleuze and Guattari, he speaks of the need to "pluralize lines of territorialization so that no single line becomes overcoded"; see William E. Connolly, *The Ethos of Pluralization* (Minneapolis: University of Minnesota press, 1995), p. 20.

102. See Pomedli's remarks on the Hurons, noted in chapter 2, in his *Ethnophilosophical and Ethnolinguistic Perspectives on the Huron Indian Soul*.

103. Michael Taussig, *Mimesis and Alterity* (New York: Routledge, 1993), p. 2.

104. Ibid., p. 16.

105. Ibid., pp. 236–37.

106. Ibid., p. 142.

107. Ibid., p. 212.

108. Ibid., p. 213.

109. Ibid., pp. 116–22.

110. Ibid., p. 122.

111. Anne McClintock, "Maidens, Maps, and Mines: The Reinvention of Patriarchy in Colonial South Africa," *South Atlantic Quarterly* 87, no. 1 (Winter 1988): 48.

112. Ibid., p. 150.

113. Ibid., pp. 149–50.

114. Ibid., p. 152.

115. There are other critical practices with a similar unmapping effect on the entanglement between the female body and imperialist cartography. For example, the Irish artist Kathy Prendergast executed a series of maps in which the cartographic conventions of grid lines are superimposed on female bodies. Prendergast's mixing of a personal geography of the body with the space of the nation constitutes an ironic reflection on the political controls over landscapes. Her body-map constructions disrupt the authority and claims to neutrality of cartography and "problematize both the discourse of geography and the representation of women and their reciprocal use." Her ironic unmappings help to unread the historic entanglements between gender and authority in the production of a national understanding of landscapes. The images are shown and analyzed in Catherine Nash, "Remapping the Body/Land: New Cartographies of Identity, Gender, and Landscape in Ireland," in Alison Bland and Gillian Rose, eds., *Writing Women and Space* (New York: Guilford, 1994), pp. 227–50.

116. Peter Handke, *Slow Homecoming*, trans. Ralph Mannheim (New York: Farrar, Straus & Giroux, 1985), p. 60. Sorger ("one who cares") is contrasted with Lauffer, his scientific colleague in the "Far North."

117. Ibid., p. 3.

118. Ibid., pp. 71–73.

119. Ibid., p. 74.

120. In the story, Sorger and "the Indian woman" both avoid the violence in their respective patrimonies in their relationship because they converse in English, which is not the "native language" of either.

121. Handke, *Slow Homecoming*, p. 75.

122. Ibid., p. 114.

123. Ibid., pp. 129, 136.

124. See Gary J. Handwerk, *Irony and Ethics in Narrative* (New Haven, Conn.: Yale University Press, 1985).

125. Handke, *Slow Homecoming*, p. 135.

126. Samuel Beckett, *The Unnamable* (New York: Grove, 1970).

# Index

Michael J. Shapiro is professor of political science at the University of Hawaii, where he teaches courses in political theory, global politics, and politics of media. Among his recent publications are *Reading the Postmodern Polity: Political Theory as Textual Practice* (Minnesota, 1992), *Reading 'Adam Smith': Desire, History, and Value,* and (coedited with Hayward Alker) *Challenging Boundaries: Global Flows, Territorial Identities* (Minnesota, 1996).